OFF AND RUNNING

OFF AND RUNNING

By Bill Corum

ILLUSTRATED WITH PHOTOGRAPHS

Edited by Arthur Mann

HENRY HOLT AND COMPANY

NEW YORK

To Mother for what she has been.
To Robert for what he will be.

Contents

POSTWAR

NEWSPAPER DAZE

THE COLUMN

GENIUS AT WORK

HEROES AND HERO WORSHIP

THOROUGHBREDS: HORSES AND PEOPLE

SCOOPS

BLUEGRASS BUGLES

AUTHOR'S NOTE

There is a chance some readers and critics will say that this book lacks organization. How right they will be! So has my life. I have known presidents and crooks, but you will find precious little about crooks in this book. I never liked bums, except sweet bums such as Toots Shor.

I have written this book the only way I know to write, so if you lose the thread of the narrative now and again, phone the Singer Sewing Machine Company. (Free advt.) Of course, it might be easier to skip a few hundred pages or more. After all, you bought the book, didn't you? Why should I worry about you now?

But I do. I think you were a sweetheart for buying the book, and I hope it won't let you down too badly.

Thanks.

BILL CORUM

Editor's Note

Meeting and knowing Bill Corum meant having another friend. For me this began in March, 1926, at Sarasota, Florida, where we first lived and traveled together while covering the New York Giants in training. It ended with his death on December 16, 1958.

Because of his daily column, Bill needed help for outside writing in research, checking, cutting and editing. He couldn't concentrate long on such a task before the unwritten column took over his thinking. Ten years ago Henry Holt and Company had expressed interest in a book by Corum. More recently, when they suggested that he write his autobiography, Bill asked me to help him with the research and the editing of the manuscript.

Confronted with actual performance, however, Bill panicked a little over the definite commitment. Leaving our first meeting at Holt, he asked me if I had heard Editor Harry Shaw talk about his grandfather taking him to see the Lewis-Speaker-Hooper Red Sox.

I nodded. "Why?"

"It means that we're in trouble already," Corum growled. "The editor has seen a ball game."

But secretly he was proud that a publisher wanted his life story. At least he boasted about it in his column now and again, and he wanted to do the book well. To expedite his writing we bought an electronic recording machine with plenty of plastic discs. I had found it ideal for dictation, but at first sight of the machine Bill drew back wide-eyed, as though it were a rattler coiled to strike.

"Granny Rice talked for four hours into one of those things," he exclaimed, "and forgot to turn it on!"

"Then say 'Granny Rice' when you pick up the microphone," I said. "That'll remind you to press the starting button."

Bill began recording early in 1958. I'd bring fresh discs and take away the full ones for transcribing into rough copy. These would be cut and edited into a first draft. Bill would then rework the draft; he always said that he was putting "the Corum back into it." This version was called "first final," but he even rewrote much of that.

During my visits to his apartment at the Park Lane Hotel, Bill would stand for hours before his writing desk with one foot on his chair, resting an elbow on the upraised knee. While I filled page after page of legal-sized yellow pads, he would answer questions, discuss new chapters and recall the endless incidents that had formed his life and philosophy. Through the recordings and these sessions we covered all the subjects he wanted to include.

One of our disagreements about what should go into the book concerned the tales of Bill's derring-do under fire in France. Each time I broached the subject, he would laugh and say, "Hero nothing, there was no other choice." So I'll simply quote from a letter written on December 17, 1919, to Bill's mother by Col. John C. Greenway:

> During our whole participation in the Great War, he was without doubt the best company commander in the regiment. When other companies were scattered and more or less demoralized, his company was always comparatively

well in hand. He not only was courageous, but showed fine self-control and executive ability to a high degree. I recommended him for the Distinguished Service Cross, which I regret very much has not been granted. However, his merit was recognized by the Commander in Chief in that he was promoted successively from rank of Lieutenant to Major and was certainly one of the youngest majors in the Army.

The first indication that anything was wrong with Bill came in mid-August, 1958. For several days he suffered severe respiratory discomfort and sweated heavily without having a fever. Although we worked regularly, he would tire easily after that. I left town in October and missed him at the World Series. Learning that he had been hospitalized, I hurried back to New York, where we began a race with the inevitable.

I felt certain that Bill was very seriously ill, but we didn't discuss much besides the work. By the day after Thanksgiving he had lost fifty pounds and was feeling weak. Yet in a long session we put together the "Taverns" chapter and he gave me specific and detailed instructions about other parts of the book.

Assailed by guilt, I sat with him for two hours at St. Luke's Hospital on Friday, December 12, working, checking, taking notes and asking questions until he asked me to go. We shook hands and he grinned as usual. "Edit the hell out of it," he said, "but leave the Corum in."

I saw him again on Monday, but we didn't talk. Thirty hours later he died of lung cancer. On Saturday he was carried to rest by a few of his boyhood friends in the Walnut Grove Cemetery, Boonville, near his father and Uncle Crutch.

Arthur Mann

BEGINNINGS

Where did you come from?
Where did you go?
Where did you come from,
Brown-eye Bo?
                    Anonymous

Distant Echoes

Every man, when he is born, may be potentially the captain of his soul, the maker or wrecker of his destiny. But he has no choice in his given names. There he is helpless, and the fellow this book is about was even more helpless than most.

The deal was that if this Corum came into the world a boy he was already named, for worse or worst, Martene Windsor. I never liked the name, and neither did my simply named father, Robert Wyan. But there was the consideration of giving a beautiful young mother her way with her first-born. Secondly, there was the pig. Martene was for a doctor friend of Mother's family in St. Louis, obviously a Dr. Martene; Windsor was for the pig.

The porker turned out to be the best business transaction of my life. All I ever got from the doctor was an engraved baby spoon, given possibly in the hope that I might soon develop the habit of taking medicine. But any illnesses which resulted in my skipping my daily sports column in the New York *Journal-American* were usually caused by the disease of laziness and a lifetime habit of staying in bed. As my Grandmother Corum used to say to me when I was a shaver and promised to get up early and mow the lawn, "Teeny, you do all your getting up early the night before."

Now, about the pig. There was a well-to-do farmer who lived near us in Cooper County, Missouri, where I was born

3

July 29, 1894, whose name was Walt Windsor. Shortly before my birth, Mr. Windsor was in my father's general store in Speed, Missouri. The store was also the post office when a Democrat was President. Otherwise the P.O. went to Mr. Harness in the "Republican store." The fact that my father had been instrumental in changing the name of the town from New Palestine to Speed—there were so many New Palestines—cut no ice in the Republican years. Political lines were hard and Father got two terms under the Democrats before the locusts descended for a lengthy visit.

Mr. Windsor said, "Bob, if it's a boy and you name him Windsor, I'll give him the best shoat on my farm when he's old enough to feed it."

Wherever I've gone in this country for years now, people who have never seen me before look at me upon hearing my voice, seem to struggle for identification of some kind and usually wind up saying, "Aren't you the fellow that does the fights?" I did broadcast the fights for a long time in the heyday of radio with Don Dunphy, so these strangers I meet look sharp and feel sharp because they recognize me.

"Ol' gravel-voice Bill," J. P. Spang, Jr., chairman of the Gillette Company, calls me. It must be that kind of voice, or so many folks couldn't tab it and say, "You talk just the same on the air as you're talking now!" If so, it almost surely traces to the pig, for Mr. Windsor was as good as his word. The black and tan shoat was put in a small pasture back of our small frame cottage at Speed, with his pen built in its most remote corner, for obvious reasons.

Almost immediately I became the town's loudest and least-loved hog caller. I can still do it and be heard from here to Yonkers: *"Peeg, peeg, sooey, sooey, peeg, peeg, peeg!"*

When the pig was full grown, my grandfather, Theodore Corum, one of the county's drovers, bought him from me for $14 and shipped him to market.

Then came a stroke of fortune that might have led me into the misspent life of a financier. Since Speed was too small to support a bank, Grandfather Corum put the fourteen clams into a savings account for me in the nearby town of Bunceton. He died a year or two later and I forgot about the pig and my money in the bank.

It wasn't until I was entering the University of Missouri a decade later that a fellow freshman from Bunceton, who'd worked in the bank there, said to me: "I won't tell anybody around here, but I know your real name. It was on the ledger at our bank."

"What's that mean?" I asked.

"You've got money there."

"How do I get it?"

"I've got a checkbook," he said. "Sign a check with your full name and send it to the bank, telling them you want to close your account. Don't put any amount on the check. Your account started and ended with fourteen dollars, but you have a little interest on it now."

Off went the letter, and that's how I got paid for my namesake pig, and was saved by the bell from being a money baron. Imagine having money lying around in the same bank all those years, getting mildewed with interest! Ridiculous!

Some people are blessed with total recall, but the sum total of my boyhood recollections consists of days and events that I either hated to leave or wanted hard to forget. In between, matters like bank balances, sports records and first names are an embarrassing blank.

Speed, Missouri, wasn't what the name implies. It was a dusty crossroads, somewhat frightening to a pioneer in the first grade. Dr. Henry Schubert, my first teacher, had a doomsday quality about him, though he never gave me anything but kindness.

I got some security from the childhood companionship of one "Pink" Allee, whose father was a doctor. But one day I realized all too well why belligerent kids weren't afraid of us. Pink was a girl! As a discovery, it was basic, but the year of my biggest awakening was 1904. First there was the new suit and a new pair of shoes, then a haircut in a real barbershop in Boonville, instead of a monthly one by a fox-hunting barber named "Coon" Williams in the back of the store. On top of all these wonders, there was the 160-mile trip to St. Louis and the World's Fair of 1904!

There were such sights as the ferris wheel, the *Pike*, the Johnstown Flood recreated, and Jim Key, the "Talking Horse." (The horse that talked was one of my top favorites of the Exposition. As a horse player, I've hoped ever since to find talking horses, instead of talkative trainers and jockeys.) The more permanent buildings and educational exhibits interested me far less, you might guess, than the world's first ice-cream cone, or the fascinating sight of Alice Roosevelt Longworth smoking a cigarette right out in public.

Those two weeks were new, exciting and memorable, but the brightest highlight was the afternoon my uncle Crutchfield D. Corum, a lawyer in St. Louis, took me to see the big-league Cardinals play. That was *the* day. Uncle Crutch was a plumed knight to me, being well-known about the city and a fellow who had tickets to the ball games. Everybody seemed to greet him, which meant an introduction to me, and I met one real live baseball writer, Louis Lee Arms, of the long-gone St. Louis *Republic*.

Among other clients, my Uncle Crutch was attorney for the (then) four Skouras brothers. Spyros, George and the late Charlie—the fourth put up his cue early and returned to Greece—saved their money as waiters in the Jefferson Hotel, bought a tiny theater on Taylor Avenue, and ran it

up and down and up again in one of the great success
stories of the fabulous motion-picture industry. For years
Charlie Skouras was best known for paying the highest individual income tax—when he should have been heralded
as the moving spirit in building St. Sophia Cathedral in
Los Angeles, the largest and most beautiful Greek Ortho-
dox Church in the United States. All this, and more, came
from the humblest beginnings on a stony Greek farm.

Later, about 1908, my Uncle Crutch was a small stock-
holder in the St. Louis Browns (a skeleton in the family's
Cardinal-rooting closet). The Browns' secretary at that time,
a great gentleman named Sid Mercer, eventually became as
fine a sports writer as any I have known in my field when he
wrote for the old New York *Globe*. Later he joined us on
the *Journal-American*.

Though that game in 1904 was my first glimpse of a big-
league ball park, I felt right at home. Like most kids of my
generation, I thought myself a baseball player. I rubbed
neat's-foot oil into the pocket of my mitt and in the summer
went to sleep sniffing the oily leather under my pillow. This
made the bed dirty and horrified my grandmother, America
Ann Corum—a wonderful name for a wonderful woman—
who helped raise me. But for a boy around nine or ten there
was no finer sight than a green cow pasture on a sunny Saturday in spring, when he had a glove and a white, new
"reg'lar big-league" ball in his hand.

The scene of my first big-league game was Robison Field,
a sprawling, almost home-run-proof enclosure at Vande-
venter and Natural Bridge avenues, St. Louis. The principals
were the Cardinals and the Cincinnati Reds. (In recent
years, some silly people have objected to the Cincinnati
team being called the Reds. But the Red Stockings are the
oldest professional baseball team; they were the Reds long

before the Russians were, so why not make the Kremlin boys stop abusing the term?)

Memory's eye has always insisted that the Cardinals still wore bright red uniforms on that first day of mine in a big-league ball park. However, such veteran fans and authorities as J. G. Taylor Spink, Fred Lieb and the former Police Commissioner of New York City, Edward P. Mulrooney (once a patrolman assigned to the Polo Grounds in the early, *early* days) have warned me off that belief on the several occasions I have mentioned it in my column. All three insist that the Cards had given up their red monkey suits before that time. Well, if the uniforms weren't fully red, be sure there was a lot of red on them. Playing first base for the Cardinals was "Eagle Eye" Jake Beckley, with a curled mustachio, probably the last "handle bars" seen on a big-league field. Eagle Eye hailed from Mark Twain's home town, Hannibal, Missouri, and eventually made 2,930 hits in the big leagues.

Who do you think was playing second base against us for Cincy that cornfield-hot afternoon? An almost runty-looking man whose toes turned out as he walked on splayed feet, he was smarter than he looked at first glance, for he was one of the very first, to my knowledge, who "switch-hit"—that is, he batted left-handed against right-handed pitchers and righty against the southpaws. This made the pitcher's curve ball break in toward him, but even so his lifetime average was only .265.

"Just imagine what it would've been," he chuckled in later years, "if I hadn't turned around?" By then Miller Huggins had become the astute and friendly manager of the great New York Yankees of the Ruth-Meusel-Gehrig era, but to me that day he was "Dusty Miller," a sworn enemy no bigger than a minute playing his first big-league season.

Jake Beckley got hold of one that memorable afternoon, so *we* won the ball game. A little boy had a tough time getting to sleep a few hours later, never dreaming that he was watching the first of more than four thousand major-league games, including every pitch of every World Series game since 1921.

Boots and Saddle

That fall the family moved to the town of Boonville on the Missouri River, the Cooper County seat named—and misspelled—in honor of the original Daniel. We took a house on the southeast corner of Seventh and Spruce. Later, after "the locusts" had gone, my father served two terms as Boonville postmaster. He was a careful and deliberate canceler, they tell me, and thought nothing of making a train wait or letting it go without the pouches. He refused to be rushed.

Boonville was steeped in all kinds of history. It had been a tug-o'-war for three years of the War Between the States and I heard the tales from eyewitnesses and victims of both sides. I listened good, too.

Old Dan'l Boone had crossed westward into Spanish-owned territory after a government survey had taken his 850 "Blue Lick" acres in Kentucky. In Missouri, Boone was granted nearly ten times that acreage by the Spanish and then lost it in the Louisiana Purchase deal. But his descendants pioneered along the lush valley.

Probably the first settler in my Boonville, or Boon's Lick, was an old lady called Aunt Hannah Cole. She built a log cabin with her own hands and settled down to grow up with the community. I was told that she feared neither Indian nor beast and very early taught folks to leave her alone, for she could lean out of her kitchen window with a rifle, whistle up a wild turkey and then shoot it through the eye so as not to spoil the white meat. That's shootin'.

The Santa Fe Trail begins at Boonville for two reasons. In the days of men with long rifles the Missouri was not navigable above that point, and it had the last salt lick on the long trail to Santa Fe. Cattle cannot live without salt, so the pioneers would bring their oxen that far and let them lick at the salt for a couple of weeks before starting the journey to the great Southwest.

The settlement also had a human salt lick, so to speak, called Cal Hager's Santa Fe Saloon, a small place on a bluff of the westward trail. It was the first and last chance worthy of the name. As I look back on this now legendary oasis on the hill above the river, it seems to me that I have never seen a neater, cleaner, more pleasant emporium of inner rejuvenation. Cal Hager was an immaculate and orderly man who would not tolerate minors in his place, though once you got your first pair of long pants it was not amiss to drop in on Christmas Day and sample the Tom and Jerry. I wonder if ever again this country will have conscientious and law-abiding saloonkeepers like Cal. He would no more have thought of serving a cheap or poisonous drink or one past the known capacity of the customer, or of breaking the law in any way, than he would have thought of trying to start a cross-country flight by flapping his stiff, clean apron.

Also located in Boonville was Col. Tom Johnston's Kemper Military School, which helped educate, among other notables, gum-chewing Will Rogers—who slept there nights when he couldn't get out of the dormitory windows.

One of the hazards of attending Boonville School in the early grades was encountering Bill Hoge who lived nearby. He won't remember me. I won't forget him and neither would that miserable fanatic, Adolf Hitler, if he were still alive. Bill's dad, Professor William H. Hoge, then superintendent of the Kemper School, had bought his son a mustard-colored cap from the Victor Clothing Store. Unhappily for me, my dad had done the same. Young Hoge resented another boy having the same kind of cap and threw mine into the street. Quick, if not strong and durable, I threw his after it. Then I did the best I knew. He did better. After that—well, it was quicker to go to school through Brockmeyer's Alley, anyway.

Football fans and Army folks will remember the Hoge brothers. Benny was captain of the West Point varsity of 1913 that also included a fellow with a twisted knee named Eisenhower, my old friend Coach Jack McEwan and a skinny mascot named Richards Vidmer, who later sank to the level of sports writing. Ben Hoge ran at left halfback in the historic first-meeting loss to Captain Knute Rockne's twelve men from Notre Dame, when forward passes from Dorais to Rockne, Dorais to Gushurst, Dorais to Pliska and others, rocked and shocked the Cadets, 35 to 13. But brother Bill helped sweeten the revenge a year later in 1914, when he played right halfback in the 20–7 defeat of the Irish.

It was Bill Hoge of the mustard-colored cap, a General thirty-odd years later, who moved his armored outfit fast enough to capture the Remagen Bridge while it was still usable, thereby shortening the Second World War on the Western Front. As a Cook's Tour correspondent in that war, I got to the Remagen Bridge while most of it stood, and immediately began a search for General Hoge. But I missed him, which was too bad, because I had a pretty good story in the back of my head about two kids who thought only of their mustard-colored caps. I wanted to find out if a many-starred general could remember what must have been one of his first fights.

We Boonville kids thought of little but the vital present.

Anything else seemed as foolish as worrying about next week's column with tomorrow's still to be written. When I wasn't hanging around the corner, I could have been located at the Jenkins' nursery picking berries for pocket money, or swimming and camping along the shore of a lazy, yellow, sluggish-looking stream with the strength of a giant and the mind of a woman. The Missouri never stays the same or behaves in the same fashion through two seasons; every few springs it can be counted on for one of those rises that sets old-timers to shaking their heads and saying, "T'ain't nothin' as high as 'twas in 'eighty-six!"

Or fishing. I pity anybody who doesn't know from experience the difference between a nice steel-blue catfish and a yellow-bellied mud cat. Taste tells you the difference. Knowledge came to me through attendance at catfish socials and festivals of the Abraham Lincoln Chapter of the Colored Ladies Aid of the Northern Baptist Church. There, thanks to the generosity and culinary magic of a gifted people, I learned about fried catfish and strawberry-shortcake eating.

There were—and still are—islands in the Missouri no more than overgrown sandbars. All we needed to satisfy another appetite was a flat-bottomed rowboat, a little nerve and a temporary loss of ethics. Big, long, dark green, red-hearted watermelons grew on those sandbars. They were guarded when ripe, but only by one man who couldn't be in two places. At least once a day he had to row himself over to town for a home-cooked meal or some eating tobacco, or to market part of his crop.

The best plan was to load the melons and whisk away, for the absent watchmen had a way of returning unexpectedly, and a big man could row a skiff faster than little men handicapped by anxiety and guilt. But a sucker can't wait. I recall once getting filled with the hearts of melon right to my Adam's apple, then loading the leaky old boat too full, with the result that it sank with us in the middle of the channel on the way back. The tough part of it was that the other kid, later a successful lawyer named Winters Martin, couldn't swim much.

Honesty is the best policy at all times. While Winters clung to the overturned boat, I managed to swim to the bank and tell the man who owned the patch that we had dropped by to purchase a few melons and, finding him away, had helped ourselves with the intention of coming by afterward and paying for them.

The slight weakness in my story was that neither of us had a dime when it came time to settle after the man had hauled Winters and the leaky skiff from the water. He wound up giving us a couple of melons apiece to take home. The Lord looks after His own.

One summer I worked in a Boonville pipe factory. My vacation job was to put the stem, which was made in the shape of a baseball bat, into the corncob bowl of pipes shaped and colored like a baseball. The pipe scarcely could have been called anything except "The Ty Cobb." Many years later, when I had caught up to little "Dusty Miller" of my first big-league baseball game, this summer of work came in handy. Manager Huggins was in his tiny cubicle off the New York Yankees' dressing room at the Stadium where the Ruths, Meusels, Hoyts, Dugans, Pipps and Pecks (Peckin-paugh) frolicked after their recurrent victories. Hug was smoking a corncob pipe, and I said, "I'll bet I can tell you where that pipe you're smoking was made."

He bridled, and snapped, "I'll bet you can't."

In those days virtually all corncob pipes were made in three small towns on the Missouri River: Washington, Pacific and Boonville. Hug had to lose.

As a child, what I hated to leave most was the happy land

of the little boy, and the people and events that formed the man.

The large, cool and lovely house where I was born belonged to my maternal grandmother, Julia (we called her Mimmy) Henderson. It is a fountain of memories to me, but I remember best the Sunday dinners. Mostly relatives came to those regular Sabbath gatherings. There were many, because Grandpa Jim Henderson reached Cooper County from Virginia as a small boy, and the Corums pioneered in Missouri long before that. So plenty of hungry folks showed up, but it was always open house.

Only once did that rule of hospitality fail, when the Civil War was in its last year. Mimmy, a bride recently arrived from Virginia, was alone in the house when at dawn one morning she heard the clatter of cavalry coming through the covered bridge near the house. With heart in her mouth, she jumped out of bed and sent a boy on the farm to see who was coming along the road. Quickly he reported back, "Feds, Miz Henderson, *Feds!*"

"Hide everything to eat!" Mimmy ordered. "I'll take care of them."

Presently the squadron of Missouri Federal cavalry, under command of Capt. Charles Leonard, cantered into the side yard. Captain Leonard was a wealthy man in our county and in later years his famed Ravenswood Farm was known nationally as a producer of Shorthorn cattle. Mimmy knew him and he knew her.

"Good morning, Mrs. Henderson," the Captain said. "It's a beautiful morning, isn't it? I trust we don't impose upon your hospitality, but we'd like breakfast."

"My goodness, Captain," said Mimmy, "but you have caught me at a bad time. I'm sorry. There just isn't a thing to eat on the place."

"But Mrs. Henderson," the Captain protested, "as we rode in we saw lots of cows and chickens."

"I'm sorry," repeated Mimmy, "but the cows are dry and the hens aren't laying."

Looking around at a yard busy with plump chickens, Captain Leonard's lips tightened and he said, "I'm sorry, too, Mrs. Henderson. But my men and I are going to come in and sit down in your dining room and we will stay until you serve us at least an omelet."

"Very well, Captain," said Grandmother.

Mimmy went out and took the eggs from under setting hens, although there were plenty of fresh ones. She made an omelet in which small, unhatched chicks were all but peeping, put her apron over her head, dashed into the dining room, plumped the savory dish in front of the Captain, and ran like hell for the milk cellar. There she locked herself in and stayed until the soldiers rode off.

Long after the war Grandmother and Captain Leonard attended the same church. It always seemed to me that when they bowed to each other in the name of the Lord across the aisle, the Captain invariably, and no doubt unconsciously, took out a pocket handkerchief and touched it to his nose. When this happened, as I sat next to my grandmother, she always seemed to smile faintly. Once a Rebel, always a Rebel.

By lucky chance, because it made me a comrade in arms of a wonderful bunch of fellows, I found my way into the 101st Infantry, 26th (Yankee) Division, in World War I. Back home after the war, it came as a shock, as well as a poignant laugh for me, to learn that my grandmother, then ninety and rapidly going blind though still stepping off a Virginia reel on occasion, had written in her own hand to Secretary of War Newton D. Baker, while I was gone:

Dear Sir—

Either get my grandson, Martene W. Corum, out of that damned Yankee Division, or I shall take the matter up with Dorsey W. Shackleford.

Julia Chamberlin Henderson

Mr. Shackleford was the long-time Missouri Representative from the Eighth Congressional District. Nevertheless, there appears to have been no reply from Secretary Baker. Perhaps our Mr. Shackleford didn't scare him.

Mimmy was a "Marse Robert" lady, who boasted that as a girl she had stroked the nose of the famed Traveler, General Lee's horse. As I have said, she remained an unreconstructed Rebel, loyal to the end.

Her Sunday dinner menu varied with the time of year, of course, but in summer we usually had fried chicken. The chickens weighed in, or out, to be more exact, for the dinner bell. Grandmother herself was clerk of the scales. She held the feeding crock under one arm, scattering the cracked corn or damp mash until she noted a young chicken that struck her as the right size. Then she would reach down, grab it with her free right hand and hold it against her chest while she felt the wishbone to see if it was fat enough. If so, she would make a deft twist of her wrist for each bird, until there were perhaps twenty fryers lying around her, each one plump and almost identical in weight. You don't see many frying chickens like that any more. Dressed until no tiniest pinfeather showed, cut into the proper number of pieces for frying—thirteen, no more or less—the meat would be salted and set away in the cool cellar overnight.

It wasn't chicken every Sunday at Mimmy's, it was real fried chicken when it was chicken. Two big platters along with the accompanying milk gravy, of course, sat on either end of the long table, for a crowd was always there. More chicken was fried in flour—not some silly sort of batter, mind—as the platters emptied. Because of the long table, everything was double-dished, like a two-ring circus, the same at both ends of the gastronomic arena. There were bowls of new potatoes and new peas, fresh from the garden, and creamed together. There were platters of corn on the cob—picked that morning—if it wasn't too early in the summer. If it was, then brian corn, which is a form of corn sauté, although it flatters all the corn sauté you ever ate.

There were bowls of green beans, cooked with ham hock or salt pork; creamed oyster plant (the square name is salsify); wilted lettuce with scallions and crisp radishes; pickled beets and piccalilli which is mostly chopped sweet and spicy tomatoes; chow-chow which is chopped everything with a sugary sauce; cottage cheese; three or four kinds of preserves and jellies, plus cold stewed apples, pears and peaches; three kinds of bread: hot biscuits, hot corn bread, and salt-rising bread baked the previous day; fresh churned butter; big sweating pitchers of cool milk; and pots of coffee strong enough to challenge Rocky Marciano.

For dessert there was fresh strawberry shortcake made on two layers of flaky biscuit crust, with the crust still warm and the ruby-red juice of the berries weeping down the sides, or homemade vanilla ice cream served with both white and dark cake.

No guest ever took as much as one bite of every dish, and even a little boy had sense enough to stick to his "special favorites." Nevertheless, there were some real good "doers" among the younger men, and they gave it a handsome try.

There was always plenty of each dish, and those who have lived in the farming sections of the Midwest, where you could get a meal comparable in quantity in a restaurant for twenty-five cents, know I am not exaggerating.

Some years later in Boonville, a man named Lon O'Neal

ran a restaurant and served similar meals for a quarter. Mr. O'Neal weighed 350 pounds, was sensitive on the subject of his size and had a temper as hot as the chili and tamales he warmed you with in winter. One day a traveling man came in, ate his fill, walked up to the desk to pay and asked the price. Lon told him a quarter.

"Mister," said the traveling salesman, "I was at the State Fair in Sedalia yesterday and I paid fifty cents to see the Fat Lady and you are much fatter than she is, and here I get a meal like I never had—"

"Midge," as we called the big man, reached around to a ham nearby, picked up the slicing knife and started hoisting himself over the counter. The traveling man took one terrified look, ran through the screen door without bothering to unlatch it, and went away from there.

Most of the relatives and friends who came to Mimmy's after church for those Sunday dinners arrived in buggies, surreys, spring wagons and even Studebaker frames with planks across the beds for seats. But there was one who always came horseback across the fields and even watching him at a distance, as he took the rail fence on his Morgan horse, you knew he was cavalry.

He was a trappy, pine-knot hard little man, the size of a compact welterweight fighter. What an Eddie Arcaro or Pete Bostwick he would have made, had be been a few pounds lighter, and how he would have loved the bright hue of racing silks and the bugle calling to the post! This was Uncle Lucien Chamberlin, who rode with J. E. B. Stuart in 'The Trouble," as he called it, the acknowledged horseman and judge of a horse in our family, all of whom had been brought up on horses.

When it came to horses, Lucien spoke the last word. Consider this bit of oft-repeated conversation among the relatives:

ALBERT (his brother): Reuben's a good horse, Lucien.

LUCIEN: Brother Albert, Reuben ain't worth a damn.

Which took care of Reuben, for the opinion got around and Albert had to sell him cheap.

When those tremendous dinners in the long dining room were over, Uncle Lucien would take his chair out under the honey locust tree in the side yard, and a little boy, his ears all but jiggling with excitement, would sit on the porch's lower step, listening to his stories of the war.

There was a strange sort of perfume in that yard. It wasn't from the locust blossoms or from the honeysuckle, or from the roses in the flower garden on the other side of the fence. These may have been a part of it, but they were not all of it. It was a faint kind of perfume of something that had been there once and was gone, which I think perhaps old, old houses have. Better than that, I can't describe it, but if I were in Timbuktu, blindfolded in the dead of night and caught that scent, I would say to myself, "I'm back in Mimmy's side yard again!"

Needless to say I have never smelled it since and never will again. Nor will I ever again see as clearly in the eye of the mind Stuart's gray troopers charging, as I did there, as the honey bees mumbled at the laden blossoms and the old man, sitting upright in his chair as though he still felt the movement of a horse beneath him, told me his tales of a fading glory that never quite had been.

There was one story about a farm boy from around Warrenton, Virginia, who, riding a little mule, captured a Federal Captain in the Buckland Races. Of course I didn't know that there really had been a somewhat comic engagement of Stuart's squadrons and Federal cavalry at Buckland on the Warrenton Road, so I almost let out a whoop of delight years later when reading about the Buckland Races in the third volume of *Lee's Lieutenants* by that splendid historian of the Confederacy, Douglas Southall Freeman. To me this seemed a vindication of all Uncle Lucien's stories, to which my elders had long since refused to listen.

I thank that old cavalryman of my boyhood for the tales that made me see the bonny blue flag with its stars and bars idling in the breeze of a bivouac, and that made me hear the sound of nickering horses, shuffling nervously on the picket line, or Sweeney and his banjo, softly plunking out "Oh, Susanna." He made me hear too, in the quiet, last weary hours of the hundred-mile night ride around McClellan's flank on the Chickahominy, the dragging shuffle of the hoofs, the protesting creak of leather, the mumbled curses of the troopers asleep in the saddle, when only Stuart, at the head of the column, still could flash a smile through his long, black beard in the rays of the rising sun.

A reason for Stuart's beard—he wasn't yet thirty then, and only eight years out of West Point—was that he was short on chin. As a Cadet this had earned him the nickname of "The Beaut"; later the adulation of the South changed the nickname to "Beauty" Stuart.

Historians seem to agree with Uncle Lucien that, trooper for trooper, when they had the mounts, there was no better cavalry than Jeb's. They did not last long, Jeb included, for he was killed almost a year before his dreams would have come to an end at Appomattox. When they wore their scarlet sashes and brass buttons against their smart, Richmond-tailored gray jackets, "our horsemen," as Uncle Lucien called them, must have made a bright, if brief, picture. Yet when the time came for action, they fought ahorseback, afoot, or rolling on the ground in silent and surprise night forays.

I was too young to think of how or why such family gatherings ended, but they did so, as families moved away and people died. Looking back, I can see the sun setting over Mimmy's side yard on my last visit. The peaceful country sounds of evening are beginning and a caressing coolness settles over the hot land. It is the last time I'll be at Mimmy's for those unforgettable dinners. I am almost nine, old enough to milk a quiet cow or drive a hayrake with a steady horse. Those carefree, small-boyhood days are behind me. Not too far before me, though their faint note is yet unheard, undreamed of, is the sound of bugles that are not echoes.

Mexican Hayride

Two things keep me from looking back as an angry young man—one the number of years I carry, the other a total lack of anger. I'm happily optimistic, maybe too much so, and I rather favor the fellow Wordsworth wrote about, the man "of cheerful yesterdays and confident tomorrows."

I learned a lesson in expecting too much the day that the last of the famed Jesse James gang visited Boonville as part of a circus and Wild West show. You can't imagine how much this meant to a Missouri kid early in this century. Jesse was born in Clay County, 100 miles or so upriver from Boonville, and his lurid career ended when he was shot down in nearby St. Joe only twelve years before I was born. I believed all the legends and the lies.

Frank James and Cole Younger, jail-free and reformed, led the approaching circus. Folks around our section used to say that Younger, a descendant of Aunt Hannah Cole, was the handiest of all with a gun, and that he'd planned the circus robbery when Jesse said to the man in the ticket wagon,

"What would you do if Jesse James came along here now?"
"Run like hell!" replied the man in the ticket wagon.
"Then get going!" Jesse ordered.

To us kids, these living symbols of such bold bravado were like Dewey coming home from Manila. I'll never forget my bitter disappointment when I finally saw them—two tired old guys in big black hats, riding a couple of bony, sleepy-looking piebald ponies and appearing about as dangerous as a couple of broken-down ex-prizefighters. What they might have been in the wild days of their reckless youth never occurred to our optimistic imaginations. It was a major let-down, but so was every hope that failed to materialize in those days.

As a teen-age debater on the "Ciceronians" of Boonville High School, I talked for posterity. The subjects were weighty and vital too. For example, my discourse one night in May, 1909, was on "Fishing." Thanks to some faded clippings forwarded by Mrs. Scott Wilson, of Kansas City, I can provide a firsthand press account of the time in 1912 when Floyd O'Rear and I debated the tar out of the Marshall School on "Resolved: That the recall of judges is undesirable." Said Mr. Van Cleve, one of the voters for us, "Their negative side was one of the strongest I have heard this year."

As a debater, I wanted to be heard, and almost was, all over the state. Once I debated in Sedalia for the Ciceronians and wound up in a draw with Schuyler Dauwalter, of the Atheneans. As in draw decisions in boxing today when the rounds are even, they figured up the points, and little Martene breezed through by 94⅔ per cent to 93⅔ per cent for Schuy.

Sedalia was a nearby metropolis and in my eyes always overflowed with newness and wonders. Among other things it was the site of the annual State Fair where I once saw a gaily painted horse-car de luxe, splashed with the name of some

St. Paul patent food concern, rolling up the Katy tracks. That afternoon they took the horse out, hitched him to a sulky and let him parade before an o-o-o-oh-h-ing crowd. Though only about my age, he was stiff and tired and horse-old. But he was the great Dan Patch (1:55), and I actually saw him pace a lap with the picture stride that time couldn't change.

There was the never-to-be-forgotten Sunday afternoon in the little town of Fayette, across the river in Howard County. A rival small-town ball team from Moberly expected easy pickings over a team composed of Boonville and Fayette players. We did have one hired hand, a pitcher who, to put it mildly, was a little drunk. Three different catchers were red-handed trying, and often failing, to hold the left-hander's stinging speed. It was no contest, no hits, no errors—except on the part of the Moberly team. The pitcher was the once-great of Connie Mack's Athletics, George Edward "Rube" Waddell.

These memorable sights as well as ushering at Stephens Opera House gave me the feeling of a cosmopolitan, which I have never been. The theater was operated by Alexander Hamilton Stephens, direct descendant of the Confederacy's Vice-President. The ushering was important, partly because I didn't have to sneak in any more to see the big shows. Don't laugh at the words "big shows"; they were the best from Broadway. Road companies, booked for successive weeks in St. Louis and Kansas City, found it difficult to close in St. Louis on Saturday night, make a slow 250-mile train trip across the state, and open in K.C. on Monday.

Mr. Stephens, therefore, could book them for Monday-night performances. So, as youngsters in our small town, we saw such stars and plays as the unforgettable Laurette Taylor in *Polly of the Circus*, George M. Cohan in *Forty-five Minutes from Broadway*, *Little Johnny Jones*, De Wolfe Hopper ($12 a seat!), Montgomery and Stone in *The Wizard of Oz*, Weber and Fields in *Hoity Toity*, Marguerite Clark, Willie Collier,

Blanche Bates, Velaska Suratt and others. The pay for ushering was small, but the fun was very big.

Parenthetically, it was an eye-opener to revisit the Opera
House in July of 1957 on the occasion of its Centennial as the
oldest theater still operating west of the Mississippi, and to
find stage facilities for scenery and productions comparable
to those of modern theaters. At that celebration I was dep-
utized as the principal speaker when former President Harry
S. Truman was unable to show up. I had nothing important to
say; after an introduction by Judge Roy Williams, I merely
recalled such things as once knowing the name of just about
every person who passed down Main Street and, in most
cases, the name of his horse and his dog. The Centennial
brought back that age when men in Boonville without a
dazzling collection of at least three barber-pole silk shirts and
two pairs of white flannel pants for the summer social season
seldom got to be guests of honor at the Japanese-lantern
lawn parties, where Lem Harris' three-piece string band
softly intoned "You're as Welcome as the Flowers in May"
back of the grape arbor.

Whatever naïveté I might have had disappeared with high
school. I had already signed up for a three-year hitch in the
Missouri National Guard and that and lesser considerations
influenced my decision to take a year of military school before
attending the University of Missouri at Columbia, 25 miles
downriver from Boonville. I could have entered Kemper,
which was just down the street from our house but Went-
worth Military Academy was a greener pasture at Lexington,
upriver 60 miles and distant enough to lend enchantment.

If military training were not more or less compulsory today,
I'd recommend the military school. It does more than prepare
you scholastically for college. No matter how much he protests, a growing boy, deep down, needs and secretly wants

leadership until he can feel the ground under his feet at all times. He gets it in a military camp or school, and he does not develop, as some people mistakenly believe, "the lust to shoot and kill." That's the by-product of actual war. Rather, he learns the value of consistency, routine and neatness, as well as respect for property, authority and degrees of rank fairly won and fairly awarded. What else is there to courtesy and good manners, or to a decent life?

As Guardsmen, we drilled regularly in Thespian Hall. We camped for a month in the summer at Nevada (pronounced Ne-vay-da) near the Kansas border. We learned and understood war conditions, and I was promoted to sergeant without much trouble.

The University was not difficult when I started in the fall of 1914, though I could have made it harder by aiming for higher grades. It didn't seem necessary because everything was meshing nicely—student life, social and fraternal (Sigma Nu) activities, a dash of the military, and an occasional foray into high finance with dice or cards.

My formal career in high finance began in the summer of 1916 through the courtesy of the Chippewa Bank in south St. Louis and a guarded recommendation from Uncle Crutch Corum. The bank paid a living wage, but failed to explain that it was for seven days of living, not three. When low in funds, which was usually, I ate lunch as guest of the Anheuser-Busch Brewing Company. The brewery, on Seventh Boulevard, a couple of blocks from the bank, conducted guided tours as a promotional stunt, much in the manner of today's trip through Radio City Music Hall, except that each tour of the brewery ended with a free lunch. Sightseers queued up and, when thirty or more had collected, walked through the vast plant. They always wound up in a cool rathskeller where sweating copper flagons of gold-colored brew were surrounded by mouth-watering cold cuts, wursts, smearcase,

pfufnagle, pickles, kraut pies and everything you've seen at a
German picnic or in a delicatessen window. It was easy to
join the line outside the rathskeller and enter, casually dis-
cussing the merits of the brewery.

For years now, no matter where I've seen him, the head of
the Anheuser-Busch Company, "Gussie" Busch, has insisted
that I tell him once more of how I used to line up with the
sightseers just in time to lunch at the rathskeller. He always
guffaws with a delight that puzzles me; had I known it was
that funny, I'd have enjoyed the free-loading more.

All this—banking career, big-city life and free-loading—was
ended suddenly by a Mexican bandit, drunk with imaginary
power. Pancho Villa was a black-bearded, grubby and strictly
minor-league Mexican bandit who had joined Carranza in a
successful overthrow of President Huerta. He failed misera-
bly when he tried to overthrow Carranza, who had been recognized by the United States government.

Being too clever and dirty for his own good, Pancho made
the mistake of raiding across the border, notably at Brownsville, Texas. You will not find the name of Brownsville on the
escutcheon of any American outfit's flag, I imagine, yet
history was made there. The "Fighting Jew," Sammy Dreben,
one of the most famous of American soldiers of fortune, was
in town on the night of the raid. Some soldiers of fortune
really sought fortunes, but Sammy and others like my friend,
Captain Irving O'Hay, an actor and Broadway soldier of
fortune, sought only to be where there was fighting. It
seemed to satisfy their craving for excitement.

O'Hay, who told me the story of Dreben at Brownsville
more than once in later years, said it best one night in his
back bedroom at the old Friars Club, as he looked over the
then low-roofed buildings at the electric signs around Times
Square. "This is the place the soldiers and sailors in faraway
places talk about and want to come to, or come back to," Cap

sighed. "But when a fellow like me gets here, he can stay only so long. Peace is a wonderful thing, I know, but God, ain't it dull!"

Brownsville was basically the reason for some 100,000 National Guardsmen, including Sergeant Corum, being in Texas under the command of a recently promoted Missourian, Brig. Gen. John J. Pershing. At Brownsville American troops fired a machine gun for the first time in anger. There probably was more than one such gun at Brownsville that night, but O'Hay always insisted that Dreben fought the one that worked. If the others jammed in inexperienced hands, it was not surprising, for the gun was the one that these first American machine gunners called "The Cranky Lady." It was a big, water-cooled Maxim, the "sewing machine of death," which in other hands—German—was to be the weapon that came so close to winning the world.

Several factors kept me from taking this Mexican interlude too seriously, and I had plenty of company. First, the hustle and preparation for a trip to the border was the same as getting ready for the usual maneuvers in Nevada, except that we carried a little more equipment. Secondly, we were going down to chase a bunch of bandits, not enemies with weapons. That they may have been much tougher than organized soldiers never occurred to me. Finally, I was well into the third year of my enlistment, and they wouldn't be able to keep me on the border after my term had finished.

With a little effort we made the whole trip, from the time we got on the train until we set up shop in Laredo, Texas, more of a lark than anything else. For reasons found only in the ego of youth, we resented the ideas of a weatherbeaten sergeant from the Regular Army being over us. Moreover, he was from Kansas City. We devised more ways of annoying that poor fellow than we did of chasing Pancho Villa (who, by the way, was never captured—just murdered seven years afterwards).

I came out of Texas some months later with two indelible memories. One was of a rain-soaked hurricane that blew down our tents, carried away some of the big platforms, soaked us and everything we owned and caused more trouble than if we had been ambushed by the bandits. The other memory was of helping to plague the sergeant—largely because my enlistment would soon be up—to such a degree that he turned me in for court-martial. I was properly shocked and subdued in the guardhouse, and my three stripes disappeared. I was Private Corum as I stood before one of the kindest and wisest military men I have ever known. He did no chewing out. I think he understood what was behind the ragging of the sergeant, a rough-speaking, hard-working guy from the ranks. This officer, a colonel, had a few words to say about silk-stocking soldiers, and some unforgettable words to say about the sergeant. "Anybody will die for his country," he said quietly, "but it's hard to find soldiers who are willing to live for it."

The colonel helped me to see the Kansas City sergeant as a courageous soldier who was determined to work and live for his army. I never forgot the words, or the colonel who had the wisdom to convey their deep meaning to a headstrong young fellow who, without realizing, needed the advice pretty badly.

Another Kind of Bugle

The fall semester at the University of Missouri was half over when I returned to Boonville in December, 1916. While awaiting the second term, I hired out my charms to merchants. I clerked for Albert Myer and Mark Jacobs and encouraged the sale of shoes at Victor's, urging the high insteppers to take bluchers, steering kids from scuffable bulldog toes to the unscuffable (and lower priced) Hard Knocks, and seeing that no lady left without a souvenir buttonhook.

After the late January inventory, I headed for the University and took a room in the big house of a distant relative, Mrs. Buckley, a widow with a son and a daughter and several empty bedrooms. She also boarded a very shy and proper girl student from Paris, Missouri, Mary Margaret McBride.

An accredited junior, I aimed at the unsuspecting newspaper world through the Walter Williams School of Journalism, then in its ninth year. It was the first of its kind, and though others may now be regarded as equal, it's still unique. Students were taught to plan, set up and produce a living newspaper. They still do; the University's *Missourian* is an afternoon paper that ranks with the best.

There was quite a lot of snobbery about the harvest from the journalism schools until graduates from Missouri began to take over. Aside from Mary Margaret McBride, Demaree Bess, Alice Hughes, Pete Brandt, Frank Martin, Jack Flynn, and Turner Catledge, all went to Missouri, not to mention that great newspaper artist, Burris Jenkins, Jr., whose only fault is that he turned down Sigma Nu for Phi Delt.

Study at college was as hard as a person wanted to make it, and the journalism work was a breeze. Unfortunately we had a campus military unit for the training of would-be officers. Drilling was compulsory and always came at the wrong time; besides, I'd done as much marching and eyes-righting as all the others combined. I think I went to a drill once, only to find them doing what we had learned the first summer in the Guard. It was a cold winter, and I resolved to attend regularly when and as the weather improved—provided, of course, that the drills were not too near sunrise.

Friday, April 6th, came before the good weather. On Saturday I packed and left that night to answer President Wilson's declaration of war on Germany. He had called out the National Guard and all able-bodied men. I was guilty on both counts.

Ninety days at Fort Riley, Kansas, was enough. It was more preparation than boys get under modern emergencies of war. After the 100-degree, wheat-baking Kansas heat, we were as ready as fresh bread, and on August 15 I was presented with a set of silver bars and a piece of paper, my only proof that I was a First Lieutenant.

"Casual officers," selected at random from six or eight training camps, were then hustled to New York City for early shipment overseas. Sight-seeing time was at a premium, so I checked into the Knickerbocker Hotel at Broadway and Forty-second Street, which was as close as I could get to Times Square.

Two things I remember about my brief stopover in the Knickerbocker. One was the fine bar and understanding bartender. The other was my first and only view of the great tenor, Enrico Caruso. I trailed him down the corridor, hoping to hear him hum at least an aria, but he didn't even whistle "O Sole Mio."

We were ordered to Governor's Island and shifted to a

hotel in Hoboken from which, one dark night, we were spirited aboard a small gray ship, with our destination sealed in an envelope. None of us on board had any outfit identification; we were part of a complete A.E.F. division to be assembled later in France. There we'd be given a choice between the Regular Army or being part of the National Guard. When the time came, I chose the Guard.

For an eternity, it seemed, we paced the deck and narrow companionways of our old British mail packet, *Orduna,* that squeaked as it wallowed through the heavy seas and fog. Actually it was only two weeks, which was also the length of the dice game in a little cubicle behind the boiler room. Play ended when somebody announced that land was off the port side. Lieutenant Corum reached the deck first, but not before picking up his substantial winnings from an unlucky Texan.

I don't know how Ireland looked to the other one hundred and fifty officers who made up our human cargo, but on that late September morning so long ago it was a sight I'll never forget—a truly Emerald Isle, like a shining green gem rising out of the darkness. Already a bright summer sun had chased away the fog and mist, leaving drops to sparkle on the green hillside of square little fields that seemed to climb away from the sea for protection. To a tight-lipped farm boy from the Midwest, really at sea for the first time, those fields looked like garden patches of lush Missouri bottom land. How easy it would be, was my first thought, to drive the cows home at night. At that early hour there weren't enough signs of life to spoil the stillness of the picture—just a curl of white smoke from a tiny cottage here and a man trudging through a field over there. The *Orduna* meandered along almost stealthily, so close to the shore line that it seemed possible to vault her railing and reach Ireland without wetting your feet. An illusion, of course, yet so near, so bright and so inviting was the land that there was a temptation to try it. After all, I had those eighty Texas dollars, enough to finance a brief Cook's Tour to the motherly security of those green fields.

But the land fell away at the *Orduna's* stern, and that evening I was in Liverpool, trying to eat what purported to be ham sandwiches, made with unqestionably the world's worst bread. It was called potato bread, and the heartless baker had dropped the poor little spuds into it, jackets and all, so that they came apart like cold marbles in your mouth when you took a bite.

Liverpool, Southampton, Le Havre . . . and soon the dawns were heralded by the stepped-up tempo of artillery, always after blood for breakfast, along the Chemin des Dames, in the Chesnay Woods, at Château-Thierry, Saint-Mihiel, Vigneulles, Wadonville, and the misty heights of the Meuse. With the brooding shadows of Verdun and Dead Man's Hill as a backdrop, shivering youngsters trembled not only from the cold and waited for what they prayed would be another day.

The dawn of November 11, 1918, was lighted more beautifully for us than any sunrise could ever be by the fires of burning German ammunition dumps and equipment that stretched away before us as far as the eye could see. Old Fritz had packed up and was going home. But do not ever believe that through four bitter, bloody years he had not been a soldier of the first class. Before I watched with swelling heart that November dawn and heard, louder than the guns, the deafening silence, I had seen more than I had come to see, and knew that whatever might befall me thereafter I would always be a lucky guy.

WAR

*". . . Valley of the Marne! . . . some of us
will not see you again . . . "*
Captain John Thomason,
U.S.M.C.

Age Is Not Years

Maturity wears many disguises, all strange and some unrecognizable though her appearance is inevitable. Meanwhile we ambled along gayly, by train from Le Havre to Valréas, near Vigneux in southern France. There we were taken under the wing of a friendly group of war-scarred Blue Devils to teach us the art of human destruction.

All wars produce good and great books, because men, even nonwriting men, are moved or shocked into self-expression. I've never read a book by those men who echoed what they had lived that wasn't good. I've relived flesh-crawling episodes with them, wept with them, and cheered the escapes that made possible their vivid recollections.

Because all of them did such a good job, I don't have even an unwritten book on the grisly subject. But I do have a few things to say. Hours, minutes, flashes of time that, I realize now, wore the mysterious cloak of maturity, taught me day by day, minute by minute, that one evening the soft and comforting goodnight will be unsaid and the child, as Robert Frost put it, "falls asleep with heartache."

Holidays in France

Next to turkey, the institution most associated with Thanksgiving Day is football. At home we think of Pennsylvania and Cornell, or Missouri and Kansas, but for our Thanksgiving Day in 1917 it was the Infantry *vs.* the Engineers, playing on a rock-strewn, goat-inhabited hillside at Neufchâteau with all the rugged intensity of a traditional college game.

The French had never seen football, or "crazee Americains" knocking each other around in the mud and snow. Maj. Frank Cavanaugh, coach of Boston College and father of nine little ones in the States, was the referee. The star, aided by the goats, was Ralph Donnelly, of Georgetown University, the first bare-legged football player I ever saw. He starred in ball-handling and scoring almost at will, as well as in his broken-field running among the displaced goats. Heads down, nannies and billys rushed in at intervals during the game, trying to reclaim their bare pasture. This amused the French peasants, who paused with their little wooden carts to laugh at the strange doings more than the bruising struggle.

An otherwise bare and bleak Christmas was made memorable by important news from the States. Until then we knew only that the Chicago White Sox had won the first game of the World Series, and the New York Giants the third. Now it was over; the clipping said that on October 15, the Sox had taken the sixth and final game. My seven weeks of wonder and worry were at an end.

Martyrs of Domremy

In the 101st Infantry, Father O'Connor said masses for the preponderance of Catholics, mostly from South Boston, led by the devout and understanding Col. Eddie Logan, for whom the Boston Airport would be named years later. Capt. Lyman Rollins held Presbyterian services, but there was no chaplain for other believers, including a Missouri boy brought up and immersed in the First Baptist Church of Boonville. This boy liked to remain in bed on Sundays; so did about twenty others who might as well have been heathens. At any rate, we were called that by Colonel Eddie.

"If those heathens think they can stay in bed while the others are at church, they're mistaken," he stormed. "They'll get up. Every Sunday. And they'll march to . . . to Domremy and back. And *march*. That's an order!"

The first trip to Domremy-la-Pucelle wasn't a great hardship, even though the round trip totaled 15 miles. We were used to hiking there and back again, so we marched to the village square, passing Joan of Arc's birthplace, turned and headed back to find the real punishment. Sunday was chicken day, and those pious churchgoers had eaten everything but a few scattered wings and scrawny necks.

Domremy lost its quaint, historic appeal on the second trip, and the third Sunday brought reflections on Joan of Arc's easy martyrdom. What's burning at the stake compared to starving on skimpy leftovers for Sunday dinner after 15 miles of marching? There is no telling how long this might have continued but for a casual remark to me by Father O'Connor. Hearing that I was a Missourian in a Massachusetts regiment, he observed good-naturedly that I seemed kind of little for a Middle Westerner. I said, "That's nothing, Father, I'm going to get smaller."

When I explained the Sunday hike and resulting hunger, he broke into the most undignified side-holding guffaws I have ever heard from a man of the cloth. The humor of our predicament blinded him, only temporarily, to be sure, to the starvation toward which we were headed.

Wiping the tears from his eyes, the good Father expressed doubt that Colonel Logan really meant it. He also promised to protest the punishment. We "heathens" compromised by attending services after that and I'm sure the others realized, as I did, what was behind Colonel Logan's indignation.

The quiet comfort of a church pew and service has a way of building a cushion against the certain travail of tomorrow. The Colonel, a smart and courageous man, knew that we would all need that cushion.

Makeshift Oasis

The town of Neufchâteau had turned over a wooden shack to the Army as a soldiers' club, and it was called the Lafayette Club in honor of the famed Escadrille. Big names came and went, leaving the initiates wide-eyed. Some paused, of course, and one that I never forgot was a thin fellow with sharp black eyes, a clipped mustache and a flying jacket. He came over to me very kindly one Saturday evening and bought a drink for a lone, lost soul in a strange place.

He introduced himself as Capt. Norman Hall. I was

thrilled to meet him; already a daredevil in the skies, he was then known as one of Kitchener's Old Contemptibles (the First Hundred Thousand). We never met again, except in print. Years later I had read *Pitcairn's Island* and *Mutiny on the Bounty* before I realized that the collaborator with Charlie Nordhoff was the same James Norman Hall who had been so gracious, and who was now doing more to popularize the South Seas than the sarong.

One cold evening a big black limousine pulled up before the club. A general got out to attend an officers' dinner in honor of Generals Pershing and Edwards. As the car drove off to park, I commiserated about the sergeant-chauffeur who had to wait out in the cold. "Would you like to meet him?" asked my companion. "He drives for Gen. Billy Mitchell. It's the auto racer, Sgt. Eddie Rickenbacker."

Who wouldn't want to meet the glamour boy of racing, the successor to Barney Oldfield? He had come out of the railroad flats of Columbus, Ohio, to create a stir on the Indianapolis Speedway. Only recently he had covered the 1-mile course at Providence, Rhode Island, in 45½ seconds, and the 2-mile dirt track at Sheepshead Bay, Brooklyn, in 1 minute and 5 seconds. Now, while he was chauffeuring a general, De Palma, Resta, Chevrolet and even Oldfield himself were cracking his marks back in the States.

We went over to meet him. I shook a chilled hand and wished aloud that he could go inside where it was warm. He shrugged it off. His face was thin, serious and young-old for a fellow in his midtwenties. The talk was small and there was little of it, because he was quiet and I was awed. With the good-by handshake, I wished him a "bon war" and left for the officers' dinner.

The chauffeuring sergeant was transferred shortly afterward to Issoudun, a plane center, as a top grease monkey, for he could take any engine apart and reassemble it without losing a purr. That was the birth of a legend. From then on, every move that Rickenbacker made was one for the book. He began flying those box kites we called planes in a day when merely returning from a mission was big news among the ground crew.

Down the street from the Club was the Hôtel d'Agriculture, where an occasional American war correspondent stopped that autumn. Three that I met there were Will Irwin, Irvin S. Cobb, and George Patullo, of *The Saturday Evening Post*. But one day in the lobby I forgot about these famed writers when I spied a pretty French girl who seemed as lonesome as I was. I asked her in English if she would come up to the Lafayette Club for a "sherree fleep." She replied excitedly, "*Jamais! Jamais!*" and then "*Jamais de la vie!*"

She hastened off, presumably to get her coat. I waited a long time, then returned to my billet where my French pocket dictionary explained everything except why I was so unattractive to the mademoiselle. Maybe she misunderstood "my French" and thought I had said "cheri fleep."

First Blood

On February 1 of each year I have a vivid recollection of a snowy path in a little wood stained with bright new blood.

Bois Marceau was just off the Chemin des Dames beside what were, by then, old trenches that ran from Belfort to the sea. Three Americans noncoms and I lived temporarily with the Sixth French Engineers in an elephant-hut encampment pitched on the right side of a hill in this wood. We were a reconnaissance group being moved by progressive

steps toward the war, and we were as safe as it was possible
to be.

The Engineers with whom we were billeted were enjoying a good war, except for the rats, bugs, the cold, and the
cloying smell of the dead and lightly buried of the great
offensives of the spring of 1915 and the autumn of 1916. It
was a dreary land. The endless bickering of artillery, now
near at hand, now farther away, echoed over the thousands
of men living underground around us. It was easy to imagine
yourself alone and lost in this desolation.

As we watched the snow flurries and restless gray clouds
of a typical February afternoon, the French captain of Engineers asked if we'd like to go out and watch the German
artillery fire over the sector. "But veree safe," he said in
his hit-or-miss English. He had been in the area for some
time and was proud of knowing just where the shells would
hit. The Boche, he explained, were stupid fellows. They
fired exactly the same number of shells that landed in the
same places each evening during the supper serenade.

When I was older, I learned that the Germans said the
same thing about the Frogs and the Limeys. A great army
in field gray lay out there not far away—methodical and
grooved in routine, perhaps, but top soldiers still for all
their losses. It was only the stagnation of trench warfare
that made the shelling predictable and, almost surely, just
as predictable going as coming.

We went along a path through the woods to the crest of
the hill. From an observation post we watched and heard
the shells fall—so many on the positions in the support line
ahead of us, then so many over our heads. The captain
counted the shells carefully and aloud in the trench where
we stood in the new snow, "Une, deux, trois, quat. . . ."
Then it was quiet in the gathering dusk, and he said, "See,
nothing to it. Nobody hurt. Silly fools, Germans."

We started back through the trench. Around the corner, lying across our path with most of his face shot away by a flying piece of shrapnel that had burst over our heads was a young French lieutenant. His almost headless body was still threshing in his blood on the snow as we reached him. Somebody had forgotten to tell him what a cinch it was to figure out an enemy on the wrong side of an 88-cannon. He did not belong to the captain's outfit, and I never heard his name. But each February 1st I remember him, my first sight of a human body torn asunder in the steady dripping bloodshed of a war.

Nor can I forget the graphic sight of the tremendous underground fortress called the Pantheon, part of what had been Fort Malmaison. Nobody was allowed in, but an officer let us look through the doorway. In capturing it from the Germans on the Aisne front, the French found an officers' mess with food from an unfinished meal still on the table. But when a French lieutenant went into the room and moved a chair, a bomb exploded and killed him. Suspecting the whole room was wired, the French put a sentry at the door and kept him there. They called the scene "the last supper."

Destiny's Acting Captain

To the French it was just another *mardi*, but to us of D Company, it was a special Tuesday, Lincoln's Birthday, 1918, and late that night it was made memorable as the outfit moved up into the front line and took over. This was it. A full company, two hundred and fifty foot soldiers from

South Boston and up the Cape, waited for trouble for the first time at Limey off the Chemin des Dames.

Some of them were younger than their captain (I was really a First Lieutenant, acting Captain, and a well-scared twenty-three). The little Poilus, going back, plodded wearily past us in the communications trench. With every forward step we took in the mud and drizzling rain, we tried a little harder not to think what an unlucky 13th might bring. As we slipped and fell and cursed under the overloaded packs (some of the kids had brought heart-shaped boxes of Valentine candy mailed from home), I could hear some of the "Southies" back of me saying "Hail Marys" in between their stumbles.

Finally we were in there at the end of the road. The last machine gun had been set up, the last sentry posted according to the instructions in French which, unhappily, I couldn't read. However, a French liaison officer who could speak a little English had been left with us.

We jumped every time a star shell rose in its lazy arc across the way and, as the night grew colder, the charged wire in front of the German positions spat and sparkled in the sleet and snow.

Never in the history of all the German armies were more troops massed against one place than they had against Limey that night. In retrospect, I imagine it might have been all of one platoon. Scared we were, deathly scared of the unexpected coming at us in the darkness, and none more thoroughly than the Captain who wasn't a captain. But we were there, ready, like all soldiers in all wars who walk to the cadence, or fly the airplanes, or steer the little ships and the big ones.

The German patrol and a few hand grenades came just before dawn. They stumbled into the wire at our left and found it rugged, but they killed one of us, wounded another and took the French liaison officer prisoner. When it was over, our D Company was no longer two hundred and fifty strong, and each of us began asking the question that real soldiers never say aloud, "Who's next?"

The ensuing weeks and months of marching and maneuvers brought a succession of high and low spots, none forgettable, because war is always a surprise whether you're walking or waiting. You're surprised when nothing happens, and astonished when it does, for it's invariably bad.

There was the attack at Seicheprey in April, a real shocker. German storm troops pulled a lightning raid and left the division with heavy losses of three hundred in prisoners, killed, wounded. But "Gatling Gun John" Parker's 102d Infantry bore the brunt. It could have been the end of our company now known as the "Dirty D"—if you smiled when you said it.

Other memories return. Aulnay, a sleepy village, where we rested in the heat along the Oise: bottle flies droned in place of the artillery, old ladies scrubbed clothes on their knees by the river, and in the gloaming the regimental band played the latest song hit from the States, "Just a Baby's Prayer at Twilight." We sang: "When lights are low . . . poor baby's years . . . are filled with tears. . . ." The band filled a few eyes with tears too.

Precision Instruments

They sent me back from the front lines at the end of June to a hospital in Nancy for respiratory examination. It was nothing serious, compared to the broken bodies that made the trip; in fact, I felt so strong after a couple of days that

I schemed and cajoled and finally got permission to rejoin my outfit by way of Paris. I might never get the chance again, and I wanted to spend Fourth of July in Paris. I watched our soldiers parade down the Champs Élysées and being in uniform, left the curb, fell in and marched until we reached the Hotel Crillon—where I fell out. The good things I'd heard about the famous bar proved to be true.

I was in Meaux, little more than a suburb of Paris, on the night of July 5th, trying to catch up with my outfit as it shifted to a new sector. The only sleeping room in the town was in an abandoned mansion with no lights but plenty of cobwebs and reconnoitering rats. But all hope of sleep ended with an explosion; a German squadron, returning from an egg-laying mission to Paris, had dropped a leftover "nuts and bolts." I got up and, reaching the street, heard people shouting, "Cinema! Cinema!"

It was well after midnight, but there was enough moonlight to see the utter futility of war. There wasn't much left of the empty little theater, or of the mother and her two girls who had been sleeping above it. All that were left of the little things that make a humble home were the twisted frame remaining from a kid's iron bedstead, some torn and bloody cloth, the remnants of what had been a movie projection machine to provide a bare living, some trinkets and pots and pans, a stove split in half, and a picture of papa in his uniform. I don't imagine the German boy who pulled that lever would have felt very proud of blowing such things to pieces.

The Germans had another implement of destruction raising havoc with Paris from many miles away. They called it "Big Bertha." I'd seen one of her occasional rounds splash into the Place de la Concorde with the noise of a million American firecrackers. Everybody rushed to the front windows and balconies of the Crillon in time to see people in the streets running first away from, and then toward, the spot where the shell had struck. Frankly, the size of the crater was disappointingly small.

It was only a matter of three or four weeks later, after the battle of Château-Thierry, that we learned the secret of Big Bertha's location. In a support movement, and quite by accident, we came upon the gigantic concrete emplacement that was far more impressive than what was no more than a long-range rifle that hurled a pip-squeak shell seventy five miles. Big Bertha was woefully inaccurate, and each barrel could stand only a few shots. The charge behind the cartridge was so powerful that the riflings were worn away by three or four firings.

Most memorable to me was a fresh grave not far from the emplacement, of a young, intrepid and really unschooled flier with the courage of his great father, an American President. The Germans had fenced off the spot with a square of barbed wire, and marked it with a cross of two scantlings and some green poplar branches. The crude inscription in English read: *Here lies on the field of honor, Lt. Quentin Roosevelt, Air Service U.S.A., killed in action, July, 1918.*

Triumph through Chemistry

I doubt that the warring nations on either side were proud of hurling gas at each other in World War I. In fact, had they known more about it they might not have used gas at all, for they didn't use it in World War II.

The Germans hurt the Canadians with clouds of it at Vimy in 1917, but they nearly destroyed themselves in a later attack when the direction of the wind changed and blew their poison doses back at them. The United States launched one hundred and fifty-two attacks with phosgene, chloropicrin and mustard between the Marne-Vesle operation and the Saint-Mihiel and Meuse-Argonne offenses. But we didn't have a coordinated Chemical Warfare Service until the end of June, 1918, only a month before our Dirty D Company walked into Croisette Woods, overlooking the River Marne and the fog-misted valley that spread beyond. There a thoroughly mousetrapped group of footsore fighters began breathing the colorless, crippling "old yellow,"—so-called from the shell identification.

Ordinarily the wind would have helped clear the gas-saturated hillside, but many days of rain and humid air had pushed it to the muddy ground, forcing it into gulleys and under leaves. There were no abandoned trenches or deep dugouts to clear and protect with gas curtains, and we found only water-logged foxholes and machine-gun pockets, each a well of trapped gas.

The woods had to be held, as part of a gigantic Allied offensive that extended along 25 miles of scarred country The burning and coughing began almost immediately and tragedy came too fast to be averted. Unable to dig fresh trenches or dugouts, the boys jumped for the meager cover, only to come up cursing and screaming from the gas, some burned so unbearably that clothes had to be stripped off and affected parts bathed. We rushed around with tin cups of boric acid solution to help the worst of them.

How I longed for the bed I had vacated in the Nancy Hospital. My chest was afire, my eyes and throat peppery hot. Scalding tears flowed freely. I wiped my eyes with the solution, knowing that if I retreated, the whole company would have an excuse to run back. We all stayed, some to regret it forever.

I'm always reminded of that horror by the thought of Alfred Gifford, the loyal orderly I lost, for soon he had to be shipped back. A Canadian, he spoke Montreal French and was long invaluable to his acting captain. "Giffy" stopped in to see me in New York long ago. He was on his way to an American Legion convention in California. Doing all right, he said, with a nice home, a camp in the country, a wife and two children. But gas had eaten away his eyesight.

"Life's all right," he said. "I'm not kicking. I can smile." He waited a long time and then added in a burst of confidence, "But the smile would come a lot easier, Bill, if I could see my kids smile back just once."

Ninth-inning Relief

There are no words or no writing skill to describe the prolonged, ear-splitting hells of Château-Thierry and Belleau and Croisette Woods. The sight of endless rubble—cathedrals, churches, homes, barns, human and animal dead, the wanton devastation of ripening fields and humbled forests—was overpowering. Between the chilling thoughts of self-preservation I used to think of this happening to Missouri, to the rolling hills of Speed, to the bluffs of Boonville and the paradise valleys below that hug the lazy river.

But imaginary horror was short-lived when reality took over in the form of mud-crawling and filth, trench foot from standing in winter water, the air heavy with mustard and burning cordite, the stink, the ever-gnawing lice, the tragic near-misses, the streaming blood, the moaning and the death of kids you wished with all your heart you could have saved.

Certainly there is no possible way to express our feelings at Fère-en-Tardenois, when the rain of death and destruction was heaviest, in seeing the blessed 42d Division at nightfall on July 25th.* Those angels of mercy who wore patches of rainbow on their shoulders were human rainbows of hope. They leapfrogged the weariest bunch of bedraggled warriors imaginable. We could only bow our throbbing heads in thanksgiving as they raced on ahead after the retreating enemy, leaving us to rest a bit before shoving off to another trouble sector in the grand offensive.

There may have been a larger and noisier birthday party but, until some old timer recalls it, the tumult that went with Gen. John J. Pershing's fifty-eighth anniversary will stand as a record. Historians call it "Reducing the Saint-Mihiel Salient," but to veterans of the 1st and 26th Divisions it will always be "The Old Man's Party."

It began for Company D at Grancey sur Ourcq on the hot afternoon of August 27th, twelve days after my double bars had come through. They had decided that I'd acted like a captain long enough. Hurried packing was followed by nights of marching in the rain and days of sleeping under a knifing downpour in deep woods and sheltered ravines.

The orders read "very secret." At night the gun mounts moving up brushed the doughboys' legs and the lead drivers swore blasphemously, demanding more of the right of way. They were veterans now, these men of the Yankee Division. You sensed it even in the darkness by the way they swung along, eating up the miles to an unknown destination.

We were five days and nights in the old front lines. Then we went over the top along Les Esparges Ridge and forward, driving deep into the salient as the day wore on. Promptly at

* *Editor's note:* M. W. Corum was twice cited for Acts of Gallantry during July 18–25, 1918; a third citation was ordered for an act near Belieu Bois, October 23–28, 1918.

1:00 A.M. of September 12th the sky screamed and spat yellow lightning, the earth rocked and the air grew thick with the acrid, smell of high explosive. American guns, set wheel to wheel, tore the night asunder. Pershing was preparing to cut his slice of cake.

It was about ten hours later that Captain McConnell of Company A, 101st Regiment, a Boston lawyer and a splendid soldier, sat with his back to a tree along the infamous Les Esparges Ridge which for four long years had defied attack. His own attack had gone smoothly, which he regarded merely as an extension of luck that had started a few nights before when he won practically all the battalion's money in a poker game.

"This one's the gravy train"—he laughed—"I'll give you fellows a chance to get your francs back in Metz tomorrow night."

We left him there with his Company which was moving on a different objective, and our Dirty D pushed on to the Bois du Something or Other. Ten minutes later a German shell dropped near the tree. They buried Captain McConnell near where he had sat and joked about his luck.

At midnight on the 12th of September the 102d Regiment, "Hiking Hiram" Baerss on horseback commanding, leapfrogged our 101st and at nine the following morning, Friday the 13th, near Vigneulles, met the advance guard of the 1st Division coming up from the south through Thiaucourt. The jaws of Pershing's pincers had clicked on his birthday. In the thumb-shaped salient behind them were 15,000 German prisoners, officers and men, and 450 enemy guns.

That night black coffee and hot stew came up in the dixies and far across the Valley of the Woëvre the Germans began their everlasting display of pyrotechnics. Red, white, blue and green went the rockets. "Here are again," they seemed to be saying. But the Battle of Saint-Mihiel was over.

Recipes for Glory

Travel a country road and you'll soon learn that the winter wind doesn't stop at the next turn. It merely changes direction. Maybe the reason for the unrelenting wind isn't quite clear, but you learn there is a reason. Thus we acquire greater understanding, we learn the meaning of endurance, and we tolerate. Through a war, the bright red blood of the living trickles away so that something, somewhere, will be better. You hope. You watch the living cease to be but you can never be casual and callous inside, just silently grim and thoughtful.

It is weird to know the last thought in a man's mind, to hear his last words and to be part of the exact and ultimate moment when his world ends like a light flashed by the touch of a switch.

Lt. George W. Foster, D Company, 101st Infantry, was young and gay, handsome and alive, with only a single unselfish wish: to know his native Vermont again. He wanted to taste the buckwheat cakes and first-run maple syrup that he often described to torture us during foodless days, and to see the general store he would own, like the one his folks operated, after he had married the girl who was waiting. He and I were in a pillbox on October 27 at Belieu Bois, within sight of Dead Man's Hill on the Meuse road to Verdun. He was firing a rifle over the top, grinning and hot with excitement. He turned and yelled, "We've got the . . . on the run!"

He turned back to aim again and there was a sudden ping. His tin hat must have gone 10 feet in the air. I yelled, "Duck!"

and did, and he fell back over my legs. When I twisted to say, "Geez, Georgie, that was close!" I saw a pink spot, no bigger than the tip of a finger just below his widow's peak, as though his forehead had been touched with the pointed end of a lipstick. A thin red stream trickled toward his nose. The eyes that had danced at the thought of the University of Vermont football team, the store he would own and the girl who wrote him so faithfully were like China marbles.

Three nights later when the 314th relieved us our favorite sergeant, the ice-cold and languid Frank Harris, stayed behind to dig a grave in the little gully behind the pillbox. He fashioned a homemade cross and hung Georgie's dog tag on it.

That day was made doubly memorable by the problem child of our Dirty D Company, Pfc. Michael J. Perkins. He knew enough to be a good sergeant, but he couldn't keep out of trouble. The poorest dress-parade soldier in the A.E.F., he shaved only on direct order and seldom shined his shoes. His leggings dragged and there was always evidence of breakfast, lunch *and* dinner on his blouse.

But Mickey was the best front-line fighter anywhere. When the advance of the 101st was held up in Belieu Bois by machine-gun and grenade fire that day, I was privileged to write this in citation for his Congressional Medal of Honor:

> He, voluntarily and alone, crawled to a German "pillbox" machine-gun emplacement, from which grenades were being thrown at his platoon. Awaiting his opportunity when the door was again opened and another grenade thrown, he threw a bomb inside, bursting the door open, and then drawing his trench knife, rushed into the emplacement. In a hand-to-hand struggle he killed or wounded several of the occupants and captured about 25 prisoners, at the same time silencing seven machine guns.

After the excitement had died a little, Mickey returned to the foxhole grinning, but holding his wrist from which blood was spurting like water from a garden hose. Sergeant Harris helped me put a tourniquet on it, and over Mickey's protests I ordered him back to the field hospital. I gave him his seldom-used razor, toothpaste and brush, and saw his head from the canvas-covered ambulance as it drove away.

Thanks to Private Perkins, we were able to move on. But he never reached the hospital. On the way back a shell fragment tore through the canvas and into Mickey's stout heart, ending his life on a note of gallantry that few heroes ever attain.

Beaumont was a badly scarred French village some 6 miles northeast of Verdun on the right bank of the Meuse River. Four days prior to November 11, 1918, it had been occupied by the First Battalion of the 101st Infantry. We had been in the front lines steadily for six weeks, since September 26 when the battalion had helped create a diversion on the Woëvre Plain to cover the opening of the Battle of the Argonne Forest on the other bank of the Meuse. Enemy shelling had hacked away at us until the battalion was now down to company strength, about two hundred and fifty men.

In the Skunk's Nest, which was just a hole a little bit deeper than the rest so that candles could be lit to read orders and give first aid to the wounded, there was a heavyhearted lieutenant colonel by the name of John C. Greenway. Yale men will remember him—he played end on the same team as Hinkey, caught Walter "Dutch" Carter, and rode with Roosevelt up San Juan Hill. Colonel Jack, however, was no more heavyhearted than the rest of us. We never knew the war waif's name; he was called only the Pigeon Boy. A little French shaver, sixteen or seventeen, he had joined Colonel Jack and all that was left of us in the Skunk's Nest about a week before and had refused to leave. In his blouse he had five pigeons. They were too gassed to fly or find food so the Pigeon Boy fed them, petted them and put them back in his blouse where they'd flop and bulge as he moved.

One by one they died. Nobody wanted him around with so much bloody business on hand, and Sergeant Murphy tried repeatedly to make him go back. But the Pigeon Boy said that he had his "orders." Nobody noticed him when the First went over at dawn on the 10th. Evidently he trudged along with us, his last pigeon stuck inside his blouse. The bird was still flapping wings stained by the blood of its host when they picked up the lifeless figure of the Pigeon Boy.

It was a strange dove of peace perhaps, but an order on a yellow piece of flimsy came down from the brigade at midnight.

Over and Out

An American plane flew over near twilight on the evening of November 10th and the occupants of the Skunk's Nest knew that something was wrong. Not, you understand, that there was anything wrong with the Allied air service, but all their squadrons were engaged on the other side of the river. Our troops hadn't seen a plane without a black cross on its belly in years. It was no wonder, then, that one doughboy was startled as he rolled over on his back and took a surreptitious peek at the ship flying low over his head. Grabbing his companion by the arm, he shouted, "Oh, my God, the Crillon's closed!"

The Crillon bar in Paris was where many of our aviators

attended ground school, and, in the minds of the infantry at that time, they came out only on rare occasions to get a look at the weather. All those animosities have since been dispelled. The doughboys learned that the fault was not with the fliers, but in a shortage of ships, and that many a fellow such as Rickenbacker, Hall, the Prince brothers and Lufberry flew crates that weren't really flyable. But it was a good crack under the circumstances, wasn't it?

It wasn't merely the fact that the flier was overhead that caused the boys to wonder. He was behaving peculiarly; leaning out of the ship, he waved and yelled in full view and fair shot of the Germans who, perversely, didn't fire so much as a round at him. A rumor started, running underground from foxhole to foxhole, as fire runs along a dynamite fuse, that an Armistice was on the way. And for the first and only time in the whole history of the war a rumor was to become a fact.

Col. Jack Greenway was a sick man that night, but a five-ton truck couldn't have dragged him from his command in that foul and fetid hole in the ground where the rats insisted on being fed first or fighting for it. However, the next morning when the last gun roared, Greenway got hold of a horse and rode back to Verdun, went from there to Chaumont to see Pershing, and was back in the United States in time to serve as an honorary pallbearer at Teddy Roosevelt's funeral.

Greenway's superior, Col. Horace Potts Hobbs, a West Pointer and a soldier, was at the Nest too, and when the last order came through it was addressed to him. It was a simple order, typed on flimsy paper, and it said only that hostilities would cease at 11 o'clock on the morning of November 11, 1918, and that the troops would remain where they were until further orders. It was signed "Foch," countersigned "Pershing" and it told the story, the happiest ever heard. When the order arrived, shortly after midnight, Hobbs issued his own instructions and returned to Beaumont—not to sleep, for nobody was sleeping that night, no matter how many nights he had been awake previously.

Dawn of the 11th found a heavy mist lying in the valley of the Meuse, and as far as the ear could tell the firing was about as usual. Three recruits marching through Beaumont with a replacement platoon forgot to duck at that sinister whine which is like nothing else in the world, and the war was over for them three hours too soon. They were laid out alongside the road under the same blanket, and all day long staff officers and aides-de-camp and war correspondents rode past them on souvenir-gathering visits to the front that had been.

By 11 o'clock the sun was trying to break through and the crew of a field piece of the 102d Field Artillery, in which Frank Cavanaugh, later coach of Fordham football, had served until badly wounded, was tying a long rope to the lanyard. At the end they hung a soiled, blood-red handkerchief, probably intended to represent the Flag. Then they took hold of the rope and waited. A young lieutenant of artillery raised his arm, then dropped it. A streak of yellow flame leaped from the muzzle of the gun. The young men who had yanked the rope sat down where they were, took off their shirts and started searching for something in the seams.

Fifteen minutes later men in heavy boots, strange little round caps, and dirty field-gray uniforms joined them, offering to trade Iron Crosses for tailor-made cigarettes.

POSTWAR

So fare thee well, wherever be,
Home is where the hat is.
                    Anonymous

The Kandy Kid

The French explorers who found the Ohio River named it La Belle Rivière, meaning water easy to look at. Not until I spent the winter of 1918–1919 on the French Riviera did I fully appreciate what they meant. Everything was easy on the eyes that winter and the shimmering blue of the Mediterranean easiest of all. It seemed to a war-sated soldier that the warming caress of the tantalizing sun had the touch of feminine tenderness. The sun, the moon and the stars were old friends rediscovered. They had a clean, crisp, brook-fresh quality that I had almost forgotten.

But it didn't take me long to exchange nightmarish memories for realistic social opportunities that enabled me to woo in my fashion an American beauty, and to meet a most remarkable athlete, Mlle. Suzanne Lenglen.

This was the period when I was the Kandy Kid of Nice, and never in my life did I have it so good. For openers during that brief interlude in which I lived the life of a gay Lothario, scattering bonbons along my primrose path, I was loaded with francs in the large wallpaper size. Never before, or since, have I had coin of the realm which I could treat as if it were confetti. (Instinctively that has been the way I always wanted to treat money, but somehow I could never get the money to treat it that way.) From the time our outfit had gone into the lines on Lincoln's Birthday of 1918, until the war ended nine months later, nobody had got a leave. That meant we had a lot of leave coming and I had due me a nest egg of four leaves, which came to eight weeks.

They moved the tattered old outfit with holes in its shoes and jackets that didn't match the pants into a little town close to General Pershing's Chaumont and said in effect: "Now boys, what's your pleasure?" There was a minor catch in this: if you had eight weeks' leave coming, you couldn't take them all at once. You had to come back at the end of every two weeks, answer a morning roll call, and possibly sign the payroll, which is the most attractive exercise ever devised by any army.

I took my first leave in December, headed for Nice and registered in the Negresco Hotel, where I had a room with a balcony of my own. The Negresco provided bath towels as long as a basketball player, and I sat swathed on my terrace at breakfast viewing the Mediterranean, a potentate wondering what the poor people in the United States were doing. To make my moment in the sun even brighter, I found that the bartender in the Negresco was the same one who had tended the mahogany in the Knickerbocker Hotel where I was billeted just before setting off for France an age ago. And what a sherry flip, which was the drink of the moment through that winter in Nice, that man could flip!

Part of being a great bartender is an infinite capacity for understanding the headaches and the heartaches of annoying clients. My own personal list, compiled with discriminating experience and taste, includes Big George, inventor of the South Side; Arthur, who stirs the Martini that sings at the Park Lane; Dick, of Shor's; Tony, a long-time friend at the Stork Club; the late Harry McElhone of the justly famous Harry's New York Bar on the Rue Daunou in Paris; and the famed six Flaherty brothers—count 'em, six—who operate the best long bar in this country in the Brown Hotel, Louisville.

The custodian of the Negresco bar was a key figure in my meeting Mlle. Lenglen, and through his good offices I managed an introduction to Miss Lillian, the Number One among the girls on the Riviera that winter. Daughter of a French doctor and an American lady, she had been born in Washington, D. C., and one of her attractions, although not the greatest of them by far, was that she spoke English. She was pretty as a Mediterranean morning and full of fun, a French-American flapper a few years ahead of the flapper era. At any given moment there were enough American army officers around Lillian to staff a regiment.

Almost every officer on leave was rich with accumulated back pay, but in addition to francs, I had candy, and candy was the pay-off. France had been sugar-starved for four long years and we Americans who had been among the first hundred thousand in the A.E.F. were by now suffering the same craving for sweets. One day at a tea dance in the hotel, I chanced to remember that I had some one-pound tins of Lowney's chocolate vanilla creams—the old beehive type, you may recall. I rushed to my room, got a box, carried it to the table and put it down in front of Lillian with some such brilliant remark as, "Sweets to the sweet, sweetheart!"

She took the top off, saw all those bonbons nestling inside, and it was love at first sight. Gosh, was she pretty, and gosh, could she eat candy! From then on life was just one sweet song of bonbons. Every two weeks I'd dash back to the outfit on the Paris-Marseilles Express, load up three or four English gas-mask covers with tins of candy and heigh-ho! the chocolate-drop soldier would be off to Nice and Candy Lil again.

When I wasn't trying to gaze into the soul-melting eyes of the Queen of the Riviera, while she in turn looked into the rapidly emptying tins of chocolates, I spent much of my time during those supernal days at Nice watching the tennis on the courts across from the Casino. I wasn't a tennis fan, but playing there was a blithe, gallic spirit with a bandeau, a different one every day around her glistening dark hair, who simply made you watch her. She was, to my mind, the greatest showman in action that I have ever seen in sports. Not even the great Walter Hagen on a golf course, or Babe Ruth or even Bill Tilden, no mean hand at the same game, could put on a show like this one.

When I mentioned to Lillian that this tennis player fascinated me, she was surprised enough to pause between chocolates and register astonishment that I hadn't recognized the athletic figure of Suzanne Lenglen, the world's greatest woman player. To confess my complete ignorance about tennis at that time, I hadn't even heard her name. But Lillian's mother graciously arranged a small cocktail party which enabled me to meet the great star of the courts, and thereafter we met a few times during the winter.

Journey's End

The 101st Infantry Regiment of the Yankee Division, Boston's Own, came home at dawn on Easter Sunday, April 6, 1919.

There are no words to describe the feelings of those of us who stood jammed against the deck railings when the gulls came out to meet us in Boston Harbor. We saw only the gulls at first. Then, indistinct in the early mists, there were blurred shapes of towers and buildings and finally, clear and unmistakable and fittingly, the Bunker Hill shaft reaching for the morning sky.

Then all hell broke loose, because suddenly there was a gray submarine chaser darting in and out and around our troop carriers with a lone figure standing at salute, palm turned out, in its crow's nest. It was the "Old Man," the picture soldier of them all, Gen. Clarence R. Edwards, coming out to meet his own again. Relieved before the war's end and sent home (age, they said), Edwards had been taken away from his boys. But they couldn't take his boys away from him. When the soldiers spotted him, standing there in salute to them, I thought we still would have to swim for it. The bands broke loose fore and aft on all decks. The stomping shook and shivered the big boats and the cheering was so frantic that some echo of it must still be there among the soaring gulls that wheel above Boston Harbor.

Never listen to talk about The Hub being a cold city. It is restrained and self-sufficient, beyond doubt, but when the right time comes The Old Lady in the Lavender Dress can swing and sway with the best of them. Every house, including those sedate, purple-windowed abodes on Beacon Hill and along Commonwealth Avenue had beckoning banners over their doors proclaiming *Welcome YD. Come in.*

Many an ancient butler's bones clicked shaking up cocktails, while hobnailed dancing shoes dented polished hardwood floors that had been petted with soft waxing cloths for hundreds of years. The old dowagers, however, were game.

That spring the uniform was a badge of admission to anywhere. I danced at the old Brunswick Hotel, whose orchestra featured Eddy Duchin, a slim young man from Cambridge who played the piano with a smile you couldn't forget. Some of us saw a show called *Sinbad* and heard a great voice, Al Jolson in blackface, sing "Swanee," the first song hit of a musical prodigy named George Gershwin.

During that Boston sojourn, by the way, I lost my first horse when they gave us infantry mounts to ride in a big parade. For a time we got along swimmingly, my horse and I. But it was a raw, cold day, and every time the parade got held up going around one of those sharp corners, or through the winding alleys, somebody would run out with a drink.

After one has ridden long enough and had enough to drink on a cold day, there arrives the inevitable moment when he would very much like to get off the horse. The parade was still going strong, with no evidence that it would ever stop, when that moment came for me. It must have been about two o'clock, I think the parade was already lost, and I know I was. Every minute it was getting colder. The shopping district through which we were parading was closed up tight in honor of the occasion, and folks were lined six deep all along the curbs. It was a very difficult situation, and much more difficult for me, because I was a stranger in a strange land. But finally through a break in the crowd I spied a tiny cleaning and pressing joint doing business as usual that was owned by a gent who didn't know the war was over, or didn't care.

I threw the reins over a fireplug and left the horse parked at the risk of a ticket. When I came out of the shop, the horse was gone and I have never seen him since. I have lost on many a horse—too many—but that's the only horse I ever lost. I took a taxi (and have been taking them ever since) back to my quarters.

After a few days of clinical fact-facing in Boston, I headed for Missouri, luckier than too many others. My oak leaves* had come through a month before we sailed, but the examining doctors in Boston said I was 10 per cent disabled. The gas had damaged my big brown eyes, though it wasn't known how progressive the damage would be. As soon as I settled anywhere, I was to report for further examination. I didn't argue; except for weeping easily, as do most victims of mustard gas, I felt fine.

* *Editor's note:* Appointed major of infantry on Feb. 22, 1919, at age 24, M. W. Corum was one of the youngest in the United States Army to hold that rank. In addition to three Silver Star citations, he was awarded the Purple Heart.

That summer was one of unanswered questions and indecision, of enthusiastic welcome, of Cooper County celebrations, of homage to those who had killed men in the war to end wars "to make the world safe for democracy." There was escape work in the Oklahoma oil fields and sweating toil in the wheat harvests from Texas to the Dakotas, tapered off with a refreshing trip to Arizona.

Col. Jack Greenway was in Bisbee, general manager of the Calumet and Arizona Mining Company. He had a dozen different plans for my future, all generous and undeserved. Since I had studied journalism, he would buy half interest in a newspaper which I could run and eventually own. No? Then I could go into mining—it was wide open, tremendous. A fortune could be made overnight. . . .

I felt I ought to complete what I had started in college and get some kind of degree. If that was what I wanted, Colonel Jack thought so too. But I shouldn't return to Missouri. I should go to New York. Didn't Columbia University have a pretty good School of Journalism?

In the meanwhile he turned over his gray Packard touring car to me for seeing the countryside. When it was time to shove off, he told me to drive the car leisurely to New York City and keep it. I said I wasn't going directly to New York, but would stop off in Missouri, and couldn't accept the car as a gift. He insisted that I take it anyway and turn it over to somebody in Missouri who might be driving back to Arizona or the Coast.

"And take this Major," he said. "You can use it in college." It was his personal check, made out to me for $10,000.

Words under those circumstances don't come easily, and sometimes not at all. I looked from the check to his kindly, sun-tanned face and the mustard gas seemed to affect my eyes. I put the check on his desk and explained that the least of my worries was money. My uncle had banked $5000 to my credit when I left for Europe, and I had sent most of my army pay to my father for deposit in my account. I had close to $15,000 salted away. Besides, the government would pay my college tuition and books, and I had been awarded a monthly disability allotment. How could I possibly take his money?

Greenway was happy, of course, to know that I had no financial worries, and he knew that I was grateful beyond words. But he didn't give up. Some time later he sent me one thousand negotiable shares of a brand new mining venture, Ahumada Lead Company, with orders to hold on to them unless I needed money.

I put the certificate where it was safe and forgotten. A few years later I found it while cleaning out my desk and turned it over to a broker friend for safe keeping. I forgot about the shares again until somebody, seeing my name on the Ahumada stock books, advised me to dust them off as they had become valuable. I got in touch with my broker friend, who stalled and finally confessed that he had been hard pressed financially and sold them. He promised to make good, but he never did. I later learned that the one thousand shares were then worth $36,000.

The Gem of Columbia

Traveling eastward by way of Boonville, my race to reach New York City ahead of registration day ended only in a tie, but they accepted me at the Columbia School of Journalism. I took a room at the Sigma Nu Fraternity on West 113th Street, and settled down to giving the old college try for one of the biggest and best of them.

Our campus was a one-block street, 116th, extending from Broadway to Amsterdam Avenue. Nestled among a group of brick and gray-stone buildings was South Field, a two-acre patch of ground where baseball, big football games and track meets were held before banker George Baker donated acres of elbow room at the northern tip of Manhattan overlooking the Hudson River. I was only a five-cent, fifteen-minute sub- way ride down Broadway from Times Square and all that it represented then. It was, a few nostalgics may remember, the locale of some pretty good emporiums of food and entertain- ment—Shanley's, Considine's, Reisenweber's, Churchill's, Rec- tor's, the Palais Royal with Paul Whiteman and The Little Club—far more than you could sample in a single evening.

Before getting around to this chore, I began reporting, as ordered by the Boston doctors, to Veterans Administration headquarters near the Battery for health and eye checks. The disability allowance was neither substantial nor important to me, for I was well-heeled. I don't recall the amount involved, but I do remember standing once before a swarthy medical major, who sat in a swivel chair with his feet on the desk. He looked up, squinted behind spectacles, appraised my civilian suit, and asked me what I wanted. I said I was reporting for a medical check-up on a disability allowance.

"Well," he said, "there doesn't seem to be very much wrong with you."

At that moment, I thought less of myself than of our Yankee Division physical wrecks who were caning their way through a darkened world, hobbling into clinics on crutches or propelling wheelchairs. Did I have to undergo this kind of monthly reception for a few paltry dollars?

"Listen, mister," I said, pointing to his shoulders, "when I wore those oak leaves, they meant something. You and the government can keep the money."

I heard his chair squeak and his feet hit the floor, but I was already on my way out. I never went back. Nor did I ever collect any more disability allowance, which was fine, because my eyes never got "progressively worse" as I had been told they might.

Journalism school at Missouri had stressed the mechanics of news production and plant operation. Columbia University majored in story assignment, interpretation, writing and editing. Each system has its merits and I had the benefit of both. When the school year ended in June, I got a job with a small advertising agency for the summer. That vacation was highlighted by a lucky break. I saw an unforgettable horse run the greatest of races.

Horses were part of our family background, and of mine from the first time I saw the trotters and the pacers at the Cooper County Fair in Bunceton. They made me jiggle with excitement. I can still hear the crunch of harness, the pounding hoofs and the whir of the rubber-tired sulky wheels, and the screaming of happy people, and can smell the perfume of horse and leather.

The sports pages had talked about the race all week and some ventured to say that Man o' War, unbeaten as a three-year-old, *might* be taken this time. My office was on 34th Street, not far from Penn Station, and I joined the 25,000 who paid their way into Aqueduct Race Track on July 10, 1920, to see the Dwyer Stakes, at a mile and an eighth, worth $4,850 to the winner. The first look at Man o' War gave me an unforgettable picture, for in the sun his coat was a striking gold color. He had a white star between his eyes and he was barrel-chested big to eyes that had seen and known horses.

There was talk that the only other entry in the race, Harry Payne Whitney's John P. Grier, had been trained to hairline perfection for this meeting, and that Man o' War was not sharp. The bettors thought otherwise. They made Big Red with 126 pounds a 1-to-5 favorite at post time; the Whitney horse, under only 108 pounds, was 7-to-2.

From the good start, with Man o' War on the rail, it was the noisiest horse race I've ever experienced. Everybody had something to shout as the pair ran almost as a team, with Big Red always a bit in front. When Grier held on, the 25,000 voices built in volume until mass suspicion became a fact at the eighth pole. Man o' War defeated Grier's first attempt to pass him at the end of the backstretch. But a drive at the head of the stretch succeeded and that was when the voices really gave out with groans, moans, stamping, screaming and actual crying, because nobody wanted to see the great Man o' War beaten.

Frankly, my view was blocked a little by the moving people, but I managed to see the miracle horse do it. In later years the jockey, Clarence Kummer, verified the pulsating moment: "John P. Grier had a head in front for an instant at the eighth pole, but I whipped that beautiful rump just once, and it was all over. It was a great race, and a good fast fight. Something had to crack after such a race. Maybe I hurt Big Red's pride more than his flank, but he sure pulled away and he was still full of run at the finish."

Full of run, yes, but no daylight showed between the two until a few yards before the finish. Man o' War had run more than a length faster than Grier in the last furlong, and set a new world's record of 1:49⅕. The incredible speed of the race can be gauged by the fact that Man o' War was clocked at the six-furlong pole in 1:09⅖, a record, and Grier, a nose in front at the mile, in 1:35⅗, another record.

John P. Grier tried again a month later in the Travers at a mile and a quarter and couldn't finish second with a fourteen-pound pull in weights. Man o' War, packing 129 pounds, ripped off the distance in 2:01⅘ and beat Upset, the Whitney horse that had defeated him as a two-year-old in his only set-back.

At the end of that year Big Red was a record-setting legend, but I had seen him at his greatest. In the years to come, it was my privilege to visit Kentucky regularly, and a further privilege to visit the peaceful Faraway Farm where this golden boy grew old with pride and dignity. He made you feel inferior when you stood at the stable door with the faithful Robert Harburt, the groom who attended his wants until the end.

After resuming school that year, I paid to see another classic which was not quite so memorable. It was the opening game of the World Series at Ebbets Field, and Cleveland won. The next year I began getting in free, but I'd have paid to see many of them—after it was over, that is—had they demanded cash at the gate. However, I do want it recorded that Corum walked up to the box office and laid it on the line to see his first World Series game.

NEWSPAPER DAZE

No evil can happen to a good man,
either in life or after death.

Socrates

Product of the Times

February of 1921 brought me a Bachelor of Literature degree from Columbia to go with my Bachelor of Arts scroll in Arts and Sciences from Missouri. The written proof was good to see, but a more material reward came from Robert W. Watt, my roommate in Livingston Hall and graduate manager of athletics at Columbia.

Bob was an ideal roommate because we were both sports fans and because he knew people in the field. Jim Harrison, of the New York *Times* sports staff, said one day, "We need a copyreader on the paper. Know of any fellow who could handle the job?"

"I'm rooming with a guy named Corum in the School of Journalism," Bob replied. "He comes in at all hours and you'd do me great favor if you'd get him a steady night job so I could get a little sleep."

That night Watt asked me, "Can you read copy?"

"Read copy! Are you kidding? Don't you realize that you are talking to a *journalist* who has attended two schools of journalism, here and in Missouri? To me, reading copy is just like brushing cigarette ashes off my coat. A breeze, boy, just a breeze."

I got the job.

On the first night that I sat down at the copy desk of the sports department of the *Times*, Capain Bernard Thomson, the sports editor, looked me over and gave me what I can only describe as a Harvard shrug. Captain T. was a Harvard man, but he wasn't scaring me even if Columbia wasn't on Harvard's football schedule at the time. I had two dozen pencils sharpened and was sitting there keen and ready.

An old pro was sitting in "the slot," a nice little man named Jack Knox, who was to wind up one night as a "fell or jumped" case in the Chicago River. He was a good enough newspaper man to get any job, but his addiction made it impossible for him to hold one. But he was a pro, a gentleman for sure and a kindly man. Though he didn't leave much when he went the wrong way he left at least one friend.

Knox tossed over to me a rousing four-line story on a college-freshman golf tournament. Until then I'd never seen a golf ball (the caddy kicks the ball and everybody else tells lies —that's the way it goes, isn't it?), so I didn't have to puzzle over the story for more than an hour or two before I had completely digested it and hit on a perfect headline. Nonchalantly, I tossed it back to Knox and pulled my green eyeshade to a jauntier angle. The headline read: VAN GERBIG WINS ON LYNX.

I am happy to say that both the *Times* and I survived that earliest effort. For the next few weeks I wasn't exactly a first-class hindrance but I wouldn't have told them what I didn't know under any circumstances. Time alone prevented that. But I was eager and friendly and after a while mastered the art of C-heads and punctuating agate.

There are times, of course, when talent begs for appreciation, and you can be sure it happened to me. In learning the rules of copyreading, I was especially aware of those inelastic regulations for style. I knew that Irvin S. Cobb was a good writer and reporter, but he violated grossly an unbreakable rule of the *Times*. Cobb had been taken on to write about the forthcoming Dempsey-Carpentier fight for the heavyweight championship at Jersey City. Big by-lines had a vogue even then. I believe the morning *World* employed the esteemed H. L. Mencken, of Baltimore, as literary *tour de force* for the same event. At any rate, it took me some time to prune out all the egomaniacal capital "I's" from Cobb's otherwise colorful copy. A horrified Jack Knox had them put back; he explained that, after all, there *were* exceptions to rules, even on the *Times*.

Beginning with Marquette and Jolliet and followed by the Marquis de Lafayette, many distinguished French people have visited America. Two at the top of my field came over from France during that first summer on the *Times*—the aforementioned Georges Carpentier, and Mlle. Suzanne Lenglen of Riviera recollections.

Fortunately word somehow leaked out that I knew the French tennis star. Captain Thomson picked up the gossip and assigned me to cover Mlle. Lenglen's arrival in this country to compete in the United States championships and to make an exhibition tour for the Devastated France Benefit Fund. Three or four city reporters from the *Times* went down the bay in August, 1921, to meet one woman tennis player; that was typical coverage on that great newspaper in my day. Moreover, the paper had bought New York publishing rights to the syndicated articles she was to write about her tour.

Although I was grass green—three months of sports copyreading comprised the total of my newspaper experience—I had a feeling of confidence that morning on the cutter churning down the bay to meet the boat. Knowing Suzanne, her speech, actions and personality was a secret weapon. It might even help me write a story that would pass muster for a very tough sports page.

But when I woke up Sunday morning, my piece was right

smack in the center of page one! It was unsigned, because the *Times* did not run staffers' by-lines then, but, glory, glory, hallelujah! What a great day in the morning! Quite naturally it was the greatest story ever printed in a newspaper. So I felt *after* I had seen it. While writing, you not only never know but you often nurse a secret fear that it is the worst, and your only hope is that editors and copyreaders won't be smart enough to detect its rank inferiority.

Even now, as I re-read that lead, after almost forty years and a number of front-page stories with my name over them in big, black headlines, the piece still seems pretty good:

> In the meeting and manner of Mlle. Suzanne Lenglen is the sparkle that is France. Those who saw her trip down the gangplank of the *Paris* on her arrival in New York harbor yesterday discovered it in the sharp angle of her big red hat, her red-heel pumps, her buoyant bearing and her smile.
>
> Seeing her then, those who had come to greet her caught some of the same spirit that has caused an American crowd to cheer for Carpentier at Jersey City on July 2. For some of those at the pier, memory went back even further, and they saw again a thin line of horizon blue as it charged the crest of a hill at dawn, sweeping everything before it.
>
> Mlle. Lenglen is here, by her own admission, to prove that all of France's victories, even on the athletic field, are not moral victories, but victories of fact. . . .

Because of this story, I seemed to be headed for a career of covering tennis. At least, I began it a day or so later, when Mlle. Lenglen, following a 24-hour postponement, was forced into a dramatic default to Molla Bjurstedt Mallory after losing the first set, 6–2, in her first round in the women's national championships at Forest Hills. She had caught cold on the boat coming over, and never regained her full strength.

Her withdrawal upset the tournament and, more important, the exhibition tour which, I suspect, I might have been assigned to trail.

I did cover a few tennis tournaments after that, pending Mlle. Lenglen's decision to start the tour, which was delayed for a few weeks. My marking time was done first at the Apawamis Club in Rye, New York, where home-towner Vincent Richards drubbed two little Japanese players, Zenzo Shimizu and Ichiya Kumagae, or "Shimmie" and "Jimmie," as I called them everywhere but in the *Times*. I accused Richards, with whom I became fast friends, of luring little fellows up there so he could beat somebody his size before the home folks.

Certainly the popular ex-child prodigy didn't want his nemesis, Bill Tilden, up there. Francis Albertanti, sports writer on the old *Evening Mail*, and a familiar figure in boxing years later, always insisted to Richards that the *Mail* employed a novel time-saving device in the form of a stock headline kept in type from year to year: TILDEN BEATS RICHARDS AGAIN.

"Saves the copyreaders and the composing room a lot of work," Francis needled with a chuckle.

Richards, who always found laughing easy under any conditions, would join in the humor, knowing that the record spoke louder than any protest he could make. In his last year as an amateur (1926) he was the only American in the semifinals of the United States singles championships with the great Frenchmen La Coste, the winner, Borotra and Cochet. Vinnie had beaten Tilden repeatedly that year and had earned top ranking for the first and only time in his brilliant career. Yet he was cruelly denied the coveted distinction by the ruling tennis body solely because he made no secret of his plan to turn professional that winter. Tilden was again ranked first, Richards not at all.

Mlle. Lenglen brought my tennis writing career to a somewhat abrupt close by announcing, finally, that she could not tour. I was saved by La Belle, you might say. But I'll always remember her as one of the five best tennis players of my time. The others were that artist of the courts, Tilden; the resourceful Richards; the girl Ed Sullivan named Little Poker Face (a subject on which he has been proved an authority); Helen Wills; and as a doubles player, the handsome Frank Hunter.

The first year of newspaper success must have gone to my head and come out my mouth, because this delightful girl I'd met at Columbia University, Elaine Kolle, said yes, she certainly would marry me. And why not? My salary at the *Times* was $40 a week and I earned almost that much more by writing stories at $8 a column.

Elaine's father, Frederick Strange Kolle, was a brilliant surgeon; Mrs. Kolle was a linguist and writer, as was Dr. Kolle between operations. They didn't object to the marriage, but I don't think they could have stopped us even if they had. Anyway, we were married within a year on September 1, 1922, and sailed for Bermuda. Except for one incident, it was an ideal honeymoon. Elaine suffered a bicycling accident, was thrown over the handle bars and hospitalized with severe internal injuries. But we returned with hopes as high as when we left, and set up domestic shop not far from the Columbia campus where we'd met.

A Man to Remember

The good fortune that has so often pursued me took charge at the start of my newspaper career. I worked under the first of two great managing editors it has been my privilege to serve. He was Carr V. Van Anda, born in Ohio in 1864 and now a legend and symbol in the history of the New York *Times*. He set a standard and pace that all morning newspaper publishers followed and few, if any, equaled.

Mr. Van Anda was a brilliant individual who reflected that luster in his life's work. When I first met him, he was in his midfifties, a quiet and thoughtful gentleman with eyes that stared, and sometimes glared, from an angular and rather ascetic face. He was a lifelong student, and an unusual scholar. With only two years of college, he was an outstanding mathematician, scientist, lexicographer and walking encyclopedia. What he could have done on those television quiz shows of bygone popularity and cash!

To illustrate, when the *Times* bought publication rights to the opening of King Tutankhamen's ancient Egyptian tomb in 1922, V.A., as he was always called, had no available authority on the subject. Being an inveterate reader of dictionaries and encyclopedias, he researched and quickly mastered a telescoped course in Egyptology. When the exhibits and pictures reached America a few months later, he could read and interpret heiroglyphics on the cartouches taken from the young ruler's tomb. In fact, he called attention to an error in the British Museum's genealogy of King Tut. The Museum acknowledged the correction and incorporated his findings into its records with thanks.

Van Anda was pre-eminent in setting the pace for news breaks, I was told when I first went to work on the *Times*. One of his biggest beats came in his first year on the paper when he got to the streets ahead of competitors with Admiral Togo's victory over the Russian fleet at Tsushima. The news broke at 5:00 A.M., but despite the late hour he got out forty thousand extras and then rode the delivery wagons to key distribution points.

Van Anda was the only editor in town who, on April 15, 1912, took seriously a cryptic wireless message at 1:20 A.M.

It came from Cape Race, Newfoundland, and read: STRUCK ICEBERG C Q D. Other editors believed advance notices that the brand new *Titanic* was unsinkable. "Perhaps it is," said V.A., hoping it was. Nevertheless, he assigned four men to do four different stories on the subject of transatlantic ships and sinkings, and printed the wireless message and all the horrible possibilities in the *Times*. The town was shocked. So were rival editors. They were even more shocked when the *Carpathia* reached New York next day with the stunned survivors and the ghastly details of 1,517 lives lost. The *Times* pioneered in news by wireless after that.

V.A. was a student of race horses and of betting. My first big racing assignment was In Memoriam's victory over the 1923 Kentucky Derby winner, Zev, in the Latonia Championship at Covington, Kentucky, in the fall of 1923. The race was over a mile and three-quarters, a half mile longer than the Derby. Van Anda sent for me after I'd returned from Kentucky. He always seemed to like me, possibly because I frequently brought him good news as his confidential betting commissioner at the New York tracks. On this occasion, he said, "That was a good story you wrote, young man, on In Memoriam beating Zev." I beamed and he added, "But you left out Magee."

I looked at him blankly, having no idea who Magee was. He explained that this English horse had sired two good distance horses, both Kentucky Derby winners, Donerail of 1913 and Exterminator of 1918. He added, with a twinkle, that they were also winners at very high odds. And Magee blood was part of In Memoriam. This detail was an indication of his thorough mind and total recall.

V.A. was a quiet and modest horse player until he left the *Times* for a well-earned rest. Joe Vila, sports columnist of the old *Sun*, once told me that long before my time when the horse players were coming across the Brooklyn Bridge on the

Bill Corum *(right)* as a ten-year-old Hal Chase

The Boonville High School debater

Crutchfield Drum Corum,
"Uncle Crutch"

At the Border near Laredo in 1916

Lieutenant Corum *(left)* in France with other officers of his regiment

Major Corum, with a short-lived mustache, sitting for a formal photograph of D-Company

Captain Eddie Rickenbacker

Carr Van Anda

Arthur Brisbane

July 4, 1923, a few minutes before the Dempsey-Gibbons fight in Shelby, Montana

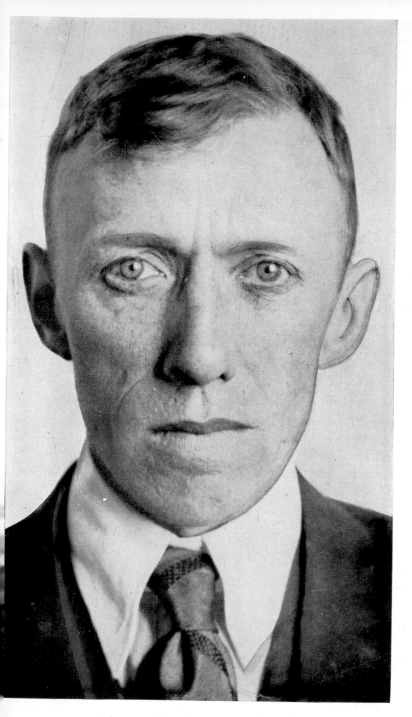

Thomas Aloysius Dorgan, "Tad"

Damon Runyon's wedding reception in 1932. Mayor Jimmy Walker married the couple in Ed Frayne's apartment. The host is third from the left, Corum next to him. Fight managers Jimmy Johnston and Jimmy Bronson stand behind Runyon, Hype Igoe behind the bride. Jack Kearns towers in the background and Bugs Baer is at extreme right.

streetcar called the Bridge Jumpers Special, for obvious reasons after some longshot had upset the last race, Van Anda, then also with the *Sun,* would pipe up more often than not and say, "I had him!" This did not surprise me because on the occasions when I handled his cash-and-carry bets in deepest confidence, he won more than he lost. It is a good trick if you can do it, and I have lost enough on the horses to know.

Unforgettable in this respect was the first of three International races in America featuring M. Pierre Wertheimer's Epinard. The name means spinach, but he was all horse flesh on the race track. When he reached America as a four-year-old, he had finished worse than second only once. He failed to win any of the three International races at varying distances, but he was never disgraced in spite of many disadvantages. It was a summer of little rain and his jockey, Everett Haynes, told me many years later that the horse had shelly and brittle feet and never got a track that suited him in this country.

The owner had been a luncheon guest of the top brass at the New York *Times* during the week. On Sunday before Labor Day, 1924, when the race was scheduled, Mr. Van Anda called me over to his desk, repeated much of what Mr. Wertheimer had told them about his great horse and suggested quite rightly that it might help me in writing about the race. Then he said, "But I'm not going to bet on Epinard." He pulled two $100 bills from his wallet. "You bet this on a horse called Wise Counsellor."

It was one of the greatest days Belmont Park has ever seen. More than sixty thousand people jammed the beautiful place, including the Prince of Wales, then scarcely thirty, golden-haired and the darling of society. My shopping trip among the bookies was a chore. They knew it wasn't my wager because I couldn't bet that heavily, a fact obvious to everybody. But they never knew whose money it was.

Sensing that Epinard, the favorite, wasn't too strong, I bet Wise Counsellor 4-to-1 to win and 9-to-5 to place, a hundred on each spot. It was a good thing because at post time my horse was the favorite at 3-to-1 to win and even money to place. The nine-horse field broke well and stayed together, with Epinard leading most of the way. He had a head lead entering the stretch. Wise Counsellor was fifth, but a hard ride brought my horse thundering down to take Epinard by nearly a length.

This acumen was typical of Carr Van Anda in all fields; he figured things out in his own way and stuck with his belief. He was one of the few managing editors I knew who, after the paper was put to bed, did not object to reporters hanging around, pampering their allergy to going home by playing cards or even shooting craps. When I worked on the *Times* and prohibition was in full flower, Mr. Van Anda took no notice of antifreeze or other nectars secluded in desk drawers or lockers to help achieve relaxation after the tension of making deadlines and replates.

Because Mr. Van Anda countenanced whatever reporters did after their working hours, even if it was in the City Room of the paper, he scored what in newspaper tradition was one of the greatest feats and beats in publishing history. On Saturday night, July 29, 1916, all Sunday papers, including the *Times*, had been locked up. The clock had passed midnight and mass relaxation was in full sway. Mr. Van Anda, as was his custom, continued sitting at his desk with his old pipe, reading and wearing a groove in the floor with round trips from his desk to the big dictionary in the center of the City Room. Over in the corner a group of financiers huddled, some backing and some bucking the unpredictable statistics of tumbling dice.

The clock hands registered nearly ten minutes after two when the building rocked. The sky lit up. Window panes rattled and smashed and all hell broke loose. A major disaster had occurred.

The cubes and money in the corner disappeared. Every figure in the huddle and in the City Room turned to Mr Van Anda for orders. Winnings and losses were forgotten as he sent the players into action. Within minutes V.A. was tearing out the eight-column front page headline on the 5,000 rioters in the Third Avenue Elevated railroad strike. He pushed the lead story to the left-hand side of the page, and cleared four full columns for whatever his legmen might give him.

The result was a sweeping headline, a half-page story on page one and three columns of continuation on page two. It was a graphic report about the fourteen barges of munitions that had exploded at Black Tom Island, perilously close to Bedloes's Island and the Statue of Liberty. Some $7,000,000 worth of military fireworks had been touched off mysteriously. Downtown buildings had rocked, windows were shattered and an estimated $20,000,000 in damage was reported in Wall Street, eastern New Jersey and far into Brooklyn. Havoc was everywhere and the *Times* had the whole story in a *regular* final edition!

Neither the *World, American, Herald* nor *Sun,* which had recently combined with the morning *Press,* made it. The *Tribune* managed a brief two-column insert by replating, and the Brooklyn *Eagle* produced a four-page extra during the forenoon. Of course the *Telegram,* an evening paper with a Sunday edition, came out with its customary Sabbath extra. But the *Times* alone, thanks to Carr Van Anda, had complete coverage on the streets within two hours of the explosion.

Go West, Young Man!

You can imagine the reaction of an editor like Carr Van Anda to the announcement in 1923 that Jack Dempsey would defend his world heavyweight championship at Shelby, a remote town in northern Montana, against Tommy Gibbons, of St. Paul. He pounced upon the story like a cat on a mouse and said with all the certainty of a man who knew, "This will be the last great fight in the West!"

He was recalling the wild and woolly affairs at Carson City, Reno, Goldfield and other places. Mr. Van Anda ordered coverage on the fight to start at once; though it was scheduled for July 4, more than a month away, he asked that I be sent into the Northwest immediately.

Since the papers for the fight had just been signed, there really wasn't anything to write about in Shelby. Nevertheless, when Captain Thomson said, "You're to go to Shelby at once," my heart leaped. I thought this was wonderful, but it was unbelievable when Captain Thomson added, "Go down to the cashier and draw a thousand dollars for your expenses."

Man! Me with a thousand dollars in my pocket, and off to the Golden West! Shelby didn't know it, but a new money baron was about to give the Old West a touch of high life it hadn't known since the Hearsts and the Crockers. Speeding out of town with that fortune in my kicks, I felt sorry for everybody back at the office. In fact, I wondered, but only briefly, how the *Times* would be able to publish with me gone West with the loot.

I was a babe in the woods, except that Shelby had no woods. Of Montana's 30-million acres of forests, not one tree could be seen from the dinky, single-story station on the Great Northern Railroad. The place resembled a cheap movie set thrown up in the middle of a gigantic pancake of prairie. A year before only seven hundred of the state's 500,000-plus people had lived in and around this county seat. Then they had the good fortune or, as it turned out, misfortune to strike oil in the nearby Sweetgrass Hills. The panic was on. The town had only two brick buildings throughout the wild, mushrooming period that saw the few slab-siding shacks spread as hopefuls drifted in, as they always will to boom towns.

Soon somebody got the idea of bringing a heavyweight championship fight to help draw attention to the bonanza burg. That news turned the place into a scene that defied the skill and imagination of fiction writers—and we had plenty on hand to give it a try.

The town was still quiet, though, when I arrived. One little building bore a sign—FIGHT HEADQUARTERS. It was empty. I went over to the Rainbow Hotel—a two-story structure, unpainted inside or out, right out of the movie set I mentioned and the only hotel in town. The clerk gave me the one room with a bath attached. I lived in state, enjoyed my bath, had plenty of money, and absolutely nothing to write about on the fight.

Otherwise there was plenty to see and report, as I learned in the evening when all Shelby seemed to wake up. The sleepy-looking shacks became beehives of activity and strained the single dynamo that fed the town's low-watt bulbs. Entertainment was strictly frontier, a real outgrowth of the Forty-Niner days. The dance halls, chili counters, dice corners and other booby traps were being thrown up and opened to lure suckers in every possible way. They had no closing hours; tinny pianos, saxophones, and human voices moaned through the night. Gambling was everywhere, the suckers stopping only when they ran out of silver dollars, and people were trooping into town round the clock by dusty flivvers, pinto ponies, burros and even on foot.

By Decoration Day the town was teeming with homeless who set up tents, or even old burlap feed bags, and slept under them. The arrival of every train brought the opening of another soft-drink stand. The biggest complaint came from debarking railroad passengers. The station was too small for commercial opportunities, so a construction gang, numbering nearly 500, sawed the two-room building in half, moved the ends out and built a connecting shed that gave Shelby the biggest railroad station in the state of Montana!

Actually, the first outlanders to reach Shelby were the Western Union supervisors and operators. Long before the first infinitive was split in the literary avalanche, the telegraphers had a big office in City Hall to handle the tremendous flow of words.

Tommy Gibbons, his manager Eddie Kane and two or three sparring partners arrived in early June, and I started living a life that Reilly would envy. One of the boxing partners, Bud Gorman, and I became good pals. He gave me good and authentic stuff to put on the wire, for serious training was still to come.

But my luxurious solitude at the Rainbow Hotel ended with the arrival of the heavy guns in the sports writing business. They were led by dour and white-haired William O. "Sheriff" McGeehan, of the New York *Herald*. My room with the only bath in the one hotel with running water was, as I recall, not just coveted—it was confiscated because McGeehan, as he politely explained, had to have the bathtub in which to keep the beer chilled for all of us. The Sheriff's aide-de-camp in this maneuver—he and Damon Runyon virtually always had one—was "Little Solly" Harris, a camp follower of sports and well known in those days.

My roommate in the new room down the hall was a bartender from St. Paul, a friend of manager Eddie Kane's. He was a sharp-eyed Irishman with a preoccupied scowl and the first name of Philip. I don't remember his last name, but I will never forget Phil; he was the only man I ever saw who slept with a lighted cigar in his mouth. Phil would lie snoring at my side in the double bed. I would lie there trembling with fear, watching his lighted cigar get frayed and wet from his nervous chewing. It couldn't burn his mouth, but everything else was in jeopardy—mattress, bedclothes, me and the entire hotel of tinder-dry pine board. When he snored, the exhalation sent sparks and ashes flying up like a Roman candle on Fourth of July. Naturally, this made sleeping hazardous, in fact impossible. When I tried a feeble protest, Phil dismissed it quickly. "I been doin' it all my life an' nothin's happened yet," he insisted.

The annoyance of Phil's nighttime fireworks was offset by his daytime generosity. He had few clothes, but an enormous suitcase, stocked from his place of business in St. Paul, contained pints of whiskey. Nothing was too good for his pal and roommate and I was permitted unlimited indulgence, even when my friends happened along. But I didn't really get to know Phil until the Saturday night when a cowboy made us blood brothers under the bed. The bronc-buster was in town for the rodeo which, like many other forms of entertainment, had come to Shelby. He and his light of love were just beneath our second-floor window in the hotel when the young lady evidently did something that displeased her swain and he socked her a solid belt. She screamed.

Phil leaped out of bed in his short, old-fashioned nightgown, his eyes blazing as brightly as his stogie over this violation of feminine sanctity. He rushed to the window, leaned out, and his cavalier tendencies getting the best of him, yelled to the offender, "You bum! I'm comin' down there an' fix you!"

The cowboy looked up and shouted back, "You won't have to come down. I'm comin' up!"

I felt this wasn't a particularly good place for me. I shoved the bureau and chair against the door, pulled on my pants and shoes and prepared to leave by the window to join the lady, who still was hollering it up pretty good on the sidewalk. When I heard the boots in the hall, I perched on the sill and got set. But the cowboy, ossified as a hoot owl, went to a vacant room next to ours and started kicking in the door.

Naturally this roused the hotel—it roused easily with its pine-board walls. Everybody started popping out of rooms, including the hotel owner who had the presence of mind to phone the sheriff. By the time the cowhand had forced his way into the vacant room and found nobody, he was rattlesnake mad. But the sheriff managed to get lover boy back to his lady friend and, as always happens, she rushed into his arms and pleaded with the law not to put him in the pokey. She won her case.

As I watched this final and touching scene of the drama enacted below the window, I heard a sound behind me. It was my brave roomie Phil, crawling out cautiously from under the bed.

"Where have you been?" I demanded.

"I lost my cigar," he said. "It rolled under the bed and I had a hard time finding it, it's so dark under there."

But that damned inextinguishable cheroot still was glowing and throwing off its usual sparks.

At least 20 dance halls operated when Shelby night life reached a peak—the Gibbons Club, Red Onion, Black Cat, King Tut and many others. Fourteen months earlier, Shelby had boasted two boarding houses. According to my count in mid-June there were 5,000 cots under canvas or makeshift roofs, 38 restaurants and a brand new soda fountain—the town's first, assuring everybody of a good five-cent soda for a quarter.

The wide-open places brought warnings from authorities in Helena, the state capital, 175 miles downstate. State's Attorney General Rankin, brother of Jeannette, first Congresswoman in Washington, issued firm instructions: if Shelby authorities couldn't handle the "public nuisance" there would be no prize fight. Straightway two of the largest joints, the Hall of Terpsichore and Days of Forty-Nine, were raided. But the whir of wheels and the rattle of chips and silver dollars were stilled only momentarily. Momentum was too great. From distant Portland, Oregon, where he was promoting fight tickets and money, Shelby's energetic mayor, Jim Johnson, denied that his town was a nuisance.

Whether it was or not, this fantastic frontier was an oasis of newspaper copy. By now all the big guns from the nation's leading metropolitan papers had checked in. To believe it, you had only to see mountainous Heywood Broun, of the New York *World*, walking under a twenty-gallon Stetson and sporting a yellow kerchief above his ample paunch. There was Richard Henry Little, the R.H.L. of the Chicago *Tribune*'s famed Line o' Type or Two. My own paper sent out a feature man, the late Elmer Davis, to write the lead story. In addition, the *Times* had my great and good friend, the late James Parnell Dawson, covering the Dempsey camp at nearby Great Falls. Dawson, along with a few others, taught me to write about boxing, but I never mastered his simple, direct style.

Each of us on the *Times* had received the same amount of expense money: $1,000. I do not vouch for this, but I heard later that Mr. Davis, an inveterate poker player, fell in with some men of skill and dubious ethics coming out on the *Oriental Limited* and did not reach Montana with his entire expense allowance. In fact, some said he had been cleaned. This seemed somewhat remarkable, since Mr. Davis was a Rhodes Scholar, a brilliant writer and commentator, a smart cookie and the only man I ever knew who carried his pocket kerchief in his coat sleeve.

These feature writers, columnists and theater critics ignored the fight news, of which there was very little. They specialized in the dramatic. There were many phenomena in this prairie village, but the star attraction was Miss Patricia Salmon, known as Patsy. We all admired her, but I regret to say that Patricia couldn't do much besides appear attractive. Hair-tinted and beauty-lotioned, she was not a bad looking girl, but she could not dance, sing or act. However, she could yodel, which wouldn't have been so bad if she had yodeled well. But she was only loud. Nevertheless, so great was the publicity given her by the feature writers that Florenz Ziegfeld put her in an edition of his Follies. She managed to stay through the one season. Following this, she continued much in the manner of a former big-league ball player working down through the minor leagues. Thanks to vaudeville and one-night stands, she capitalized on her fight-camp fame for years.

Before Shelby could reach a peak of the comic and bizarre, tragedy took over. Unbridled enthusiasm had dominated from the time in early spring when Mel McCutcheon spawned the innocent idea that the fight would put their town on the map in a constructive way. Roy Mullomby was appointed to handle the impossible task of producing $300,-000 as a guarantee to Jack Dempsey and his manager, Jack Kearns. Mayor Jim Johnson heartily agreed that the money could be raised. The first $110,000 was collected, but mid-June brought the big cash crisis. Ticket sales were carelessly handled in several cities to the east and west. Lumber for the half-finished arena was pledged to protect a bill of nearly $80,000. Workmen hadn't been paid. Local banks were straining under the demands of backers and promoters and bankers from Great Falls were called in.

Of course the pride of the entire state of Montana was involved here, but this wasn't enough to make anybody rush in from other sections with a saving amount of money. However, a young lawyer from Butte did come over to remonstrate with the pernicious Jack Kearns to make him see the light, lighten his demands, and perhaps take a smaller cut for Dempsey's end of the purse.

I can still see Kearns, hard and unyielding, standing in the doorway of the office. He wore a light, pullover sweater and looked as dressy as he always does. He was adamant about changing the articles of agreement for the fight, especially in the matter of the guarantee. The money was owed for agreeing to risk the heavyweight championship, which had become a multimillion-dollar commodity. He wanted the dough or there would be no fight; he didn't care who got it or how. His blue eyes were steel cold.

The young lawyer from Butte, Mr. Frank Walker, who was later chairman of the National Democratic Committee and Postmaster General of the United States in 1940, finally said indignantly, "We have trees out here in Montana for fellows like you!"

Kearns, leaning nonchalantly against the door jamb, peered out, looked up and down the muddy street and across the steaming prairie to the distant blue Sweetgrass Hills, shrugged and replied, "Mr. Walker, I don't see any trees."

That was Kearns' position and attitude until a few hours before the fight which most of us believed and predicted might not come off. In addition to the financial crisis customers and promoters had the bad luck of terrific rain that lasted more than a week. It knocked out the few roads, one of which was a brand new highway leading into town that had been counted on to accommodate the heavy vehicular traffic. The road couldn't be completed. Visitors expected by train simply never showed up.

But Shelby had three things in profusion: mosquitoes, panhandlers and lemonade stands. All three were busy night and day. You couldn't go down the street for a meal without passing a hundred grimy, outstretched hands that left you too full of guilt and shame to enjoy food or drink.

Through the week before the fight good tickets appeared by the bushel-basketful. Local backers of the project who had been given batches of tickets to sell to help recapture their "investment" couldn't give them away. A tribe of Blackfeet Indians left their reservation about 25 miles to the west and wound up with some of the best seats in the arena. Perhaps the biggest single group at the fight was the crowd covering the Dempsey camp in Great Falls, about 90 miles to the south. When they arrived, more newspapermen were on hand for the fight than customers from out of state.

This is typical of our business. The heavyweight champion is royalty in sports—whatever happens to him, however small, is important. In the old days, during radio but before television, a heavyweight championship fight sold more papers than any peacetime event.

The Dempsey crowd couldn't believe what they saw in Shelby. Being accustomed to citified Great Falls, they agreed that it was even wilder and woollier than we had pictured. They believed the rumors of danger and gunplay. On the day of the fight, which broke warm and sunny and grew very hot, there was open speculation among the Dempsey crowd as to when the muffled anger and stifled tempers would erupt.

The local law gave fuel to this rising apprehension by ordering everybody to strip himself of firearms before entering the arena. All of this was a joke, because everybody was as peaceful as my noncombatant roommate Phil. The nice, quiet folks of this prairie village were too numb for retaliation, too broke and beaten to fight back. Guns couldn't bring back their squandered money and mortaged properties. They looked on in silent horror at the shambles of their town, now filled to overflowing with bums and grifters, thugs and thieves, bankrupt lemonade stands and carnival itinerants with nobody to sell anything to but each other.

Nevertheless, the fear persisted with Dempsey and his entourage. Kearns, the "villain" of the cast, "Jerry the Greek" Luvadis, his head trainer, Joe Benjamin, Leo Moore and Mike Trant were all extremely unpopular and had to expect rough stuff. I can remember One-Eyed Connolly, the incurable gate-crasher, who got in by masquerading as a water boy on that hot, stifling afternoon, casting apprehensive glances around Dempsey's corner. So did Mike Trant, the Chicago policeman, who was bodyguard and umbrella-holder when the champion, swathed in an old blue sweater and towels, entered the ring at 3:30 P.M. to wait eight minutes for Tom Gibbons to appear.

Never was Grandmother Henderson's Biblical warning, "The wicked flee when no man pursueth," more evident that an instant later when a Fourth-of-July firecracker exploded somewhere in the pine bowl. It had the effect of a six-gun outburst. The reaction was sensational and, for one ghastly instant, panic threatened among the seven thousand cash customers. With that, some four thousand who had crashed the gate by scaling the perimeter of the arena stormed the ringside successfully for better seats.

But the firecracker was louder and more damaging than any punch landed in the fight. Tommy Gibbons, outweighed by nearly 13 pounds at 175½, boxed at a fair pace for ten rounds. Then he decided to hang on for the full fifteen and be the first challenger to carry Dempsey to a decision since he had become champion four years before. Of course Dempsey was awarded the decision. It was virtually guaranteed, because he couldn't have had a better friend than the referee and sole judge of the fight. He was Jimmy Dougherty, the "Baron" of Leiperville, Pennsylvania, who, around that time, managed a heavyweight fighter named George Godfrey. The good Baron, about whom Damon Runyon wrote so entertainingly, was an intimate friend; Jack couldn't have been safer if his own father, Hiram Dempsey, had judged the fight.

When the fight was over, the Baron, who had also seemed unduly apprehensive, hurriedly grabbed Dempsey's arm, raising it in victory and at the same time appearing to clutch it for support. Maybe it was for comfort. At any rate, both of them slipped through the ropes and down the steps. They were running up the aisle as fast as they could when the cushions and debris began to fly from a disgruntled, angry mob. Dempsey's handlers didn't bother to cover him again with the old sweater and the towels—he left the ring so fast that there wasn't time. Within three minutes the entire Dempsy crowd, Kearns included, was out of sight. They headed for a railroad siding where two private cars were attached to a steam locomotive that was warmed up and ready to roll. They climbed aboard and an instant later the heavy chugging sounded as the two-car special headed for Great Falls. There the Dempsey party evidently felt safer, though they didn't remain in that part of the country for long.

It's to be doubted that any of them, especially Kearns, ever returned to pay their respects to Mayor Johnson, Matchmaker Collins, Promoter Mullomby and other ill-starred victims, including a few bank executives. Kearns took all the money, some $210,000. Only $15,000 was taken in on the day of the fight, and the cost of staging the battle totaled $316,000.

Sports history has produced nothing like it, before or since. The town went bust, and took thirty years to come back—if it ever actually did. Recently, friends passing through on the scenic Great Northern route say that many of Shelby's 3,000 people today claim they can't remember the financial nightmare. If that's true, they're lucky.

So ended the last great romance of the West in the fight game. Certainly I'll never forget my baptism as a sports writer in Shelby, Montana. Every now and then to this day I bump into somebody who was in Shelby at the time and who remembers the fight, but the ranks of those I knew personally who were there are thinning.

The Big Switch

Ford Christopher Frick has not always been Commissioner of Baseball. Some years ago he was president of the National League and, prior to that, manager of the League's Service Bureau. There also are those, I suppose, who will remember him as a radio broadcaster. But only the oldest settlers can remember when he was a sports writer who wore pince-nez glasses and composed poems that not only rhymed but scanned.

It was in this long-ago period, when he was a young baseball writer on the New York *Evening Journal,* that Frick attended a six-day bicycle race at the old Madison Square Garden during the first week of December, 1924. Whether or not Ford approved of six-day bike races, I don't know, but he visited this one by appointment only. He wanted to see a

Times reporter, Jim Harrison, the chap who had got me my job on the paper.

"I have good news for you, Jim," Frick said eagerly, for they had become friends while covering the baseball beat together in the summer. "Mr. Brisbane wants to see you about working for the *Journal*."

In those days, it was a command performance when the great A.B. sent for a reporter. Such an offer was good news for anybody's ego. Jim was pleased, but before he had time to think about it, Frick began explaining the reason for Brisbane's interest. A baseball story in the *Times* had caught the eye of the famed editor and writer. It was written after the final game of the recent World Series in Washington. Brisbane had given Frick a clipping of the unsigned piece and, because Harrison was the *Times'* top baseball man, Ford assumed that Jim had written it. It read:

WASHINGTON, Oct. 10—Dreams came true in the twelfth—Washington's dream and Walter Johnson's—and when the red September sun dropped down behind the dome of the Capitol, the Senators were the baseball champions of the world.

Washington waited twenty-five years for a World Series, but when it came it was the greatest one in history, and the king of pitchers waited eighteen years for the sweetest victory of his career. . . .

Somewhere, perhaps, in that little patch of sunlight that was filtering through the shadowy stands and down in front of the pitcher's mound, the once-mightiest arm of all was finding the strength to do the thing that twice before had balked it. . . .

Harrison nodded as he read the half-column story that had been tucked in the lower part of page 9, column 5. He peered over his rimless spectacles at Frick and said, "There's only one hitch, Ford: I didn't write it."

"Who did?"

"A young fellow in the sports department named Corum."

"Who the hell is he?" Frick was part of a vast and contented majority who had never heard of Corum. He apologized to Harrison and retired to form new lines for his report to Mr. Brisbane.

Naturally, I knew nothing of this at the time, but an inkling came my way a short while before when I was at Princeton to see the football Tigers tear Harvard to shreds by a score of 34–0. I was walking across the campus to Palmer Stadium with Heywood Broun, of the *World*. He had traded the twenty-gallon Stetson and yellow scarf of Shelby, Montana, for a mammoth raccoon coat that made him resemble a Kadiak bear about to hibernate. He said, "I hear you're going to get a big offer from Arthur Brisbane to work for the Hearst papers."

"I haven't heard anything, Heywood," I said. "And I don't think there's any truth to it."

"Yes, there is," he insisted. "And you'll hear about it."

Actually, there was some mention of it in the press box that afternoon, but I didn't take it seriously until Ford Frick talked to me during the National League meetings in December at the Waldorf. When he reported the mistaken identity incident to Mr. Brisbane who, by the way, had discovered and brought Frick from Colorado Springs a few years before, the editor had said, "I don't care what his name is. I want the fellow who wrote the story."

But as Frick started out of the office, Brisbane decided not to hurry the matter until spring, since the baseball season was over. I thanked Frick, reminding myself, however, that nothing actually had happened. I was still a *Times* man, quite happy with what was now a $50-a-week salary, plus almost that much more from space-writing assignments parceled out to staff writers.

March found me on my second Southern baseball training trip. I covered the Brooklyn Robins (so-called then for their jolly manager, Wilbert Robinson) at Clearwater, Florida, and managed to pick up the Giants and Yankees for a few games before reaching New York. But with the assignment to cover the Brooklyn opening at Ebbets Field, I felt there was no reason for not having my daily story identified with a by-line unless, of course, the *Times* was ashamed of what I wrote. All other New York papers were by-lining staffers.

My sports editor thought the appeal valid and suggested that I take it to a higher court, which turned out to be Joseph Tebeau, assistant managing editor and a Brooklynite partial to the Robins. He not only agreed with my argument but said that the lack of a by-line was an insult to Brooklyn fans, and carried the battle from there. So April 15, 1925, became a red-letter day for me, because the sports page of that date carried my first by-line:

By M. W. CORUM

Vance, victory and visions of a pennant served to mellow the otherwise chilly opening of another baseball season in Brooklyn yesterday. Some 20,000 hopeful fans of Flatbush gathered at Ebbets Field to see the Robins beat the Phillies, and that is what they saw. The score was 3 to 1.

From the Yankee Stadium, the story was *By Harry Cross*, and the Giants' opening in Boston read *By James R. Harrison*. Thereafter no *Times* sports writer could be blamed for someone else's literary shortcomings.

It was the busiest of seasons for Brooklyn baseball writers. Charles H. Ebbets, president and half-owner of the Robins, died four days after the April 14th opening. Within a few weeks, Ed McKeever, the younger of the two brothers who owned the other half of the club and who was to be Ebbets' successor, also died. For the next fifteen years, the ball club's occasional turmoil on the field was exceeded only by the constant chaos in the front office.

About midseason a little blue envelope from Arthur Brisbane reached me with a request to see him at his office. He was a short, compact man of sixty at the time, bald, with sharp blue eyes and crisp speech. He didn't take long to reach the point, and asked if I had anything in the paper that day. When I said I did, he picked up the *Times* from the untidiest mess of litter, turned to the sports page and studied my piece.

"M-m-m," he murmured and nodded. "Nice short sentences."

When he asked whether I was interested in working for the Hearst papers, I sparred a bit by saying that the *Times* had treated me well and. . . .

"Would you be interested in a contract for three years at one hundred and fifty dollars a week?" he asked pointedly and reached toward a stack of papers.

I murmured that it was quite a liberal offer. Naturally, I thought of what good news it would be for the fair Elaine; the sum was almost double my current earnings and definite every week for at least three years. You know the stuff that whirls around your head and before your eyes like giant pinwheels when a situation like that confronts you. I was still trying to bring things into focus when Mr. Brisbane said, "If you'll just sign these three contracts—" He was pointing to the dotted lines. Of course, the contracts had been made out in advance. I'm sure he felt there was slight chance of my refusing, or even haggling.

I signed, shook his outstretched hand and left the comfortably littered office, wondering what words would best explain my departure from the *Times*. To my relief, Mr. Tebeau was most understanding, though I had no reason for expecting any other treatment. I've never forgotten the words he used: "I'm sure Mr. Hearst's dollar will buy as many groceries as Mr. Ochs'."

By M. W. CORUM

Is the number 13 unlucky?
Ask Eppa Jeptha Rixey.
Eppa's a college graduate with a string of degrees almost as long as he is, and he is six feet six, if he's an inch. . . .

Take it or leave it, this, on July 21, 1925, was the first of untold, and too often unread, millions of words that I have written for the same paper for more than half my sixty-four years. Rixey, a good left-hander with the Cincinnati Reds, had lost twelve games when he started that day at the Polo Grounds against the Giants. He was winning until the home half of the ninth, when the Giants scored and handed him his thirteenth.

My regular assignment was the New York Giants, and I succeeded an institution on the paper, Samuel Newhall Crane. Sam had been a big-league manager and second baseman in the 1880s and had even played for the Giants. He had long been a close friend and confidant of John J. McGraw and had written for the *Journal* until a few weeks before when he was stricken in St. Louis. They brought him home, but he passed away in June.

The responsibility of following this almost legendary baseball figure was heavy, and I could feel it. However, from the start I tried to be not a "second Crane" but a "first Corum." Nobody could duplicate Sam. He knew more baseball than most writers and could draw upon two generations of big-league players for parallels and anecdotes. He was close to McGraw, having ghosted that fine volume, *My Thirty Years of Baseball,* a source of material for newspapermen for the next thirty years.

Thanks to John McGraw's intelligence, help and understanding, I had no problems about covering the ball club under the shadow of the beloved Sam Crane. In fact, at the end of the season which found the Giants finishing second after four pennants in a row, I got spring-training fever. I couldn't wait to get to Sarasota, Florida, and start my first full year as a New York Giants' correspondent.

THE COLUMN

I pray thee make my column read,
And give me thus my daily bread.
                    Don Marquis

Only Yesterday

The telegram reached me at St. Louis in late July, 1926, as the New York Giants were ending the second of their three swings through the West. It said: STARTING IMMEDIATELY YOU ARE TO WRITE A DAILY COLUMN—W. S. FARNSWORTH, SPORTS EDITOR.

This milestone called for a quick huddle with myself and with a few other baseball writers making the trip. Somehow the content of the first column was thrust aside for the more important matter of the pillar's title or masthead. It had to be breezy, good, different, big-league—like Joe Vila's "Setting the Pace," or Granny Rice's renowned "The Sportlight," or "Down the Line" with W. O. McGeehan. Ideas and suggestions were plentiful as we toasted the future of the project. They included, "According to Corum," "The Sportscene," "Take It from Me," and, when somebody came up with "Corum's Forum," somebody just as quickly cracked, "What will you call it when Corum's *not* for 'em?" All suggestions, feeble and strong, were jotted down and sent on to New York for consideration. Then I got around to thinking about the first column itself.

The origin of the sports column is unknown to me, and I'm sure it's clouded. Long ago, newspapers covered sports as a necessary evil and permitted no such lavish use of space. I imagine when space was expanded the idea materialized to relieve the succession of headlines and news stories. For that reason, most sports columns were usually light-reading, off-beat, or opinionated because they weren't actual news items. Thus, sports columnists have "iffed" their way through billions of words, and no one has made greater use of the second guess.

While I was pleased and flattered to be chosen, I knew it wasn't for my deathless prose, because I couldn't remember writing anything worth repeating since the first piece on Eppa Rixey's thirteenth loss. Besides, the *Journal* sports pages had, and would continue to have, columns by the entertaining William F. Kirk, Sid Mercer on boxing, Ford Frick on a variety of subjects, Tad's Tid-Bits, and others. Since I was probably a trial horse, I could write as I always had. I wouldn't burden readers with heavy-handed stuff that might chase them to another page or, worse, to another paper.

July 28, 1926, was the day of the first column. With it came two jolts. Mr. Brisbane discarded all those fine suggestions for titles and called it "Sports," and Bill Farnsworth, the sports editor, whose Christian name was Wilton, decided to call me Bill too.

So the first milestone went like this:

SPORTS

Too Much Red Meat	*Snyder Good Catcher*
Case of Hornsby	*Crusader and Sande*
Vegetables Better	*Pop Bottle Barrage*

By BILL CORUM

The red meat for he-men campaign has foundered. Rogers Hornsby, most recent champion of the double-sirloin, sits supinely in the shade these warm days while his ball team fights for a pennant. Too many steaks tell the sad story.

While the great Hornsby sulks in the shadow of the dugout, Billy Southworth, an athlete of the salad school, hits home runs and suffers from no boils. Hornsby is learning what Babe Ruth learned before him, that a man cannot live by steak alone.

In Hornsby's home, a palatial one in the exclusive section of St. Louis, they serve each evening a sumptuous six-course dinner of steak and potatoes. On this diet, the Rajah has led the National League hitters for half a dozen seasons, but not because of it—in spite of it.

That was ten thousand columns ago. The piece continued with a variety of topics, all calculated to catch the eye. To my surprise, the lead caught the eye of Mr. Brisbane for an odd reason. The topic of food, he said, was of universal interest; he believed that almost everybody liked to read about it.

Since that day I've written about ten million words under that "Sports" masthead and participated in at least two endurance records. One was by me as a fixture on one paper; the more important one is the record patience of the publication and its tolerant readers. For, let's face it, if all 10,000 columns were laid end to end there would be one big cry for a match to light either or both ends.

But the columns remain to laugh at me, indict me and, though they are far too few, to flatter me. And I'd willingly swap the few good ones to have the bad ones obliterated, just as we'd all like to erase our shortcomings, however minor, from the record.

The status of a sports columnist is widely envied, sometimes for good reason. Admittedly he is privileged in things like subject matter, viewpoint, crusades, mobility and reasonable expenses. And while some have been fired, I don't recall any who quit except those who may have reformed to take up general columning, like Heywood Broun, Westbrook Pegler, Jack Kofoed, Bob Considine, Bugs Baer and Ed Sullivan.

But all the so-called advantages of sports columning are more than offset by the many responsibilities that must be

assumed on this freedom road which, take it from me, is
paved with pitfalls. A well-intentioned writer can land flat
on his face, and often does. The lucky ones get up before the
nose dive is noticed.

The columnist must persuade the reader subtly that he
knows it all. This isn't easy, especially for a new sports columnist plagued by the fearful fact that he knows very little.
Such was my predicament beginning in August, 1926, when
I faced the job of getting on the inside of situations, and
writing to conceal the fact that I wasn't. It called for a real
cover-up job. Fortunately there was plenty to write about in
those days. Postwar sports activities had rolled to an interesting peak. In boxing, for instance, in the year 1926 new
champions were crowned in five of the eight standard divisions—heavyweight, light heavy, middle, welter and lightweight.

Though we didn't fully realize it, baseball was undergoing
a thorough change of operating methods in the front office
and on the field. The swashbuckling era of John J. McGraw
was over. The ministerial and meticulous Branch Rickey of
St. Louis had taken over. French tennis had caught up with
and was about to pass that of the United States. Man o'
War's sons and daughters were taking charge of racing. And
a woman, America's Gertrude Ederle, had conquered the
English Channel in record time!

Prosperity, which later disappeared around the corner, was
then zooming to a peak, along with prohibition violations and
their inevitable by-product, heavy spenders. In fact, you
rarely asked your neighbor or bar companion how he earned
his living for fear he might tell you.

Much of my nocturnal ruminating, at that time, was done
in walks up Broadway, a habit I had started when copyreading on the *Times* sports desk. After work, I liked to stop at
the first Lindy's (Runyon's Mindy's), near the Rivoli Theater

for a pre-dawn snack. Whenever I dropped in, I always saw two familiar faces. One, in a booth at the rear, had more furtive visitors than a political leader—which he was, in a shabby fashion. He was Arnold Rothstein, the gambler, who was implicated in the 1919 Black Sox baseball scandal, and later murdered up the street. The other fellow was the exact opposite. He sat alone in the third booth, reading the papers, and jotting things down that I liked to think were deathless melodies or lyrics. He was Irving Berlin, maker of America's music, and a pleasant fellow who would smile when we exchanged glances.

While I wasn't exactly anonymous, the majority happily unaware of Bill Corum was still vast. My acquaintance with the top brass in the sporting world was small. I caught up with them through the help of the more knowing writers, particularly my boss, Bill Farnsworth; Vince Treanor, of the *Evening World*, at the race tracks; and my former coworker on the *Times*, Jim Dawson, who knew and had the confidence of more big shots in all walks of sports than any other writer. The reason, of course, was that he was a good listener and never broke a confidence.

In no time I learned that a sports columnist is never without friends of all kinds. Because some of them had more angles than a busy architect, I often listened to feedbox information from all stalls in the stable, leaving me worse off than when I had only outside information, or none at all. Such was the case just before the first Dempsey-Tunney fight less than two months after I'd started the column. Rumors mushroom in size and numbers before every big fight, but one in Atlantic City where the champion trained had special authority.

"Dempsey hasn't got it, Bill. He won't win—can't win, because he's just not there any more." This came from one of the all-time great fighters at any weight, Harry Greb, the Pittsburgh Windmill. We had become good friends after a chance meeting in New York a year or so before. Out of the ring he was a pleasantly disarming fellow with a soft, sincere voice that belied his profession and a record of more than two hundred and fifty fights. He had lost only six or eight of these, two to Tunney whom he had beaten badly in their first meeting for Gene's only defeat.

Greb had boxed a few rounds with Dempsey in training to help ballyhoo the fight. He used all his persuasiveness each time we met in Atlantic City to urge me to pick Tunney. While I may not have followed his advice, I felt out my elders who scoffed at the idea of Tunney winning. "Stick to the champ, kid," they counseled. "You can lose only once."

So with Greb's plea still ringing in my ears, I picked Dempsy, thereby missing fame and the tangibles that were heaped upon the only experts, to my knowledge, who picked the 4-to-1 underdog, Tunney. Harry Grayson, of the NEA Service, was received on the Pacific Coast as a conquering hero for picking the winner. The late Ed Van Every, then of the New York *Evening World,* gained permanent stature among boxing writers and a 100 per cent raise in pay.

My failure to heed Greb's plea was even more regrettable a month later when this fine fighter and fellow, only thirty-two, died in Atlantic City while undergoing an operation to remove defective bone growth over his eye.

The Dempsey-Tunney fight itself, terrible as a boxing exhibition, produced drama in every other way. It also produced revenue—nearly $2,000,000—and the largest crowd, more than 120,000, to attend a heavyweight championship fight. The customers were packed into a concrete horseshoe in south Philadelphia, about five miles from the center of town. Rain fell as early as the second round, let up and fell again. In the last two bloodstained rounds, there was what the weather bureau calls a mean precipitation. The downpour flooded the sunken ringside area and drenched everyone at the scene. There was no doubt that Tunney had won; Dempsey was a battered and bloody one-eyed spectacle for the first time in his career. But the crowd had only one idea: to get out of the place and into a change of clothing before the late September chill could do its worst.

The storm had knocked out most of the ringside telegraph wires, bringing a rush to the temporary press room under the stands. But the wires were short-circuited there too, and the few still usable were prorated among the frantic writers for morning papers.

I was in an archway on jam-packed Broad Street, screaming into the bedlam for a nonexistent taxi, when someone on the back of a passing truck yelled an invitation for me to ride downtown. Lucky Willie hustled over, handed up the portable typewriter, and was hoisted into a tarpaulin-covered truck where it was warm and dry. After battling five miles of crazy traffic, it stopped within a block of Western Union's downtown press room.

There a small prairie of typewriters, direct wires, and idle telegraph operators stretched before me. A lone writer, Bill Cunningham, of Boston, disturbed the eerie quiet of the place. Without asking how he'd made it, I called the most frustrated sports editor in the world. Bill Farnsworth had a whopping staff headed by New York City's mayor, James J. Walker, covering a heavyweight championship fight won by a native New Yorker, and he couldn't get a word from any of them.

"Words!" he wired. "Just give me words. I've got a mail edition to fill. I just need words. . . ."

I wrote:

PHILADELPHIA, Sept. 24—The Marine has landed and the championship is in hand.

In one of the wettest and worst heavyweight title battles in the long history of the prize ring, Gene Tunney, the Marine of Destiny, knocked the coveted crown of gold off the battered, bloody head of a tired and worn old man—Jack Dempsey.

I don't know how long my copy was. I just wrote words. Somebody kept taking half pages, paragraphs and even single sentences from my machine. It was nearly 2:30 A.M. when Farnsworth flashed that time had run out, but that he had enough copy to fill his mail edition and the early city edition in New York. By this time many writers had managed to get in from the Stadium, every one of them soaked to the skin and shivering cold. Cunningham and I were dry, but we soon remedied that.

Countless out-of-town fight fans, damp in body and spirit, refused to risk pneumonia by leaving Philadelphia. They fought through the night for shelter, taking anything that would protect them from the damp chill, and many paid twenty-five dollars for a cot in a hotel hallway or storage room.

Offhand, I'd guess that 100,000 wet and wrinkled suits went to the cleaners, apart from gamblers who had laid 4-to-1 against Tunney. This rush of pressing business bottlenecked the tailor shops and hotel valet services around town. Moreover, it kept the one-suiters, including many sports writers, in their rooms awaiting the return of reconditioned raiment. But I was able to be up and about quite early, wandering here and there with only a few of the usual competitors. I was one of the first to see the new heavyweight champion at fight headquarters in the Bellevue-Stratford, and showed Gene a telegram that seemed to give him as much pleasure as the title. It was a congratulatory wire from my boss, Mr.

Brisbane, who knew and admired Tunney, saying ". . . you have always believed in your destiny, and a man who believes firmly in himself cannot be denied his goal."

Again because I was alone, another break of sorts came back at my hotel, the Adelphia, where the Dempsey party also was staying. One of them, recognizing me from training camp, confided, "Something big's on tap for this afternoon. Why don't you come up?"

Somehow I, a lone reporter, didn't feel comfortable in the parlor of the defeated champion's two-room suite, awaiting the arrival of his beautiful wife, screen star Estelle Taylor. Dempsey was in the darkened bedroom behind a closed door, a battered tiger licking his wounds. No sports writer had seen him, and I didn't want to see again the cuts, the bruises, and the lacerated, closed eye. Dempsey had been badly hurt. When Mrs. Dempsey and her escorts arrived on the service elevator, I heard them in the hallway. I heard her ask, "Which way?" I glanced out, saw her and saw them open the door to Jack's room. She went in alone.

A good reporter would have had his ear to the closed door in the parlor. But I felt that a young wife and her once-invincible pugilist husband in the depths of pain and defeat were entitled to that moment as their own. It wasn't news.

But I was wrong. The murmur of voices, as the world learned a few days later, became one of the most famous quotes of all times. As she entered the room, Mrs. Dempsey said, "Hello, Ginsberg, what happened?" "Ginsberg" was a humorous reminder that Jack had employed plastic surgery to remove the dent in his broken nose.

"I forgot to duck," he replied.

Well, I missed it. But I think I'd pass it up again, because I've never peeked over transoms or listened at keyholes for news.

Ringside Reports

Ten months later I picked Jack Sharkey to beat Dempsey in fifteen rounds or less at Yankee Stadium and win the right to meet Gene Tunney for the heavyweight championship in Chicago. Dempsey was thirty-two and the all-important spring had left his once lithe body. His reflexes were dull, making him easier to hit, the tragedy that comes to all aging fighters. Sharkey was twenty-four, youthfully supple; he could punch and he was strong and skilled as a boxer. It was my business to meet and know him, and I could see no reason for his not winning.

The fight, the fourth of Tex Rickard's million-dollar promotions thanks to Dempsey's drawing power, ran true to expectations. Sharkey outboxed and outpunched Dempsey through four of six rounds, even staggering him a few times. The former mauler, cut and bleeding again, was headed for another beating from a fighter he could have taken in his prime.

Sitting next to me at ringside was Murray Lewin, the late boxing expert of the New York *Daily Mirror*, a fierce competitor of the rival tabloid *Daily News* for early-edition readers. The outcome of the fight was so obvious to Lewin's managing editor, Phil Payne, that he suggested a "Sharkey Wins" story in the fifth round. Lewin demurred. When Payne persisted and urged that the story be sent, Lewin pleaded for time, but the editor wanted his papers on the street ahead of the *Daily News*. Finally, at the end of the sixth round, he ordered Lewin to write the story as a flash and send it.

Both of us turned to hear two voices calling up to Dempsey's corner only a few feet away. They were influential friends who had come down the aisle without being questioned. "Give it to him, Jack! Now! Give it to him!"

Whether this had anything to do with what happened is not for me to say. I only know that Murray Lewin, a smart cookie, failed to send the "Sharkey Wins" story, and 35 seconds after the seventh round had started Sharkey was writhing on the ring floor as Referee Jack O'Sullivan counted ten.

Dempsey had rushed from his corner and hit Sharkey with three hard punches that were unquestionably foul. I was less than 10 feet away and I saw them land, one high on Sharkey's thigh and two higher, but below the belt. When Sharkey turned to gasp an appeal to the referee, Dempsey clipped the unguarded jaw with a sharp left. Sharkey sank to the canvas and rolled over on his stomach, clutching his groin. He was not unconscious.

A day or so later Sharkey wanted to show me the damage that Dempsey had caused with the foul blows. I declined with thanks and no interest, since the State Commission doctor announced that he had found no evidence of damage. Dempsey, in a signed story for my own paper, swore that he had never intentionally fouled a fighter in his life. That was good enough for me.

The managing editor, Phil Payne, by the way, was a passenger five weeks later on one of the several tragic transatlantic flying efforts that followed Lindbergh's historic flight in May of that year. Neither of the two pilots nor Payne was ever seen again.

Another New York editor had something to say at the same ringside three years later with a more positive result. Sharkey was beating Max Schmeling, the German, for the heavyweight title vacated by Gene Tunney. In the fourth round, Sharkey tattooed Schmeling with both fists and plainly had the German groggy. Then, coming out of a clinch, he hit Max with a left to the body and Schmeling, writhing and holding himself around the middle, fell to the canvas and claimed foul.

In the confusion, only two persons among the wild and excited 80,000 seemed to be sure of anything. One was "Cigar Joey" Jacobs, manager of Schmeling. Promptly he rushed a handy man to the dressing room to get one of the metal protectors that fighters wore then, dent it, dunk it in water and bring it back to Schmeling's corner. The idea was to make the elastic part of the protector look as though it had been soaked in honest sweat.

The other man who had his mind made up was my editor, Arthur Brisbane. He was sitting just behind one of the judges in the second press row. In a loud, clear voice he announced, "If the German doesn't get this fight, there'll be no more boxing in New York State."

The judge didn't know his own mind, but he knew who Mr. Brisbane was. He called the referee over and told him what the influential editor had said. With Jacobs following the referee around the ring like a snarling, snapping terrier, the official, rather tentatively, declared Schmeling the winner on a foul, and another Dempsey-Sharkey "scandal" was averted.

The Tunney-Dempsey fight in 1927 was the crowning achievement of Tex Rickard's promotional genius. Though it drew 15,000 fewer than the Philadelphia meeting a year before, the setting was classical. More than 105,000 people poured $2,650,000 into the Grecian structure called Soldier Field on Chicago's lakefront. The late September night was clear and perfect, and the glow from the busy Loop a mile

away silhouetted the stately columns atop the concrete horse-
shoe.

My ringside seat was directly beneath Tunney's corner.
The only ones closer than I were his four corner men, headed
by his chief second, Jimmy "Bow-tie" Bronson. In that trigger
moment just before the opening bell, I stood up to ease my
own tension and take one more look at that fabulous sea of
faces surrounding us on all sides. Then I heard a voice above
call, "Sit down, Bill, there's nothing to get excited about."

I looked up and saw Tunney's grinning face. If he was
nervous, he didn't show it. Nor did he appear to be when the
bell for the first round brought him to the center of the ring.
A desperate Dempsey made a good fight from the start. A
foolish Dempsy later made it historic. Midway in the seventh
round, Dempsey got Tunney against the ropes and clipped
him with two hard rights. The champion went down on the
seat of his pants and 105,000 people came up off of theirs.

No matter what's been said or what you've read, Gene
Tunney wasn't "out" in the pugilistic sense of the word. I'm
sure he was stunned by the two punches, but his head turned,
almost instinctively, to look at his corner. I glanced quickly
and saw Jimmy Bronson motioning for him to stay down.
Tunney didn't nod, but the look in his eyes indicated that he
knew what the score was. So did Bronson, because he could
see the referee, Dave Barry, using priceless seconds trying
to make Dempsey obey the rule agreed upon, that "The
fighter scoring a knockdown shall go to a neutral corner."

Barry had started to count. Seeing Dempsey hovering near,
he stopped and shouted into the din, "Go to a neutral corner,
Jack!"

"I stay here!" Dempsey panted savagely.

For the first time in his fighting career, Dempsey was prevented from standing over a stricken opponent and bashing
him as soon as his gloved hands left the canvas. He had bat-

tered Bill Brennan that way in 1920, and before him Billy Miske. He was a couple of feet from the rising Carpentier in Jersey City, and in September, 1923, I saw him club Luis Firpo once while the Argentine was rising, and again before Luis' padded fists had pushed his body from the ring floor. I might add also that Dempsey, punched and pushed through the ropes by Firpo, was out of the ring more than ten seconds and should have been counted out.

By refusing to obey Dave Barry immediately, Dempsey gave Tunney at least four precious seconds when they were needed most—at the start of a knockdown. By the time Barry reached nine, Tunney, counting along, sprang to his feet and hopped "on his bicycle" for the rest of the round. Dempsey, leg-weary and raging mad, stopped at one point, beckoned and snarled, "Come on an' fight!"

But he who hits and runs away can win and fight another day. Tunney won, quite handily, I thought, in spite of the most dramatic knockdown in all heavyweight history. At the end of the ten rounds, waiting for the decision, I again rose to ease my tension, and again heard that voice just above my head, "Sit down Bill, there's nothing to get excited about!"

Tunney was grinning, even though the verdict in his favor was still to come. My report went:

CHICAGO, Sept. 24—The Thinker won. Gene Tunney beat Jack Dempsey in one of the most brutal, primal, blood-lusty battles in the history of the resin pit because his brain was sharper than the scathing claw of the "Tiger Man."

If the Manassa Mauler's wits had been as nimble as his hooks, he would again be champion of all the world this morning instead of a beaten, bruised and broken has-been in a darkened room of a Loop hotel.

While a million dollars and all the spoils of victory lay at his feet in the twisting form of a dead-game champion, Dempsey forgot to think.

"Go to a neutral corner, Jack," commanded Referee Dave Barry.

"I stay here," announced the sullen, savage Dempsey.

And he did stay while three or four precious seconds ticked away and with them the only chance to regain the ermine mantle of the heavyweight throne that had slipped from his shoulders in the rain at Philadelphia a year ago last night.

End of an Era

Few of us, if any, realized that the end of Jack Dempsey either as heavyweight king or pretender to the throne closed a chapter of ring history in the late Twenties. The million-dollar gate had come and gone with him. Five of his six fights (the Shelby fiasco excepted) pulled more than a million each time he stepped into the ring, and the gate of all five totaled well over $8,000,000.

Most of us made the mistake of believing that the heavyweight title itself was the main factor. Not until a few promoters including the best, Tex Rickard, had lost a few dollars, did we realize what had left our midst. Jack Dempsey had brought a predictable savagery into ring technique. He lifted the hope and expectation of every fan who paid to see brutality. Like him or not, call him the greatest if you wish—and I don't—Dempsey best typified the real fighter. He was a brutal, unrelenting punisher when desperate, he carried a punch in either hand and he had a magnetic fistic personality to a degree unequaled by every fighter before or since.

The other fighter contributed to the gate, of course. Receipts were also helped by the promotion, newspaper discussion, contrived publicity and assorted ballyhoo. But it was Dempsey's promise of corporal punishment, to himself as well as his opponent, that drew the extra fans and sent the bloodletting extravaganza over the million-dollar mark at the box office.

Tex Rickard learned those facts of financial life by losing a fortune (he admitted to $155,000) on the Tunney fight with an Australian punching bag named Tom Heeney in 1928. Not only was Tunney woefully lacking in color and provocative angles; both fight camps were without incident and rumor, natural or manufactured. The most "important" piece of news to come out of either camp, I suppose, was my announcement that Tunney would definitely retire after beating Heeney. It wasn't official, but I had enough information to be certain two weeks before the fight when I sprang the news. Promoter Rickard was considerably upset, but my conclusion was obvious.

Tunney's guarantee of $600,000 for meeting Heeney gave him a take of more than $2,000,000 in two years. Income taxes at the time were only 5 per cent on $100,000, and a surtax of 19 per cent on everything over that. After beating Heeney, millionaire Tunney made me look good by formally announcing his retirement and leaving the heavyweight championship a wide-open affair.

Tex Rickard turned this grab-bag situation into a fabulous plan of Florida conquest. Basically Rickard was a dreamer and a fearless gambler. He had dreamed up Madison Square Garden five years before and built it out of the warp and woof of a vision with other people's money. But once he had built it he needed a hard business brain to keep it going, and that he didn't have. Though he had turned in a profit of more than half a million dollars on the second Dempsey-Tunney fight, Rickard had committed the sin, unpardonable in cor-

porate operation, of sustaining a big loss on Tunney and
Heeney not just in cash but in prestige and wasted time and
effort.

It was whispered at the time, and later became a known
fact, that Rickard was already on the way out of the Garden
he had built at the same time that he planned an all-winter
gambling headquarters, playground and fight capital at
Miami Beach. The new dream was to be launched with a
heavyweight "elimination" fight between Jack Sharkey and
William L. "Young" Stribling, of Georgia, for late February.
But a long-neglected appendix ruptured in December, 1928,
and Rickard died shortly after the first of the year. He left a
wife and a small daughter in modest circumstances. Two
years later the money for his $15,000 bronze casket, for which
everybody was going to pay and nobody did, was still owed.

The so-called Six Hundred Millionaires, who had backed
Rickard in building and operating the Garden, named one of
their own to take over the maze of unfinished business left
by the promotional genius. He was a florid-faced engineer
and contractor with iron-gray hair, William F. Carey, a rural
New Yorker from the Grandma Moses country near Hoosick
Falls. No man was less qualified to succeed Tex Rickard than
"Cyclone Bill," for he was as gentle as a zephyr. No more
modest or self-effacing human being ever lived. As an example, there is the story of what happened when the family was
located temporarily near a big construction job Carey was
doing on the Hudson River.

His young daughter, Francesca, home from boarding
school, reached the dinner table in a state of high excitement.
"Daddy," she gasped, "there's a man with the same name as
yours building the Bear Mountain Bridge. I saw the name
on the cars and he has the same initials too. Isn't that funny?
Do you know him?"

Having no escape, Carey admitted it was funny, and also that he "knew him."

"The Bear Mountain Bridge—" mused Mother Carey. "Why, dear, aren't *you* building that bridge yourself?"

Unmasked at last, Carey had to break down and confess responsibility for constructing the half-mile-long, ten-million-dollar suspension bridge over the Hudson.

As titular head of the Garden promotion in Florida, Carey put on five weeks of Arabian Nights that are best described as a Rich Man's Shelby. It is remembered today as the last of the really colorful fight camps, a wing-ding to end all wing-dings.

No promoter spends $10,000 a week on sports writers any more. Carey leased one of Carl Fisher's homes, "The Shadows," a 30-room affair facing the Atlantic Ocean, on Collins Avenue. Then by letter, wire and word of mouth, invitations went out to sports writers throughout the hemisphere to bring their wives or friends. A total stranger to the sports field, Carey didn't know where to stop. Not every ink-stained, overworked sports scribbler got a chance to visit Florida in those days, and certainly not by invitation on a nice, clean, expensive cuff. Before two weeks had passed, writers were trooping in from everywhere by train and jalopy, accompanied by wives or girl friends—and some had one of each.

Prohibition was, in theory, very much with us that winter. Which may explain why the "libation du maison" was a little number called a Golden Tornado. Its components were equal parts of gin and raw egg, and the fact that the head bartender (who worked in a clothes closet on the main floor in sight of everybody passing along the beach) was in the egg business and that gin was the easiest alcoholic beverage to obtain may have had something to do with the recipe. No matter what drink a parched guest requested, he invariably got a triple Golden Tornado—unless, that is, he liked to hear corks pop and wished to bury his beak in the bubbly, of which there was no shortage either.

Francis Albertanti slept in the adjoining cot and became a sort of combined night clerk and concierge of the joint after a time. He was always busy, going or returning, much to the curiosity of Bill Carey. Mr. Carey liked to rise early and greet the sun from the spacious porch of this winter paradise while reading the stock tables of the *Wall Street Journal* or the *Times*. Almost daily, he would be greeted by little Francis wearing only a Coney Island bathing suit and a large cigar.

"Good morning, sir. How's steel?"

Carey would react instantaneously, running an eye down the column and reporting the closing price, number of shares sold and any other pertinent item. Whereupon Francis would nod approvingly and trot off.

The next morning it would be, "Good morning, sir. How's General Motors?" Carey would respond and Francis would raise an eyebrow.

Francis was only one of dozens sleeping in the same cottage with Carey, who, at first, didn't know anyone well, and who was almost completely ignorant of such colloquial terms in fight-promotion jargon as "the nut," "the take," "ice," and so on. It was natural, then, after a half-dozen mornings of Francis and his big cigar for Carey to ask me who he was. Not wanting to spoil a good thing, I simply said he was Mr. Albertanti from New York.

"He must be quite an investor," Carey mused. "He only asks about the best issues on the Big Board."

I kept quiet about the fact that Francis, having come South with only winter clothes, was wearing my light attire, including my best linen knickerbockers and Argyle stockings.

Those golden days and nights on Miami's lotus sands couldn't be kept secret. When members of the Six Hundred Millionaires in New York got wind of the free-loading, they left suites in expensive hotels for the privilege of sleeping on cots in The Shadows and taking part in the fun. Broadway playboys, gigolos, actors at liberty, movie stars, ex-prize fighters, sleight-of-hand gamblers, horse players and male members of the chorus mingled freely and on even terms with those newspapermen who could struggle to their feet to grace the groaning board three, four and five times a day. Guests dropped in for lunch and spent a month.

The climax was reached when the conglomeration of guests included the Chicago gangster "Scarface" Al Capone, known to many of us in New York as "Al Brown." He and his wife made a grand entrance and sent the wives and girl friends into twitters because Mrs. Capone looked as though she had dived into Tiffany's window and come up with everything. She sparkled so that we called her "The Walking Chandelier."

Following the rules of Emily Post, Capone invited everybody over to his joint a few nights later. It was quite a joint, a beautiful bungalow surrounded by the Atlantic Ocean in the front and Venetian swimming pools in the rear. The place was full of swank rooms and jewelry of all description. The lady visitors had never seen so much jewelry; it was lying about in open boxes, on dressers, in bathrooms and within such easy reach that about $30,000 worth of it left with the visiting ladies in the form of souvenir trinkets that "wouldn't be missed."

But it was missed eventually, and Capone complained to Bill Carey that a joke was a joke but that some of the stuff had sentimental value. Carey made a quiet canvass among the boys who, with considerable coaxing and promises of replacement, managed to pry loose from the girls all but about $5,000 worth of the baubles. This satisfied Capone, but there was no other exchange of visits, owing to a protest by one of the sports writers, Joe Williams, who refused to attend the

Capone party. His reason was, "If I want to visit guys like that, I can go to Sing Sing."

Somehow in the reports from this Babylonian splendor the heavyweight prize fight was mentioned now and then. But you couldn't blame the writers; even the Stribling training camp was more of a circus side show than anything else. It contained nine Striblings, from ninety-year-old grandpa down to "Young" William's six-month-old Mary Virginia. Ma and Pa Stribling had long shared equal publicity with their phenomenal son who had started boxing in his early teens. The tone of the camp was best reflected by a clown who refereed the training bouts and occasionally "kayoed" himself with a wild swing.

The training extravaganza produced a couple of mysteries, chief of which was why Stribling was ever called a heavyweight championship contender. Another was the "shooting" of Jack Dempsey. The old Mauler was thought, mistakenly, to be a partner of Rickard's in the project; Jack simply helped out a bit with his presence. But everybody was getting more publicity than Dempsey, who got none at all, which may have been the cause of the so-called shooting.

The story was broken one morning by Sergeant Fred Tapscott, a detective of sorts, to a sports writer who arose at seven on doctor's orders. The report spread like wildfire before anybody could get a detail—after that, you could find only discrepancies. Floyd Fitzsimmons, a promoter friend of Dempsey's, showed us a flattened bullet from a .38 revolver (a gun used by detective sergeants). But there were no suspects, revolver, corpus delicti, or hole in flesh or wall. Since Fitzsimmons and Dempsey had been involved in a similar shooting affair, also harmless, at Benton Harbor as ballyhoo for the Miske fight, we drew our own conclusions and washed them away with Golden Tornadoes.

The fight was a fistic failure but a social success. The glow of

Gold Coast jewelry vied with the glare of the incandescent floodlights over the ring, and when Jack Dempsey came down the aisle with his beautiful wife Estelle Taylor, every other jewel and glow was outshone. She was simply stunning, her natural beauty enriched by a sequin gown with a triple rope of orchids extending from one shoulder to the hem of her long, glistening robe.

Half the people in Flamingo Park couldn't take their eyes off this picture of pulchritude, and they were better rewarded than those loyal wretches who had to watch the fight. Sharkey won easily on points in ten rounds because Stribling's only weapon seemed to be indifference. Whether William L. could fight or not, I never knew. He was a fine and handsome young man from a resourceful Georgia family who gained fame and fortune by making people believe he could fight. I hasten to add that he took far more punches in the ring than I ever would. The star performer of the Stribling Circus, as it was called, was listed as having had two hundred and nineteen fights prior to meeting Jack Sharkey. Then only twenty-four years and two months old, he fought forty-eight bouts in the next four years and died in a motorcycle accident in 1933 before his twenty-ninth birthday.

The happiest result of the Florida Fantasy was that Bill Carey emerged as a successful promoter. He was a smart one too, because he met and got to know Francis Albertanti whom he later hired as a right hand and secretary. Few knew the fight game better than little Francis. Carey turned in a profit of $40,000 at Miami from a gross gate of $400,000 paid by 35,000 people. The profit would have totaled $100,000 had it not been for the cost of Carey Cottage, lavish entertainment and Hertz-private-limousine service for everybody.

But without all that, we wouldn't have had anything to write about. And so ended an era (sigh).

Object Lesson

The lesson began with the fight between a Negro heavy-weight, George Godfrey, and the mountainous Italian importation, Primo Carnera, at Philadelphia in mid-June, 1930. I wasn't covering the fight as a news story, so I sat several rows back from ringside.

Protests were bitter and vitriolic when Carnera was called the winner on a foul in the fifth round. Everybody in ancient Baker Bowl, then home of the Phillies, seemed to rise in anger. They had good reason. Godfrey lost on what seemed to be as intentional a foul as ever was seen in any ring. When he passed my aisle seat I hopped out and joined the rush of policemen and angry fans that was sweeping him toward the dressing-room runway.

Never have I seen an athlete get such a booing, cussing, and catcalling as Godfrey did from those bleacher fans; in their displeasure they threw pop bottles, old newspapers, cuds of chewing tobacco, cigar butts, cushions and handy debris. This kept all hands busy running, ducking and dodging, with the result that when we reached the door of his dressing room, there remained only a couple of coppers, Godfrey and yours-in-haste. The policemen shoved big George and me inside, slammed the door shut and promptly placed their broad hulks against it.

A Negro helper, Godfrey and I were the only ones in the room. The helper, overlooking me entirely, quickly produced a noble-looking bottle of ale for the beaten gladiator and then returned to a corner to resume packing some liniments.

I had met Godfrey on a train ride several weeks before. I liked him; he was a big, genial fellow, getting on in years as a fighter, with a good record that was significantly marred several times with the notation, "Lost on Foul." We had talked fights on the train and also discussed a subject of mutual interest, because I had written some time before that he was a champion fried-chicken eater. He had enjoyed the story and recognized me as an authority on the subject—which I was, thanks to Grandmother Henderson's groaning board.

Alone with this solemn, Alabaman pugilistic chattel, who would have been tarred and feathered in some parts of this country for what he had done to Canera, I took quick advantage of the situation. "George," I said, "I want you to tell me just one thing and I want you to tell me the truth. Can this fellow Canera fight?"

"Mr. Kome," he replied promptly and earnestly, "the man cain't hurt you. He's big as a house, an' he kin box a little, but he cain't punch . . . he cain't punch."

At this juncture, Godfrey's manager, Jim "The Baron" Dougherty, rushed in and dragged the sweating fighter off into a corner where they conferred briefly. By the time the rest of the sports scribes had got inside, Godfrey was rolling his eyes and saying, "Mos' terr'bul man I ever did see; man kin knock your hed reight off; man's dangerous, goin' to be champeen shuah!"

I held to the belief that Godfrey, alone and free to speak, had told me the truth.

Primo Carnera, then twenty-two, was born in Sequals, Udine Province, Italy. Because of his abnormal lateral growth —chest, feet, hands and bones—his actual measurements were exaggerated. First reports from Europe had him six feet, ten inches tall and weighing three hundred pounds. After one glimpse of him any figures were believable. For the record, he was six feet four and a half inches and scaled about two hundred and sixty-five pounds.

Leon See, a Frenchman, saw him first in a circus, and took him on as a fighter. Having no confidence in Carnera's fighting ability, See saw that most of the earlier fights were "bagged." Primo never knew. The profitable practice of meeting only cooperative opponents was continued in America. Of all Carnera's fights in this country, not more than half a dozen were honest. A happy and jovial fellow, he did his best, provided good entertainment and, even after his managers took most of his purses, lived like a king compared to the squalor of his youth.

Primo was Exhibit A in the Great American Sucker Tour of 1930. From January 24 through September 18, he scored twenty-two knockouts in a total of fifty-six rounds, or an average of about two and a half rounds per man. The only opponent he failed to kayo in that period was Godfrey, who fouled out.

In Chicago, Elzear Rioux, a January opponent, was told, "If you hit this man even one punch you won't get your money." The result was that Elzear left his corner at the first bell poised for a one and a half gainor, grabbed his nose so that it wouldn't draw water, and executed instead a full swan dive at the feet of his astonished conqueror. Elzear got his money.

When he met Jack Sharkey in Brooklyn in October, 1931, Carnera had lost only two of fifty-one fights, plus an early disqualification. One loss was to Young Stribling in Paris, the other to Jimmy Maloney in the Irishman's home town, Boston. Sharkey gave Primo a bad beating. At the bell ending the fifteenth round, Sharkey left a bleeding hulk reeling and helpless on the ropes. But when we got back to the dressing room, Manager See's surprise seemed to be not that Primo had gotten a good beating but that he hadn't received a worse one. I can hear Leon yet, repeating over and over, as though astonished beyond words, "Is *that* the best they've got? Is *that* the best they've got?"

To operate in America, See had to work through Louis Soreci and Bill Duffy. Duffy was associated with Owney Madden, known as the beer king of metropolitan New York during prohibition. Madden's office boy, by the way, was the late Joe Gould, who wound up managing a heavyweight champion, Jim Braddock.

All this, and much more, was behind the lesson I learned in the Madison Square Garden classroom in early February, 1933. Carnera had been matched against a promising young heavyweight, Ernie Schaaf, the winner to meet Jack Sharkey in June for the championship. Sharkey had won the title from Max Schmeling in the fifteen-round decision that brought forth the cry from Joe Jacobs heard 'round the world, "We wuz robbed!"

The catch lay in the fact that Sharkey was part owner of Schaaf. He and his manager, Johnny Buckley, had paid $12,-500 to Phil Schlossberg for Schaaf's contract. How could Sharkey possibly make a serious defense of his title against his own fighter?

In addition to hearing from three different sources around town that the fight was a fake, I received an unsigned letter, mailed from downtown Boston, that Schaaf was scheduled to lose. There was a fight hangout and gymnasium just off Scollay Square in Boston where such news could easily be found, along with information about when the next convoy of bootleg liquor would be trucked from Boston to the Madden-Duffy crowd in New York.

If there is truth in the rumor [I wrote on Feb. 7, 96 hours before the fight] no purpose will be served in locking the boxing larder after Carnera's dogs have carried away the bone. One of the weaknesses of boxing officials and fans alike always has been that they have contrived to control their indignation over crooked bouts until after the thievery was committed.

It has been customary, in other words, to wait until the thief had a good running start before setting up a cry of "Stop Thief!" But in this instance, thanks to the warning herein contained, they have four whole days in which to guard and insure the precious jewel of the fair name of fisticuffs.

In spite of my warning (and I was not the only writer who issued one), some twenty thousand fans packed the Garden for the fight, which went according to warning. Carnera, big and unusually fast for a big man, threw his butterfly punches and light jabs at Schaaf for twelve of the scheduled fifteen rounds. Ernie was slow, undecided and far from aggressive. Less than a minute of the thirteenth round had passed when the obviously tiring Schaaf fell from the lightest of Carnera's countless left jabs. He slid against the ropes and down to the canvas, landing first on his left elbow and then on the seat of his pants, slumping like a roly-poly baby stumbling over his toes.

Still leaning on his elbow, Schaaf tried to rise at the count of three, grimaced dramatically and changed his mind. Instead of trying to rise, he became more horizontal. When the counting ended, Buckley and Sharkey hurried through the ropes and carried their fighter to his corner. I felt that he couldn't be unconscious because he could hold up his head. When I reached the dressing room a few minutes later, Schaaf lay naked on the rubbing table, covered with a black cloth. To keep him from biting his tongue, a man stood at his now-slumping head with forefingers caught in either side of the fighter's limp mouth.

"Is he faking?" somebody asked in a stage whisper.

"How the hell can you tell?" came an audible reply.

A priest joined the group at the head of the table, adding a somber touch. A big man in an oddly striped jersey looked at me with clear blue eyes, smiled faintly and winked. He was heavyweight champion Jack Sharkey, half-owner of Schaaf.

"What's wrong with him, Doc?" a writer asked.

The official physician, Dr. William Walker, a brother of New York's former mayor, shrugged. "We won't know for sure until we have a chance to give him a thorough examination. He may have a concussion."

"Which will be the first time," chuckled a skeptic, "that a man ever got a concussion of the brain from sitting down." The babble of voices went on endlessly. "Lousy fight." . . . "I told you so." . . . "Before the biggest crowd since Delaney and Maloney, too." . . . "How much you win, kid?" . . . "Great! Just like money in the bank." . . . "And Carnera will do the same thing to Sharkey, too." . . .

I could hear a distant echo from another dressing room after a Carnera fight. "Mr. Kome . . . the man cain't hurt you . . . he's big as a house an' kin box a little . . . but he cain't punch . . . he cain't punch" . . . and I could still see Sharkey's faint smile, and the wink.

My column a few hours later read:

JUST A SCHAAF AND A HAIRCUT

Unless there is something organically wrong with Ernie Schaaf—in which the writer starts out by offering the most sincere apologies of which he is capable—the fight in Madison Square Garden last night was the fake which so many have been insisting for ten days that it was going to be. As this is written, Schaaf lies in Polyclinic Hospital across the way from the Garden, to all intents and purposes still unconscious.

If he is actually unconscious, as nobody in his dressing room apparently knew for sure, then he collapsed either, as I said above, from some organic weakness, or because he was a sick boy as a result of a recent attack of flu before the bout and, therefore, in no condition to be in the ring.

Nothing that Carnera did to him before a tremendous crowd of 20,000 persons could possibly have accounted for the desperate condition in which he appeared to be as he was carried away on a stretcher. If he was not actually in bad shape, which continues to be my private opinion, then it looks as though the boys are beginning to include the dear old Polyclinic in their act. It's so handy, you see. If this keeps up they won't be able to get an ordinary run of the mine patient a room because they will all be occupied by swooning pugilists who are trying to prove something or other. This may or may not be the case with Schaaf. Any disinterested physician should be able to tell after a thorough examination, which, naturally, cannot be made in a dressing room crowded with skeptics and pleaders for the fair name of fistiana.

As for the tearful pleaders, methought, as somebody may have said before, they did protest too much.

"Look at him!" they begged you, "could anybody put on an act like that? And would they?"

My answer to both questions was "yes." If I were going to stage a phoney, especially one that had been branded a phoney in advance, it seems to me that the hospital is exactly where I would want the victim taken. It makes it, somehow, look so authentic.

But Schaaf *was* unconscious, in the dressing room and later at the hospital. All signs, physicians said, indicated a brain hemorrhage. The fighter's skull was opened and closed late in the day, but he remained in a coma.

I went through a hell that equaled anything I have ever experienced. The sight and memory of Schaaf's mother,

father and sister, who stood in a heartbroken little group outside his door when we reporters left the hospital after the
evening operation, remained to taunt and mock.

The column which follows came awfully hard. It was
clumsy, but sincere:

In writing my report of the Carnera-Schaaf fight in Madison Square Garden last Friday night, I prefaced what I had
to say with the statement that if it turned out that there was
something organically wrong with Schaaf, I wanted to begin
by extending him the humblest apology of which I was capable. It was developed that there was something seriously,
possibly fatally, wrong with the boy and I hasten to make
the apology publicly.

In believing that Schaaf was feigning injury when carried
from the ring and later in his dressing room, I was as wrong
as it is possible to be and I am deeply sorry to have been
unfair to the stricken boxer. Doubly sorry because, so far as
I know, he has always fought fairly and honestly.

Nobody has asked me to make this apology and nobody
has, or can possibly change my opinion that the Carnera-
Schaaf prize fight was, on its face, a fishy-looking affair.
Knowing no more about it than I knew at the time, seeing
the same fight fought over again tonight, I would have to
sit down and write the same story. That was the way I saw
it and, therefore, that was the way I had to write it.

But in view of Schaaf's critical condition and the delicate
operation performed on his brain yesterday afternoon, it is
obvious that what looked spurious in the ring Friday night
could have been the honest efforts of a badly hurt and thoroughly game youth. Indeed, the very injury proves not that
the fight was all right as it was fought, but that there was
something radically wrong with it.

Had it been possible to look into Schaaf's brain as he lay
on that rubbing table after the bout, none of us would have
blundered. But if it were possible to look into the minds of all

about us, how many mistakes we could save ourselves! . . .

There is one more thing we want to make clear. . . . Our opinion that the fight looked bad was not based on our selection of Schaaf to win . . . or our pre-fight question of its honesty. . . . The fact that he is fighting for his life brings home to me again the necessity of trying to be as fair as possible in a column such as this. I do try to be fair, and so I say again that I'm sorry to have suspicioned that Schaaf was shamming.

But Ernie Schaaf had been dead several hours by the time this reached print.

The report of the post-mortem examination by Dr. Charles Norris, New York County medical examiner, made public a week later completed my lesson. Schaaf had suffered no skull or brain damage, or any harm from a single punch. The emergency operation the day after the fight was made necessary by cerebral compression.

The Norris report said in part:

> The deceased had a chronic or subacute meningo encephalitis characterized by lymphocytic infiltration around the blood vessels in the subarachnoid space and adjacent cortex. The cause of the inflammation cannot be known with certainty, but it may be referred to a recent attack of influenza.
>
> This condition would have been difficult to detect at the time of the physical examination before the fight. In the ring, however, it interfered with Schaaf's boxing skill so that he was unable to avoid blows.

We also learned that Schaaf had done little or no training for the fight, not because he had no fear of Carnera but because he had been in the hospital with influenza until ten days before the fight.

From time to time since that fight I have been chided by

indignant readers for my tendency to "see no evil," or at least for failing to denounce it in print. Of course I know there's evil, perhaps right under my nose, but I feel it's a matter for the district attorney, not for me. Once I called a boy a faker, a dishonest fighter, a fraud, in black type that cannot be erased or called back. I labeled him that while he lay in a hospital, unable to fight even for his life. It was not a pleasant experience, and please excuse me if I don't care to risk those hours again.

I have leaned more to reporting the facts as I saw them, and interpreting only those facts, interesting or intriguing. I have left the "exposé" to others. I didn't utter a word of protest or criticism four months later when Primo Carnera became heavyweight champion of the world by "knocking out" Jack Sharkey in the sixth round.

Rose Bowl Bill

Writers have devised many good ways of saying, "A fool may now and then be right by chance." My turn to prove the adage came on Armistice Day of 1933, the Saturday afternoon I stumbled into some kind of poor man's immortality by visiting Baker Field in upper Manhattan.

The Columbia Lions were to play a strong Navy eleven that had beaten Notre Dame. I was unable to spare the time for an out-of-town game; in fact, by rights I shouldn't have been watching at all. Along with others, particularly Tim Mara and his sons, operators of the professional football Giants, I was helping to promote a football game at the Polo Grounds on Sunday to benefit the widow of a great soldier, football coach and friend, Frank W. Cavanaugh, the "Iron Major."

Neither Columbia nor Navy drew me to the game, though I had a reportorial duty to see the Midshipmen in action with the annual Army-Navy game coming up. But I had suffered through Columbia's 20–0 defeat a month before by a Princeton team brought to an early-season peak by Fritz Crisler. What really attracted me to the game, I think, was the way I felt about the Columbia coach, Louis Lawrence Little. Lou was then in his fourth year at Morningside Heights, where, he had said at the start, "I did not come to fail."

This tremendously sincere and likable fellow had reeked of failure when I happened to see him on Friday. He carried on like a professional mourner—which is exactly what he was. "I just don't see how our boys have a chance, Bill," he moaned.

Little could cry the biggest pre-game tears since the lachrymose Gilmour Dobie, who wept in direct proportion to the devastating power of such great teams as Cornell of the early Twenties. So even though I shouldn't have spared the time, there I was in the Baker Field press box ready to join Coach Little at the wailing wall after the final gun.

Then my eyes were opened wide. Before the second quarter was half over, you could see that this Navy team didn't belong on the same gridiron with Columbia. Speed, precision, maneuvering that seemed intuitive, cohesive effort, and intelligence were all there. They showed more dash and fire than any Lion eleven I had ever seen. There may have been greater Columbia teams, or would be later, but up to that time there never had been a better looking one.

Cliff Montgomery on this particular afternoon was as fine and cooney a field general as any college team ever boasted. The final score was 14–7, but it might have been 27–7, so completely did the speedy Blue and White dominate the field. All this was written in my daily column with a slight feeling of guilt, because Columbia was my school. Nothing delighted me more than to see them produce a fine team, but also nothing could make me say it was a better team than I really believed. I'm a strong rooter for my convictions, but I've always thought too much of my few loyal readers to think I could fool them.

Though I had other things on my mind, that Columbia-Navy game jumped through my mind all week. Another Blue-and-White victory on Saturday left me with little else to think about over the weekend. By late Sunday night, I had developed the idea, believed it, and wrote it for the Monday column under the heading of "A Little Trip to California."

Why, in all the Rose Bowl game talk, I asked, has nobody suggested that Columbia represent the East? Right out of the ever-loving dope book there were only two teams on the Atlantic seaboard that got a higher rating on the year's play than the roaring Lions of Morningside. I wrote:

> One of these is Princeton, unbeaten, untied and unscored on, but only once peaked for a game, and that was with Columbia . . . the only game, by the way, that Columbia lost. The only other team at this writing with a higher ranking than the Light Blue and White is Army, and Army must still go to war with Notre Dame. And chances are Army wouldn't be permitted to go.
>
> Columbia might also have trouble getting sanction. But now that President Butler's long fight against prohibition has been crowned a success, he should be in a lenient mood. It would be a wonderful thing for Columbia's athletic prestige even to receive the bid. And with the extra dough they might buy some band uniforms, instead of those white duck pants they have been parading around in on these cold November days.
>
> But Columbia has something to offer the Far West, too. It is one of the oldest major educational institutions in the

country. It is truly Eastern, and its campus lies along a fairly
well-known street—Broadway, New York City . . . It is one
of the strictest schools about scholastic standings, and over
and above everything else, it has a honey of a football team.
A team with a smashing, diversifying attack that is something to watch. My memory is that it has lost only three or
four games in three years. And if Cliff Montgomery isn't as
sensational a back as Red Franklin, who ran wild against
Fordham and is called the Coast's best, take my overcoat.
. . . Perhaps this is only a dream . . . but of such stuff are
dreams, and columns, made.

Naturally, the horse laughs reverberated through the terra
cotta canyons of Los Angeles at the mere suggestion that
New York represented *anything* nationally, least of all football. Even Hollywood couldn't picture this one. Why, Fordham in its greatest years of "the seven blocks of granite" had
been snubbed; there was even a saying referring to Fordham
as "Unbeaten, untied and uninvited." How then could a light
team of "scholars" qualify?

They qualified with me. I not only said so in print and in
public, but a few days later I wrote an open letter to "Tiny"
Thornhill, coach of Stanford, the Rose Bowl selection in the
West, explaining the whole Eastern football situation. I said
that, with the exception of Princeton and Army, Columbia
represented us best. "They're so good," I wrote, "that no team
in the country right now can go out and beat 'em to music.
They might not have the man power to stand off the likes of
Michigan and your team and Southern Cal, and then again
they might. . . . For some reason they have decided they
are good—and four Saturdays in a row they have proved it.
. . . If it should work out that you should invite these New
York boys out there and they should accept . . . if they
don't give you a better game than Pitt gave the Trojans last

year (Southern Cal 35, Pitt 0), and draw as many people, sue me. . . ."

Columbia *was* invited. But the red tape of official consideration occupied a whole day while thousands of excited kids sweated it out on the campus. The student body whooped it up on Broadway and produced three thousand signatures demanding acceptance. A hastily organized detachment of fifteen hundred undergraduates stormed the office of Dean Hawkes. Finally, Dr. Elliott, director of athletics, announced that Columbia would go to Pasadena—and that's how I came to be called, among other things, "Rose Bowl Bill."

Ended there, the story wouldn't be complete; the best and most meaningful part would be missing. It wasn't just another football team that crossed the country to play in the Rose Bowl on January 1, 1934, but a group of determined and dedicated students—dedicated to an unusual coach and his unusual methods. A football squad, small in number and stature by ordinary standards, believed so implicitly in Lou Little and in what he was trying to do with them and for them that they rose to their greatest heights of accomplishment. They have never stopped believing in their coach whom they revere to this day, twenty-five years later.

The team had to be unusual to bounce back from the depths of a midseason whitewashing. On the night we rode back to New York after the Princeton shutout they were as far from Rose Bowl aspirations as a vacant-lot team near your home. Morale was so bad that a well-known football authority whispered to me, "This will just about ruin Columbia's football season. They are not the sort of team to come back off a defeat like that."

But they did. We crossed the country with many of the "experts" still unconvinced, and a few of them insisted on saying for publication that "three or four teams rated the invitation over Columbia." But they didn't know Lou Little as I did, which made it almost possible to read these foolish remarks with a smile.

Lou had telephoned me right after receiving the invitation from Stanford, and he said words that I'll never forget. "You got me into this, Bill, but if we go, we're not going to lose. I know these kids. I know 'em like a brother, and no football team that ever wore cleats can outfight them."

There were light moments on that trip to California, the best of which came from my roommate. From the time the Columbia argosy pulled out of New York's Penn Station on the great adventure, I bunked with "Uncle Harry" Grayson. It is always a privilege to be with Grayson, but the price this time was heavy. I listened to the life story of his distinguished nephew, Bobby Grayson, the backfield star of the Stanford team, exactly one hundred and forty-two times in ten days. It finally came down to the question of whether it was preferable to stay awake and listen to Uncle Harry snore, or try to sleep and listen to the story of Bobby's life. It was a fifty-fifty proposition, and you'll appreciate what that means when I tell you that his snoring was terrific. (Hal Coffman, the cartoonist, was the only man I ever shared a room with who could carry Uncle Harry's typewriter as a snorer.)

Until you have heard a Grade-A snorer wake up from a sound sleep, yelling, "Bobby, take it around! Watch the blockers! Take it over!" you will never know the true meaning of sleeplessness. Also you will never know the family pride of which man is capable—though every ounce of it was justified by one of the nation's greatest backfield stars. Nephew Bobby was a unanimous All-America selection for two successive years.

But Uncle Harry's pride, deep as it was, couldn't match mine on that rain-soaked January 1, 1934, when my boys "did it all." The Lions of Broadway exceeded my blue-sky hopes, partisanship and prayers. In the press box I saw a few other lips whispering prayers too, especially when big Stanford, trailing 7–0, was only a few feet from the Columbia goal line, soaking wet and raging mad. I sat next to Bob Harron, then of the New York *Post*, and later a Columbia University publicist, and we could only stare in unbelieving silence, carefully keeping our fingers crossed.

It was my joy and privilege to wire home:

PASADENA, January 2—They'll remember this one.

Great football teams come and go and mighty California teams will one day lead the big parade again. But out here on the majestic Pacific Coast, vaunted home of the vaunted elevens, and sometimes sunny days, they'll remember how a great-hearted little Columbia team from the sidewalks of old New York leveled mighty Stanford in the mud of the Rose Bowl on January 1, 1934.

Oh, yes, they'll remember this one. They'll remember how the little Lion roared through the murk and mist beneath the storm-blanketed Sierra Madres on this New Year's Day.

They'll remember how, not once, but three times, with their cleats dug deep in those last white lines, a great football team that was outnumbered, outweighed, and out-manned, but not outfought, rose up and threw back one desperate Cardinal-clad charge after the other while 35,000 looked on in wonder and dismay.

They'll remember how the black-haired, black-browed Al Barabas, the Austrian howitzer, spoke once early in the second period, and on the most perfect play of the ball game, raced 17 yards to the only touchdown. They'll remember, too, how Luke Wilder place-kicked the extra point that at the finish had the Stanford side on the field rooting its heart out for a tie.

Stanford, with a team that answered the opening whistle a four-to-one favorite, and on which its supporters had blithely given from 12 to 20 points, rooting for a tie with Columbia! Imagine that! What a shock that must have been.

Even former President Hoover, most distinguished Stanford Alumnus, who saw the game, must have looked on unbelieving and incredulous at the sight. There was the ball game play, if it is this reporter's opinion you are asking. Let me try and set the picture for you.

It was the third period. The big scoreboard, its white letters and numerals standing out in sharp relief against the gray of the day, told an amazing story. Back of the big S there was a zero. On the other side there was a C with this tantalizing 7. Through fleeting sunshine and shadow and gusty windblown spatters of rain, the little Lions had held their giant foes in check.

As one Columbia rooter said, "The game seemed all wrong. Every time Stanford sent in a replacement, he seemed larger than the man he relieved, and every time a substitute trotted from the Columbia bench, he seemed smaller.

I could go on and in fact I did, because it was the sports event of the season and year. That gang of gallant kids was symbolized to me by little Tony Matal standing in the dressing room after the game with the tears still streaming down his cheeks because the club doctor had forbade his playing the second half. Over and over he blubbered, "I wasn't made to sit on any bench."

Tony Matal missed the second half, but the thirty minutes he played right end was enough to clutter up the whole Stanford offense. The one hundred and eighty pounds of redheaded dynamite shook their bones and teeth as they had never been shaken before. Only one inactive player suffered more than Matal. Joe Ferrara was ineligible to play on the slimmest of scholastic technicalities. He had good marks, but not quite good enough for Columbia requirements.

The returning party of sixty reached Penn Station a few hours late, but three thousand students in an overflow crowd of five thousand men, women and children swarmed beneath the floodlights in a bedlam of acclaim while three hundred police struggled to get the weary travelers into waiting cars. Motorcycle outriders flanked the cavalcade and sirened the path to Morningside Heights where the sidewalk at 116th Street and Broadway glistened with soft winter rain. The old bronze Alma Mater sat proudly on the Library steps under the inscription that reads, "Founded as Kings College in the Reign of George the Third" and powerful voices rose in the dripping darkness singing lustily, "For this is old Columbia's Day."

The "day" might be called endless, because it's still going on. The victory served to weld as one the hearts and minds of the whole Blue and White squad. For a quarter of a century now, that 1933 group has symbolized what all coaches, educators, and even sports writers like to see in a football team— better men and better lives through study and play. Those Rose Bowl boys went out into the professional world as individuals and in separate ways, but always they kept in touch with each other as a team. I'm proud to boast that whenever they've assembled to resurrect the glory of Pasadena, Rose Bowl Bill has been invited to help celebrate.

The last reunion was in 1954. We swapped tales of military service, but soon got around to the classic with Stanford and the films of the game. At the end of the first half, the touchdown-scoring Al Barabas turned to Coach Little and said, "Lou, let's not show the second half. They might beat us!"

As this is written, twenty-five years after the game, the players had been contacted again by their unofficial secretary, Cliff Montgomery, now a magazine advertising executive. The response was quick and heartening, for all the squad's survivors (four or five, including Doc Barrett, the trainer, had died) were doing well in a variety of professions. There were happy marriages and many children, and a couple of sons were playing football at Columbia. Most of the correspondents referred to the lasting influence of their coach, Lou Little. They wrote things like, "I am trying to live as Lou taught me"; "I taught our 'K-79' Rose Bowl touchdown play to my high-school team and it still works"; "My experience under Lou Little was a high privilege." None of them seemed able to forget.

These men formed the only team from a New York City college ever to play in the Rose Bowl; Columbia was the last of the Eastern teams to qualify. All things considered, we never developed a better one, or even one as good, in my book.

GENIUS AT WORK

*It is true greatness to have
in one the frailty of a man . . .*
Francis Bacon

The Big Year

Newspaper life is made exciting by the stories you cover, but memorable by some of the people you meet. Greatness often camouflaged beyond immediate recognition walks at your side, sits at your dining table, or sips with you at the bar.

Pre-eminence may be concealed in a coworker or competitor, or in a newsworthy character that you have been paid to watch, understand and explain to the reading public. Outstanding people are interesting chiefly because they're like the rest of us—mortal under the skin or the camouflage. The story develops as you see what makes them click, and understand enough to write about them. Occasionally, and always surprisingly, you find what I like to call genius. I've never met many who qualified, but I can recall a few. There was no push-button answer to any of them and they could drive you nuts by their inconsistencies of mind, manners and method.

Definitions of genius differ, and I've never bothered to look up the word. But to me a genius is one who can do something so well that the end product has a timeless quality of perfection and leaves an indelible mark on those it touches. This accomplishment outshines all its creator's mortal shortcomings, making them not so much forgivable as forgettable. Errors and faults on the human side are obscured in the glow of pure achievement.

These definitions occurred to me early in 1934, a milestone

year for me which began with that Rose Bowl victory by Columbia. There was the sudden appearance of a boxing great, Joe Louis, to lift a shattered sport from the sleazy depths to which it had fallen. There was also the second All-Star Game, single-handedly turned into a classic by a great left-handed pitcher, Carl Hubbell, who tingled our spines at the Polo Grounds by striking out Babe Ruth, Lou Gehrig, Al Simmons, Jimmy Foxx and Joe Cronin in a row. And there was the flight of my St. Louis Cardinals to the peak of baseball supremacy again, and the full emergence of the Branch Rickey farm system. This totally new concept of baseball administration was to influence the entire structure of the game for the next quarter century.

But far more important than these and other events that year was my own emergence as a father. I hasten to assure you that I'm not claiming genius for this achievement; I merely wish to record that, after twelve years of marriage, Elaine and I had a son. We named him Robert and Strange for our fathers. Some medical genius was required to get him launched, because the little guy began life in an incubator.

Giant among Men

The methods and achievements of John J. McGraw, who died in February, 1934, are best described, in my opinion, by the word genius. He was identified in the headlines as "manager of the Giants," but that title didn't tell the story. McGraw *was* the Giants, and for more than two decades he was virtually Mr. Baseball.

From the time he entered New York as manager, on July

19, 1902, McGraw began making the big leagues big league. No other man did more to change the game from a hit-or-miss sandlot pastime into a great national sport. Every ball player that ever walked in spikes owes him a debt of gratitude he cannot pay.

I'll never forget, in one of the several celebrations of McGraw's Silver Jubilee year as a Giant, 1927, what the National League president, John Heydler, said: "When John McGraw came from Baltimore to New York, the National League was tottering. It was close to bankruptcy. The fight being waged by the new American League threatened the very life of the old circuit. But McGraw saved the situation. He put New York back on the baseball map. He built the Giants into the most powerful machine in baseball."

This was public acknowledgment by a high official that one man had just about saved the game. One man cannot do such a thing, in any line of endeavor, unless his whole mind, being, and flesh and bones are part and parcel of the endeavor. After meeting him, it did not take me long to recognize this all-consuming preoccupation with baseball in John McGraw. His every thought and move in baseball was second nature, and all else was secondary.

McGraw was sharp-tongued, sarcastic, even brutal, when any person or thing threatened his purpose in baseball—which was always concerned with winning a game or a pennant. Yet he could be human enough to take a young sports writer aside to ease his tension and make him feel like a big man by saying, "Don't let the fact that you're new with the Giants stop you from telling what you see as you see it. And if you have doubts, about any thing or player, don't be afraid to come to me and ask about it."

This was said to me in the same, soft voice that could become razor-sharp and cut to the heart of an enemy. The kindly brown eyes were the same beady eyes that I have seen glare with fiery anger. Unless you could evaluate and distinguish between one mood and the other, you couldn't understand McGraw. A lot of people didn't—some by choice.

Being mortal, McGraw made mistakes, and with them he made enemies. Off the field, he was not my concern. My interest in him centered on a knowledge of every rule and angle and method of baseball so fantastic that it left every other pretender behind him. He knew the game and pioneered it; since earliest childhood he had lived it, dreamed it, breathed it and sacrificed every other interest to master it. You could like McGraw or you could hate him—and in those boisterous days some hated him so that it would have shamed a dyspeptic rattlesnake—but you could not be unaware of the fact that McGraw and his Giants were there. He taught his players to think as he did, to regard themselves as the very best. They became the scourge of the National League by either playing you or fighting you—preferably both.

Once McGraw and his players were sitting out on a twelfth-floor fire escape on a hot summer night, drinking a little cold spring beer. Below them was a courtyard bathed in sable darkness, and the fire escape, loaded down with rare old baseball ivory and Pilsener, did not seem any too secure.

"If this thing breaks," Larry Doyle laughed, "here goes the Giants."

"You mean here goes the National League," Art Fletcher corrected.

McGraw took professional baseball players out of Mrs. Murphy's refined boarding house (bring your own soap and butter), out of the lodging house overlooking the railroad tracks, and into the best hotels in town. The best was never too good for him or his teams. In return he demanded the best from them, and tongue-lashed them mercilessly for falling short of their best.

The steaming vitriol of McGraw's temper was well known

and not exaggerated. I once saw him turn it on full blast and chase a whole squad of reporters from his room. It was during spring training at Sarasota, Florida, in 1926. Mac had called one of those Thursday-morning meetings with baseball writers, an innovation of his to take advantage of space available in the bulldog, or early, editions of the Sunday papers in those days when newsprint was $40 a ton. We New York writers were in McGraw's room on one of the three finished floors of the Sarasota Terrace Hotel. Still in silk pajamas, he held court sitting on the edge of the bed. His main topic was Bill Terry, the young first baseman; as a holdout, Terry was delaying Mac's team-building plans. While he castigated the absent player, McGraw kept trying, and failing, to cross his legs. He was roly-poly, his legs were short to begin with, and the silk of the pajamas made it an impossible task.

"Pardon me, Mac," said Bozeman Bulger of the *Evening World.*

"Yes, Boze, what is it?"

"If you'll wait a minute, I'll run downstairs and get you a slab of sandpaper to put behind your knee so you'll have some traction. Won't take but a minute—"

"You can all get out of here and find your Sunday story—" The outraged manager recommended a far hotter place than Florida as a source of news, and you'd have thought we were heading for it to see us stampede out of there. McGraw continued the outburst behind the slammed door and returned to bed. All of us enjoyed it, but Boze and I laughed loudest, perhaps because both of us worked for six-day evening papers and had no use for a Sunday story.

During that spring we saw one facet of the McGraw genius make baseball history. He told a teen-age, left-handed-hitting catcher to take a fielder's glove, go to the outfield and "watch Pep Young." The teen-ager, Mel Ott, sat at McGraw's side through the season and wore the Giant uniform for the next twenty-two years, appearing in more than 2,750 games as a player and about 1,000 as manager.

I always associated the decline of John McGraw's influence with the year 1926. Bickering with his veteran players began in Sarasota and it was obvious before midseason that he had "lost them." A manager in any sport must have complete respect, even admiration, from his players to make his leadership effective. The tension snapped in midsummer when McGraw's favorite player, Frank Frisch, declared himself fed up with criticism from "the old man," bolted the team and returned home in violation of his contract. He rejoined the Giants, but McGraw never forgot it and traded him to the St. Louis Cardinals for Hornsby that winter.

Long before McGraw retired in 1932, his personal physician, Dr. William Walsh, the old Fordham pitcher, warned him to slow down. He even advised him not to travel, for McGraw was a sick man several years before retirement. But his mind remained bright, and so did his memory, especially of old friends, the has-beens and the never-weres. I saw the proof. McGraw was always noted for his generosity and unwillingness to say no to a touch. On occasions when he wasn't socializing or was feeling too miserable for any company, he'd leave envelopes at the hotel desk for the ones he couldn't forget. They inquired of the clerk, who selected an envelope from the stack to tide them over for a little while. No man in my memory was more understanding of such things than John J. McGraw. And few men were more misunderstood.

Tad

Thomas Aloysius Dorgan, "Tad," was a great cartoonist who was equally accomplished as a lexicographer in slang. He spoke and wrote in slang; it was as natural to him as breathing. To my regret I never knew Tad well. Many who knew him longer made the same complaint, but at least they had met him. I never did, for by the time I began writing for the old *Evening Journal* Tad had been working for a few years at his Long Island home to favor what he termed "a bum ticker."

He didn't like to talk about it. "It's one of those dime-a-dozen tickers," he confided. "But nobody's going to laugh about that in the paper." Still, he was well enough to write me notes frequently, or call me on the telephone, especially when I wrote something pleasant about John McGraw.

Tad's intense dislike of McGraw was no secret around the old office at 200 William Street. There was no mistaking the meaning when Tad expressed his feelings. That's why his slang was so natural when he spoke of someone as "a phony," "a hardboiled egg," "a rummy," "full of chin music," "a finale hopper," "the cat's meow," or "the cat's pajamas." Each phrase rang with specific meaning, as did everything he said.

The origin of Tad's hostility toward McGraw, however, was clouded. Some charged it to a legendary insult by the manager when Tad, supposedly a timid young man from San Francisco, tried unsuccessfully to interview McGraw at the Polo Grounds. I doubt that any real newspaperman—and Tad was one—can be that thin-skinned. None of those San Franciscans who migrated to the East scared easily. Besides, Tad was twenty-seven in 1904 when he began work on the *Journal* and McGraw, in his second full season with the Giants, was only thirty-one. It was one of his greatest years; he won the National League pennant and refused to play the Red Sox, winners in the American League, for the baseball championship. Tad drew a whimsical seven-column cartoon of the victory celebration at Klaw and Erlanger's Theater.

I'm inclined to trace Tad's feelings back to McGraw's unfortunate and unforgettable repudiation of some baseball writers in June, 1917. It sprang from McGraw's claim of interference when Hal Chase shouldered Fletcher to prevent a double play in the ninth inning of a game at Cincinnati. Quickly McGraw stormed at the umpires, harsh words were exchanged, and McGraw replied to an insult by Umpire Byron with a punch on the jaw. A good-sized riot followed, after which McGraw was suspended indefinitely by Tener, president of the National League and former governor of Pennsylvania.

"I'd give a hundred dollars," McGraw stormed to New York reporters, "to tell that Tener to his face what I think of him and his National Commission."

In a formal hearing McGraw was obliged to sign a statement of repudiation in order to save libel suits and a few heads—his own included. Possibly President Tener might have resigned, but baseball writers who had quoted the enraged McGraw with his permission were out on a limb.

Tad took a definite stand in the matter of defending the published truth. He showed pity for nobody, including his own coworker, Sam Crane, who had not quoted McGraw after the heated outburst. Within a week Tad drew and published four cartoons that bared his feelings. In all four he took McGraw to task as only his incisive pen could. So nearly ten years later, whenever I happened to write anything that was complimentary, or even favorable, to McGraw, I could pretty well count on getting a note from Tad saying, "Well, I see you're boosting that old so-and-so again."

I don't want to give the impression that Tad was always carping and criticizing, or that his dislike of McGraw caused him to dislike me. He was bigger than that, and the stories of his drolleries in the old hangouts—the Battling Nelson bar at Jack's, the old Madison Square Garden, at Jack Doyle's pool room, and at Tim Shine's Restaurant—proved it. Yet he had the makings of a first-class curmudgeon. When you knew his background, you could understand why.

Tad was born in Frisco, south of the Slot, in April, 1877. Eight years later, the story goes, he was hitching a "sleigh ride" on a house-moving job by standing on a shovel, guiding the handle with his left hand and gripping the towing rope with his right. He turned to look at something, the right hand slipped into a big pulley, and four fingers were chewed off. With only the thumb and a stump of knuckle remaining, he had to become left-handed.

Like every red-blooded Frisco teen-ager in the Gay Nineties, Tad was thoroughly sports-minded. In spite of his mangled mitt he could box and play baseball. He hung around the livery stable run by the father of his pal, Joe Corbett, a year older than Tad and a baseball nut. Later, at twenty, Joe was pitching for the Baltimore Orioles of McGraw, Robinson and Keeler, but at that time big brother Jim, ten years older than Joe, was already a boxing star and a hero of the exclusive Olympic Club. Midway in their teens, Tad and Joe saw Jim box a four-round exhibition with the great John L. Sullivan when the heavyweight champion reached Frisco as an actor in *Honest Hearts and Willing Hands*. You can imagine how they rooted a year later when big Jim kayoed the great John L. at New Orleans for the world's heavyweight championship.

Tad's main interest was drawing. He had learned to sketch with his left hand and he hero-worshiped Jimmy Swinnerton, a great cartoonist of the Hearst papers. When Tad landed a job in the art department of the *Bulletin* at $5 a week, it was inevitable that he would combine sports and drawing.

One "first" that Tad liked to relate, I was told, came in August, 1901. Boxing promoter Jim Coffroth took some sports writers across San Francisco Bay to Alameda where Kid Carter was training at Croll's Gardens to meet George Gardner. Coffroth was trying to build up interest in the light-heavyweight division, then unrecognized. After the usual gym workout, Carter boxed with a tall, graceful colored sparring partner, Jack Johnson, twenty-three, just up from Texas.

According to Tad, Johnson at the time was a happy-go-lucky young fellow who would rather tell jokes than box. The sports writers used to sit around and listen to him spin yarns after each workout. But on this Sunday afternoon, Johnson made a mistake in the third round and hit the boss a bit harder than a paid employee is supposed to. Carter got mad.

"Tryin' to show me up, huh?" he muttered, lowering his head. "I'll show you who's boss around here!"

Carter did his best to knock Johnson stiff, Tad used to recall, but instead nearly disgraced himself. If it hadn't been for Coffroth, who stopped the bout when Carter was groggy and all in, the big fight with Gardner four days later would have been a flop.

"Coming home on the boat that evening," Tad said, "we talked more about Johnson than we did about Carter. We knew that a new, big man who could fight had arrived. It didn't take Johnson long to be recognized after that Sunday workout."

While I never met Tad, I saw many pictures of him besides

the one published with his box of comment running below his daily cartoon. He had been described to me in detail, and over the telephone I had heard the sharp, light voice, the occasional laughter, and the frequent snarl. I feel I could have recognized in any crowd the tall, spare figure, the gaunt face and the sad, very light blue eyes.

As almost everybody knows, Tad coined the popular name, hot dog, for the frankfurter on a vienna roll. The comestible had long been a staple at Charles Feltman's restaurant in Coney Island and I'm told it was actually introduced there by the German-born baker to sell his rolls as early as 1888. The combination was presented for the first time at the Polo Grounds by the late Harry M. Stevens, the caterer and concessionaire, in April, 1914. The event was important enough to be recorded on one New York sports page as follows: "Hot frankfurters have been added to the lineup at the indigestion counter at the Polo Grounds. They are served between the peanut course and the lemonade, and those who tried them yesterday recognized several old friends who were on duty at Coney Island last summer."

This whimsical approach was later enlarged upon by Tad. He named them "hot dogs" and dramatized them in the corner of his popular "Indoor Sports" cartoon by drawing a small sausage and adding four toothpick legs. These little figures talked and danced and Tad often used them as trial mouthpieces for his original words and phrases in slang. The phrase, "Gimme a hot dog," is only one of the countless contributions Tad made to the English "slanguage." He had a genius for what higher education calls euphonic jargon that came from years of association, observation and absorption of human nature.

"Indoor Sports" was a mirror of human frailties, frauds, and harmless windbags. The caption in the corner often carried much of the slang: "Listening to the cake-eaters lamping the skirts on a windy corner"; "Facing the ball and chain after a night of merry mucilage and kelly pool"; "Watching the drugstore cowboy waiting out the nickel nurser in the phone booth"; "Watching the hard-boiled egg trim a fall guy who has forgotten his cheaters"; "Barnum was right—there's one born every minute, and two to grab him!"

To all sports writers, Tad's recorded speech was music. It could be duplicated, but with effort, and it was never bettered, because it was natural to Tad's Irish senses of humor and of word-music. A whole volume could be written on the terms that Tad created or popularized. Most of them became part of our speech, in spite of protesting educators. But show me a better way to express the overbearing ostentation of a heavy spender than to call him a "big butter and egg man." What is more explicit than "the bum's rush"? Or "Twenty-three skiddoo"? Or "This is no place for a minister's son"? To Tad a straw hat was a "skimmer," an overcoat was a "benny," and untrue stories were "the bunk" or "applesauce." His senseless declaration, "Yes, we have no bananas" became a popular song hit from which he received nothing.

"Dumbell," "Dumb Dora," "Solid ivory" and "nobody home" were only a few terms Tad coined to convey benign mental shortcomings. His slang, devastating in accuracy and reflection, was always in good taste. By that I mean nobody was hurt, which was another facet of his genius.

Few in the newspaper business have influenced or impressed me more deeply than Tad. I remember him as a little Frisco kid with a mangled hand who grew up to be an institution. I welcomed Tad's notes and his telephone calls. They meant he was interested enough to read my pieces, which was flattering because he was a giant in our business. I always enjoyed the feeling that he thought of me as a protégé who misbehaved now and then by speaking well of John J. McGraw.

The D-Man

Tad induced another Aloysius, Bert A. Igoe, cartoonist and writer, to leave San Francisco in 1907 for New York City. When an elevator operator observed, "That skinny kid in your department looks like he needs a hypodermic," Tad nicknamed Igoe "Hype." The nickname appeared thereafter on the brilliant Igoe sports cartoons which had the quality of a dry-point etching.

A second Tad protégé, Charles Emmet Van Loan, thought by some to be the best of all sports fiction writers, was a Tad discovery in Frisco in 1903. Through the cartoonists's recommendation and urging, Van Loan reached the New York *Journal* and remained until 1910.

While in Denver, Van Loan met and liked a skinny kid named Runyon, who landed on the New York morning paper, the *American*, thanks in part to Van's recommendation. My good friend Gene Fowler explains that a corpse, never identified, was partly responsible for Runyon's eastward journey. Railroad rules called for an extra ticket when a corpse was shipped and, thanks to a tip-off, Damon used the spare ticket. In his early New York days, Runyon supplied plots for some of Van's sports stories. Van Loan always insisted that Damon could and should write fiction, but he never did until long after Van died in 1919.

Tad called Runyon "the ten-minute Egg." I called him the D-Man, because he had a lot of the qualities of the FBI about him, particularly in his power of observation and ability to listen and then relate in detail what he had seen and heard.

Once I ate with him on a train and, leaving the dining room, whisked a fistful of those paper-wrapped quill toothpicks into my pocket without changing stride. Three hours later in the drawing room, Runyon said, "You practically broke the New York Central grabbing all those toothpicks. Now give me a few."

It was foolish, almost insulting, to begin a comment with, "Did you see that—" Runyon had always seen it, and would add what your own eyes had not caught. This uncanny faculty was, of course, the backbone of his greatness as a reporter, fiction writer and storyteller. His blue-gray eyes, which looked unusually large because of the strong glasses he wore, were always working, drinking in the little things that lesser writers missed or dismissed at a ball game, race track, prize fight, or in the person he was talking or listening to. He did a lot of listening.

Runyon's actual birthdate, like mine (Boonville records were loosely kept, or not at all), was open to argument. Some insisted that his first appearance was October 4, 1884, in Manhattan, Kansas, where his father happened to be working as a printer. He was named for his father, Alfred, and his mother, Elizabeth Damon. However, the Court House in Manhattan, Kansas, has long since burned down, destroying the record of his birth. It could be true that Damon was, as he claimed, a drummer boy in the Spanish American War, but how old he was as a boy drummer is another matter. If, as is said, he went to Minnesota where he wasn't known and joined the 13th Minnesota Volunteers, he was only fourteen. He was in the Philippines for two years, then, because his journeyman father had shifted to Pueblo, Colorado, began work as a reporter for the *Chieftain*. After that came San Francisco and Denver.

Damon looked ageless and in many respects he was. He had sallow skin, thin light-brown hair that never seemed to gray, a set jaw that emphasized the unusual jowls, and the sleek, springy figure of a yearling. Since Runyon was a star writer on the *American* while I was on the *Journal,* we naturally moved together covering the World Series, the big fights, the racing classics like the Kentucky Derby, Preakness, Belmont and other top items. We fell to traveling together, often in the same drawing room or hotel room when only one was available.

Runyon answered my definition of a genius in a dozen ways, all fascinating and some exasperating as well. This man was the hottest and coldest—and the quickest hot-and-cold—character that I ever met in my life. One day at lunch in Lindy's Restaurant, which he referred to in his stories as "Mindy's," he said to me, "I've got a great idea. You and I covered the Hauptmann trial at Flemington, New Jersey, together. Tomorrow is Sunday. Suppose we get together, go out to Flemington and look around the town and see what changes have taken place since we covered the trial."

To me Runyon, much my senior in years and experience, was a kind of elder statesman in the business, so though I wasn't very enthusiastic I said, "Sounds great."

"I thought you'd like it," he said. "Tell you what I'll do. I'll get Leo [meaning Lindy] to pack a big basket of sandwiches and soft drinks and beer. [Runyon never drank anything stronger than soft drinks; the beer was a concession to me.] We'll get out of town in my car early tomorrow morning to beat the traffic. We'll see Dave Wilentz [one of the prosecuting attorneys in the Lindbergh kidnaping trial], the old Court House, and the old hotel where we stayed, and we can picnic along the way and have a big day for ourselves."

The next morning I dragged myself out of bed at an unaccustomed hour, shaved, bathed and had half-dressed when I decided to telephone Runyon. The phone rang and rang. Finally he answered.

"Damon," I said, "I'm almost dressed and I'll be over in about fifteen minutes."

"What the hell are you talking about?"

"Aren't we going to Flemington this morning?"

"Flemington what?"

"Flemington, New Jersey. At lunch yesterday you told me you'd like to go on a picnic to Flemington and we arranged it."

"Are you crazy?"

"No, Damon, but I wonder if you are."

"Well, I guess one of us is. What do you want? I want to go back to sleep."

"I want to go back to sleep too. What about Flemington?"

"Who in hell cares about Flemington when he can sleep?"

We were good friends, but it was a friendship that demanded a lot of understanding on both sides. Damon Runyon was what he was and, to paraphrase Shakespeare, "they that level at his abuses reckon up their own." He was self-conscious, suspicious and so sensitive that you could almost make him mad just by poking your finger at him.

He was particularly conscious of his personal appearance. He was probably the best-dressed man in New York; certainly he had more suits, sweaters, hats and shoes than anyone else. I recall the time Bill Cunningham, the renowned Boston columnist of the "New England Breakfast Table," went to Damon's suite, then in the Vendome apartments. Cunningham, a cane-carrying dresser of taste, was overwhelmed by the sight of a great glass case of winter suits, fall suits, spring outfits and summer combinations. All the colors in the rainbow were in that wardrobe, with hat boxes across the top and shoe boxes—each shoe preserved with trees—across the bottom. There were even typewriters to match the hats and suits. Cunningham called this touch "the doggonedest collection of sartorial splendor since Beau Brummell."

Runyon actually had colored typewriters in dyed leather cases to match any outfit he might select to wear on an assignment. Cunningham said, "This is the first time I've seen the Louvre outside of Paris."

If you happened to meet Damon three different times in a single day, it was not unusual to see him in as many costumes —complete to hat, suit and shoes, different in color scheme down to the shirts, ties and, of course, tie-matching socks.

Like most writers, Runyon was both sensitive and defensive about anything he wrote. He often made a dozen false starts—half pages or more—in writing his lead for a story. Wonderful writer though he was, he wrote bad things, wrong things, as do most of us who write from day to day and meet deadlines. But he was proud of his writing and his pride was justifiable, because he worked so hard at it. A fellow who ever told Damon he had made a mistake or had written something badly had to beware.

In September of 1935, Runyon was standing in the lobby of the 48th Street Theater on the opening night of *A Slight Case of Murder,* which he had written with another newspaperman, Buck Crouse. Enter the late Mark Hellinger, a columnist and short-story specialist on the *Daily Mirror.* Hellinger carried his own supply of needles for all occasions, and said to a nearby ear, "This will be a slight case of getting out of here as quick as I can."

Runyon's rabbit ears caught the pointed remark and he never forgave Hellinger. The play, by the way, received lukewarm notices, but had a fair run before the sale to Hollywood. Hellinger never mentioned the play in print, but the crack in the lobby began a feud between two swell guys with razor-sharp tongues and wits.

Some weeks later Jimmy Cannon, who felt as badly about Runyon's dislike of Hellinger as their other friends did, made a "meet," as it is called on Broadway, between Damon and

Mark to patch up their differences. This was never hard to do with Runyon, because he could get mad like a flash of light and be over it just as quickly. Cannon took them to Lindy's. They shook hands and over a good dinner discussed sports and the theater and reminisced about Broadway. It was a pleasant meeting and all were smiling as they left the restaurant.

Hellinger went his way, Jimmy headed for his hotel and Runyon apparently hurried over to his hotel apartment. Cannon said he had scarcely reached his room when Damon called him. The dialogue went something like this:

RUNYON: What I told you about that so-and-so goes. And I knew it all the time. He's no good.

CANNON: But, Damon, I don't understand. Everything was pleasant at dinner. You liked him. We had laughs. What are you mad about now?

RUNYON: Jimmy, I told you before. He doesn't go, and I say it again. And all the things I said about him go double now.

CANNON: But Damon, please tell me why. What did he do? What made you mad?

RUNYON: Why, didn't you see what he did?

CANNON: No, I didn't see what he did.

RUNYON: Why, he tried to pick up the check in *my* joint!

Then there was the time that Bob Considine, one of our best and nicest reporters, came to New York from Washington to work for the Hearst papers. Whether he actually said it or not, word got back to Runyon that Considine had admitted coming into New York "to take over Runyon's place" on the Hearst papers as soon as Damon left for Hollywood to write and produce motion pictures. That was enough to make Runyon unsheath his claws and bare his fangs and for the next several weeks he never missed an opportunity to make a crack at Considine. Once, after he had lost his voice and was jotting little notes on pieces of paper from a pad, Runyon wrote and handed me this comment: "There are three guys in our business that I don't like." I nodded.

He wrote: "Bob Considine, Joe Williams, Bob Considine."

Like most writers at the head of their field, Runyon had a high degree of self-preservation—and this was the key to my understanding of him. He enjoyed a lofty and enviable position in the sports-writing world, but he hadn't reached it easily or without great personal sacrifice and struggle. A Spanish war veteran as a teen-ager, he was the product of a broken home, a scattered family, and other trips to the wars in Mexico and Europe, and he knew more domestic drama than he could ever put into his great fiction stories.

Runyon was consistently inconsistent in all the years I knew him—and I knew him in the bad years as well as in the good ones. I don't think he had too many real friends, because far too few people had the patience to understand him. Yet he was a kind of toast of Broadway in the last years of his life when, his larynx removed and unable to talk, he wrote some of his best columns for the papers.

Many years before, Damon had been a gutter drunk, an undependable lush in Denver. When he reached New York he was known as a fellow that you wouldn't see for three weeks if he had three drinks. But sometime, somehow, he had said to himself, "I'll never take another drink." And he never did. Runyon had annoying idiosyncrasies, yes, but he also had great character and the inner courage of a lion.

I've received hundreds of letters from fans who wrote, "Well, I saw your teetotaling friend Runyon tottering out of the Stork Club at four o'clock the other morning and he was in great shape." I suppose such canards are the price of fame. Once Damon visited my little suite at the Chase Hotel during a World Series in St. Louis between the Cardinals and Yankees. This was either in 1926 or 1928 and prohibition was in full flower. Understanding restaurateurs from the East had dropped by to slip me a bottle or two of liquor to help entertain any "show me" friends who would surely visit. The bottles were on the mantel of one of the fireplaces when Runyon arrived to keep our dinner date. He eyed them and said, "What have you got that stuff here for?"

I explained that I had Missouri friends, a lot of them.

He walked over to the mantelpiece and surveyed the assortment—scotch, gin and what I've always called "red" whiskey, a rye-bourbon mix. He took down a bottle of red, pulled out the cork, smelled it, studied it, and shook it. I've never seen a man want a drink more than Damon did then. It wasn't my place to say, "Won't you have a drink?" On the other hand, I didn't think it was my right to suggest, "Why don't you put that bottle back?"

I said nothing. Damon took another sniff. With a sigh he replaced the cork, replaced the bottle and said, "If I started drinking that, it would be no good."

"What do you mean, Damon, it would be no good?"

"That wouldn't even warm me up. Unless I had a case under the bed, I wouldn't dare take a drink of that."

While dying, Damon Runyon still carried a torch that burned hotter than his cancer. This torch of emotional involvement had a tremendous effect on him; in speaking of it earlier in his life, he had said, "You walk forty miles and don't know you've been around the block."

Once, tragically smitten with a lady who did not reciprocate, he was so close to a nervous breakdown that the Hearst organization had to send him around the world on a semireportorial chore with the United States Navy. I'm not sure he was cured when he returned because the torch, as far as I could see, burned as bright as it always did in Damon.

In the last years of Runyon's life his wife, the former

Patrice Amati, divorced him and married a younger man. I have in my mementos some of the scraps of paper on which he wrote after he'd lost his voice. One I find reads: "Pat has married a guy twenty-four years old. Ha-ha." Then: "She'll come back to me."

At this time—the year before he died—Runyon was living at the Buckingham Hotel, on 57th Street, just west of Sixth Avenue, in what I thought was a gloomy apartment. From time to time I went over to see him and bring a little creature comfort. The only person with him, more or less constantly, was a fight manager named Eddie Walker, Runyon's "Walking Around Man."

Walker was a nice little guy and it was about him that Runyon coined the phrase, "crying all the way to the bank." He said, "Eddie is a manager whose fighters always lose and then he cries all the way to the bank." In those days of loneliness and deepening despair, the great writer needed Walker. Eddie was a life-saver, though there was only half a life to save.

I did a little, less than I might have of course, but what I thought a friend should do. I used to drop over to Damon's rooms at the Buckingham, knowing that just being there would help. He had usually read the papers. Little could be said and there was nothing to plan. You couldn't speak honestly of hope or of his future.

Once when I was there Runyon rose and picked up a chair in which he was sitting, moved it to a corner, turned his back on me and began to cry. Nobody knows what to do under those circumstances. Certainly I didn't, so I did nothing except smoke a cigarette and wait. After a while, he turned around and resumed writing his little notes. I started talking again and everything seemed all right, except that every once in a while Runyon would get up from his chair and cross the room to a table by his bed. There was an old-fashioned scarf on the table and Damon would pick up the corner of the cloth, look under it and then return to his chair.

Perhaps I am not as curious as a reporter should be, and one of the things I resent most is having people meddle in my business. For that reason I've tried all my life not to pry. Nevertheless, I couldn't help wondering what was under the cloth. When Damon left the room for a minute, I said—truthfully, because I had to call the paper, "Is it all right to use the phone?" He nodded and disappeared. I sat on the bed, placed my call and, having normal curiosity, lifted the corner of the tablecloth.

I saw a sad and moving thing. It gave me a memory that I'll never be able to erase. There was a full picture of Runyan's former wife, Patrice, who had remarried the year before. The photo was obviously arranged by the bed-light so that he could pick up the cloth at any time he wished and look at her picture.

Two or three weeks after this visit to his rooms I walked into the Chatham Hotel where I lived and saw a headline in the late evening paper, "Damon Runyon Dies." The shock was much greater than I would have expected. I had known that his days were numbered, but he was wiry, Middle Western tough, a determined, gutty man, and I'd had tremendous admiration for him as a writer and as a person welded to his convictions, screwy as they might seem at times.

My column on his passing stressed the fact that very few people knew or understood him. It must have hit home better than anything I've written before or since, because I got congratulatory messages about the piece from all over the world.

An example of people's feelings when Damon died was the man who walked into Toots Shor's restaurant after hearing the news and sat at the circular bar with tears streaming from his eyes. Shor came over, laid his ready hand of compassion on the guy's shoulder and whispered, "What's wrong with you, pal?"

"Haven't you heard?" said the weeper.

"Heard what?"

"Damon Runyon's dead."

Shor thought an instant, and asked, "Did you know him?" The fellow shook his head sadly and sniffed, "No."

That was a perfect illustration of how Runyon affected people at the time of his death. His greatness as a writer coaxed tears from people who never knew him.

The real Runyon, strangely enough, was best reflected by his last, tragic days. There weren't many people around him —only Paul Small, his agent, and of course the faithful Eddie Walker. In the last hours, Small was there when the doctor came to the hotel and said, "We'll have to take him back to the hospital."

Runyon had been in Memorial Hospital before. He knew about his affliction, of course—he had even written humorous columns about it—and he knew that complete removal of his larynx hadn't arrested the cancer. By this time he was in great pain, but he was dead game; I never met anybody with grimmer determination. He had written a peculiar codicil to his will, publicized after his death, asking that after cremation Eddie Rickenbacker, president of Eastern Airlines, scatter his ashes upon Broadway from a plane.

The doctor gave Runyon some shots to ease the agonizing pain, then Small and the hotel bellboys helped him downstairs and put him in a taxicab. Paul rode to Memorial Hospital with him. Runyon was in such shape at the time that it seemed that no one could possibly have known or noticed what was going on. Reaching the hospital and helping him from the cab and across the sidewalk, Small felt that Runyon had no idea of where he was or what was happening.

But the large man with the deceptive name reckoned without his charge. They got into the elevator and went up to the reserved room. Pausing at the door, Runyon shook his head. Small patted the wasted shoulder and said, "What's wrong, Pop?" Runyon's head shook again. They sat him on the bed and Small pulled up a chair and sat close. Damon rested awhile and then asked for his little pad to write on. He scribbled in a now-wavering hand: "This is not as good as the old room."

Paul read the slip and looked at him, bewildered.

The D-Man scribbled again: "The old room had a nice view."

Those were the last lines Damon Runyon ever wrote.

No Littleness in the Big Man

I always considered Babe Ruth in a class by himself—with only Jack Dempsey a respectable second—as an outstanding popular sports hero. This feeling, which existed before I knew him well, was thoroughly confirmed when I got to know Ruth personally in New Orleans during my first base-ball training-camp trip in 1924.

There was much to understand about Ruth over and above his baseball prowess as a super slugger. He had color, a quality easy to recognize but hard to define. He had a certain flair in human relationships, especially among kids, and his timing in all things was remarkable beyond words. Yet none of these things, singly or in the aggregate, is enough to explain the hold that he plainly had on the public mind—and on the sports writers too. I don't think this hold can be explained; Babe Ruth had the kind of genius that defies precise analysis. The product of his achievement had the required timeless quality of perfection, and it certainly left an indelible mark on those it touched. Ask any big-league pitcher who faced him—he was unique and special.

When our advance party of Yankee players (mostly rookies like Hinkey Haines, Mike Gazella, Benny Bengough and a stocky kid named Lou Gehrig), officials and baseball correspondents reached New Orleans in early March, 1924, the Babe was still in Hot Springs, Arkansas. Veteran players, especially those with winter waistlines, used to go there for a process of weight reduction. For ten days we writers had trouble finding news. It was rough on a conscientious young reporter taking his first whack at covering Spring training, and it took much of the fun from one of the easiest touches in the newspaper business.

Then the big fellow arrived! I wired to the New York *Times:*

> Babe Ruth is here. That word, starting from the lobby of the Bienville Hotel and spreading rapidly over the whole of New Orleans, roused drowsy bellhops, stirred complacent newspaper correspondents, sent a horde of schoolboys scurrying toward the ball park and a chill along the spines of a score of rookies at practice there. Baseball's reigning sovereign arrived from Hot Springs accompanied by a court composed of Deacon Scott, Bullet Joe Bush, Sailor Bob Shawkey and Wally Schang.
>
> Greeting the slugger there was Mrs. Ruth and their daughter, Dorothy. The Babe seemed to have benefitted from the baths, and his weight was 218 pounds.
>
> "I was too light last year," he explained. "I tried to get down to 200 and it sapped my strength. I will hit harder and better at my present weight, and I am going to try to stay right around this figure."
>
> Asked if he expected to win the home run title or the batting championship, Ruth exclaimed, "Both!"

And he did. Ruth hit forty-six home runs in 1924 and his batting average, .378, gave him the first and only hitting championship of his fabulous career.

But within a few months of the next year, through unwise living and disregard of his athletic well-being, Babe had become a physical wreck. He collapsed on the way North during Spring training. He was later hospitalized, rejoined the team and hobbled through a dismal season made more so by his "leadership." Many players, including stars, used him as a model and staged open rebellion against "Dusty Miller" Huggins who saw his once-invincible championship team become a shambles on the field and off in 1925.

The powder-keg situation exploded at St. Louis in late August when little Huggins brought the big fellow to his room in the Chase Hotel. There he literally begged Ruth to realize the damage he was doing to himself, to his family, to the team, and especially to the youth of America who looked up to him as to no other figure in sports. Ruth's reply has never been printed, and never will be, owing to its character or the lack of it. It was accompanied by derisive laughter and followed by an exchange of heated remarks. Hug said that only his own size prevented throwing him out the window. Ruth replied that if Hug was twice as big, he'd dare him to try it.

Overnight the nation was shocked by the manager's action which was backed by his superiors, Jake Ruppert and Ed Barrow. Huggins met the new low in replies with a new high in fines, $5000, plus indefinite suspension.

I was in New York when Ruth came home spouting defiance, and I covered the sweating-out period that Ruth endured. "There will be no living with the team, if this sort of thing is repeated," Huggins said, "and this has got to be the end one way or another. I'll not put up with the worry Ruth has subjected me to again."

After he had finally let Babe put on his uniform, Hug said, "The big fellow was helpless, pitiful, and really a sorry sight. He was like a fish out of water, completely useless and unable to express himself. But I had too much at stake to weaken. We had no trouble with him after that."

The incident helped me to understand Babe Ruth. He was helpless, yes. But put that big and graceful figure into a uniform and a bat in his hands, and he could express himself as could no other baseball player before or since. It was his single channel, the sole outlet of his genius. Blessed with grace, rhythm, supereyesight and marvelous reflexes, he was an instrument of pure artistry, unbridled, as are almost all artists of motion, by thinking or planning. He performed his feats of greatness unconsciously, and did his thinking—if any —later. It explains the observation made by many players and writers alike, that they never saw him make a mistake on the ball field.

A good illustration is the story the late Ed Barrow liked to tell about Ruth starting the first game of the 1918 World Series between the Boston Red Sox and Cubs in Chicago. The Babe was a great pitcher, smooth, graceful and with pin-point control, but Barrow, as manager of the Red Sox, had already started experimenting with him in the outfield because of his hitting. Ruth had hit .300 in 95 games, and tied Tilly Walker for the American League home-run championship with eleven.

"Watch Leslie Mann," Barrow cautioned as Babe started out to pitch the home half of the first inning. "He's a plate-crowder. Don't let him dig in and get a toe hold on you. Brush him back a little."

Well, nobody was going to crowd the Babe. He dumped the lead-off batter into the dirt not once but three times, then completed the first of his nine scoreless innings. He reached the Red Sox dugout with a wide grin of triumph, and crowed, "Well, I guess I took care of that Mann fella, didn't I?"

"Not yet you didn't!" Barrow roared. "You knocked down Max Flack. Mann was the third batter and he crowded you good before you got him out."

That Flack was a left-handed batter who was duck soup for Babe's left-handed curve, and that Mann was a plate-crowding right-hander who could murder a curve were un-important details to Ruth—he had knocked somebody down and gotten out of the inning. By pitching seven more score-less innings in a second victory, added to the thirteen he had pitched in 1916, he set a record of twenty-nine consecutive scoreless World Series innings still unequaled at this writing, forty years later.

Babe Ruth couldn't do anything small, even when he in-sulted his manager and almost threw away a career. His rise from those depths was even more Ruthian in size and scope. Less than two years later, in 1927, he was drawing a record salary and putting the home-run mark at sixty, beyond reach of all. By now he had a business adviser, Christy Walsh, who showed him how to salt away some of his $70,000 yearly salary plus outside income. The Babe was never in financial straits again.

I'll never forget the luncheon held by the insurance com-pany to publicize Babe's down payment on a whopping an-nuity. The company president, a distinguished looking gentle-man with white hair and a neatly trimmed mustache and goatee, made a great to-do from the dais about how lucky the Babe was to have this policy. He was really "a fortunate young man, to be congratulated on his stroke of luck."

"There's no doubt about it," Ruth said bluntly when his turn came to speak. "I got all the luck, but you got my thirty-five grand."

Ruth's masterful hitting and slugging sparkplugged the

Mr. and Mrs. Bill Corum and his mother, Mrs. Robert W.
Corum, in Florida about 1934

Bill in his office at the Chatham Hotel in 1939

With Jimmy Walker, Eddie Eagan, Toots Shor,
Carole Landis, and Bob Considine after a war
benefit

The war correspondent in 1945

The finish of the '49 Derby and the four horses which made Corum
an expert: Ponder, Capot, Palestinian, and Old Rockport

Robert Strange Corum at the age of seventeen

Bill and his mother at Churchill Downs. Colonel Matt Winn's picture is in the background

The twentieth anniversary reunion of the 1933 Columbia football team which won the Rose Bowl game on January 1, 1934. *(Left to right)* Joe Rich, Al Ciampa, Al Barabas (holding football), Paul Jackel, Corum, Jim Davis, Cliff Montgomery, Owen McDowell, Anthony Matal, Steve Dzamba, and Bill Nevel

With Don Dunphy at their ringside microphones
before a fight

After the second Marciano-Charles fight in 1954
Charlie Goldman stands at left, Al Weill to the
right of Marciano, while Bill waits to interview the
champion

Photograph by Bill

After a luncheon honoring sports personalities. *(From left)* Guy Lombardo, Gertrude Ederle, Corum, Ty Cobb, Jake La Motta, Rocky Graziano, Bugs Baer, and Gene Tunney

The Derby host with Mrs. Frank Conniff, Mrs. Robert W. Corum, Red Smith, Mr. Conniff, and Senator Alben Barkley

Photograph by Bill Mark

Photograph by Ben De Broc

Bill Corum at work on *Off and Running* a few months before his deatl

Yankees to American League domination in 1926, 1927 and 1928. With six pennants in eight years, Miller Huggins was now undisputably one of the leading managers in the game. He had big plans to rebuild the Yankees again in 1929, but died near the end of the season.   A month later, when Ruppert and Barrow were still considering a new manager (Eddie Collins, Athletics' coach, was first choice, and Art Fletcher, Yankees' coach, second), Ruth left the Yankees' 42nd Street offices with Bob Shawkey who had made a routine call.

"Did you hear anything about who's gonna manage?" Babe asked.

"No, I didn't, Babe. Did you?"

"No." Ruth grunted and puffed his cigar. "But if it's not me, whoever gets it is gonna have a helluva lot of trouble." Two weeks later Shawkey was surprised with the offer of the job which both Collins and Fletcher had refused. Ruth's promised "trouble" failed to materialize during Shawkey's year of directing the team, but it began a year later, in 1931, when Joe McCarthy left the Chicago Cubs to take over at the Stadium.

Stories of Babe Ruth have filled many books and a couple of feature-length motion pictures, but nowhere will you find tales of how his gullible nature and his priceless popularity were used and abused by selfish interests. This genial and moon-faced fellow was involved in situations that were wholly foreign to his happy-go-lucky personality.

In the early twenties the Huston faction of the Yankees' owners wanted Miller Huggins replaced as manager by Brooklyn's popular Wilbert Robinson. Ruth was talked into being a pawn within the struggle to help split a powerful team. Huggins' authority was flouted. Private detectives mingled with the players, and at one point a drunken outfielder held the little manager at arms' length off the rear platform of a speeding train as a "joke." Huggins finally demanded and got a vote of confidence from Jake Ruppert. A year later Ruppert bought out the Huston interests to become sole owner.

Ten years later it was Manager Joe McCarthy "they" wanted out and Babe Ruth in. Don't ask me who or why it's not important to me or my story. What is important is that a fine manager and man, Buffalo Joe, was driven to drink and worse by a behind-scenes struggle to make Ruth, the good-natured behemoth of baseball, manager of the Yankees. Fortunately for everybody and for the game itself, Joe McCarthy remained on. Though embittered and ridiculed by a hostile press, he led the Yankees to their greatest successes.

It was the Babe who finally left the Yankees, but I had a few anxious moments before he did. On October 25, 1934, the *Journal's* first page read:

BABE RUTH WINS POST
AS BRAVES MANAGER

Ruppert Won't Get Cent
for Home Run King

By BILL CORUM

The Babe goes home—to Boston.
Babe Ruth, greatest ball player of all time, will manage the Boston Braves in the National League.

My information, from the best possible source, embarrassed and angered the Babe. It didn't last long; he never held grudges, even against the few pitchers (Hub Pruett and a kid named Dick Coffman are a couple I remember) who could fool him. Winter months came, and the Boston deal failed to go through. But I knew that Governor Curley, of Massachusetts, had talked to the Babe. Hiring a name like Ruth's was the only way of bailing out the unfortunate Braves' owner, Judge Emil Fuchs. While Ruth left the country for a world tour, I sweated it out and printed the story again on February 6th.

Three weeks later my four-months-old story stood up. Sure enough, the Yankees "gave" Babe to the Boston Braves. There he would be "vice president and assistant manager" and a lot of other things, all meaningless except for the salary of $35,000. Thus the greatest of all sports personalities left the New York scene, but not the hearts of the fans and writers. You simply couldn't forget him, once he had bestowed upon you that "Hi-yah kid!" accompanied, if you weren't careful, by a bone-rattling slap on the back. People were interested in him because he lived in a seemingly endless high tidal wave of life and excitement. He was no angel, but innately fine in the final reckoning and a true friend— even if he seldom remembered my name in meetings over a period of twenty-four years.

Ruth's popularity was fixed once he had been seen anywhere in the world, and this was due largely to the fact that his unbridled words and actions were always sincere. There never was anything spurious about that feeling of his for youngsters. He never bothered to find out their names— whose name ever troubled him?—but he understood them instinctively. With them his touch was perfect and, if they were hurt or sick or frightened, as gentle as a mother's. Kids understood Ruth just as quickly and surely, of course, and why not? Though it has been said a million times before, it remains true that he always was just a big kid himself. He gloried in his strength and in his achievements as the most natural and unerring player in his instinct for the game that ever lived.

It was no shock or even surprise to me when Ruth died in mid-August, 1948. His numberless well-wishers all over the world knew that the Great Umpire for some time had his thumb pressed against "strike three" on the final and inescapable indicator. But the announcement, which I heard from an automobile radio, sounded unreal and untrue. I could think of him sick and worn—as he had been for too long—but still with us. Alive, he always found a way to enjoy life, for there was no bitterness in the real Babe we all knew. He had no time for prejudice or meanness. There was no littleness in the big man.

He made his full share of life's mistakes, but he never whimpered about having to pay for them. He was without jealousies, and no one ever heard him do anything but boost the DiMaggios and Williamses and Musials who shared his mantle, because no single player could ever fill it.

Babe Ruth's lack of smallness in his hey-day or in the long-suffering of his untimely end helps to explain his unbelievable popularity. Few men ever bade the world good-by in a ceremony comparable to that at St. Patrick's Cathedral, New York. Cardinal Spellman's memorable prayer, the open weeping of many who filled the nave to overflowing, and the miles and miles of mourners along the route to his final resting place were lasting testimony.

Perhaps the Babe was a bigger man than even those of us who knew him well on the sports beat realized. Surely his life must remain an inspiration to the youth of the land. Look where only a kid at heart wound up!

HEROES AND HERO WORSHIP

The history of the world is
but the biography of great men.
                              Carlyle

Heady Stuff

Hero worship is an outgrowth of envy in persons of limited talent, and I speak from experience. In awe of the truly accomplished, I'm a pushover for the fearless darers and doers, especially of some athletic artists I've watched and written about over the years. But I've learned to be careful. Admiration sometimes grows into reverence, which can be fatal for a newspaperman. The idol usually takes care of that by developing feet of clay, which means he probably had a head of the same substance long before you noticed it in his shoes.

Heroes and heroism have taxed the abilities of far better writers than I. We've done a lot of explaining, but heroes remain a mystery. The substance that makes for greatness in one and not in another is a mystery.

Here is an interpretation of the hero's qualities that jibes with mine: "The hero is a mind of such balance," wrote Emerson, "that no disturbances can shake his will. . . . There is somewhat in great actions that does not allow us to go behind them. . . . Heroism feels and never reasons, and therefore is always right. . . . It is the avowal of the unschooled man, that he finds a quality in him that is negligent of expense, of health, of life, of danger, of hatred, or reproach and knows that his will is higher and more excellent than all actual and possible antagonists."

That is exactly the way I feel about heroes. I wish I could

say that Ralph Waldo took the words right out of my mouth, but he was a little ahead of me in time and in many other things. However, this particular explanation of heroes appeals to me as a definition for my own particular listing. Read the Emerson lines again and you'll understand why. They are a pretty good description of a washed-up hero, too, and one of my earliest idols qualified on all counts as a no-account.

Prince Hal

When the strange cavalcade drifted into my room at Phoenix, Arizona, many years ago, I had not yet read Scott Fitzgerald's caustic observation, "Show me a hero and I will write you a tragedy." But there it was, written and edited in final form, a reunion in the desert twilight with a dilapidated human being who was once a symbol of athletic perfection. Now beady eyes squinted in a leathery face beaten and seamed by sun, wind and weather; the man seemed to have been beaten by a scant fifty years of life.

He wore a floppy old white hat, a baggy pair of pants that plainly had seen better days on somebody else, a dirty blue sweat-streaked shirt and a broken, dusty pair of shoes. In the enthusiasm of the meeting I was ignored for a time. Finally the figure in the white hat spied a bottle on the bureau and went for it like a homing pigeon. At that instant Doc Barrett, trainer of the Columbia University football team, grabbed my arm with an eager strength, spun his quarry by the arm, turned him toward me and exclaimed, "Hal, I want you to meet Bill Corum. Bill, this is Hal Chase. Did you ever see him play first base?"

Ever see him? Ever *see* him? What a question! Especially to one who had so often dreamed of Chase's poetry of baseball motion in youthful reveries of future athletic triumph. Hadn't I sat with my eyes glued on him at old Sportsman's Park, St. Louis, until I could go back to my little country town and see him with my eyes shut? Hadn't I put my smelly glove under my pillow at night and dreamed of the time when I would spear 'em out of the dirt with one hand like Prince Hal? That gossamer goal had been mine through countless baseball games won and lost, a shimmering mirage of fame and fortune which all of us have in one form or another at one time or another.

Chase had left the baseball scene by the time I entered it as a writer in the early twenties. Behind him were fascinating legends of matchless skill, many exaggerated but all serving to confirm my early opinons. There were other legends, too, ugly and unseemly, but they couldn't alter my memory of his magic. The whisperings, the secondhand tales of his moral inconsistencies and sleight-of-hand career off the ball field could not dim the radiance of my youthful vision. I saw the luster of legends, never the unflattering truths.

Now this relic of professional baseball, this wanderer of self-made wastelands who had shuffled through one-street mining towns playing baseball with itinerant Mexican teams for a buck or a single shot of rye or tequila when the game was over, was the mortal remains of Hal Chase of my early baseball hopes and dreams. Such a wind-up for an athlete so perfectly coordinated was all but unbelievable. But now I could see that the skill had been entirely physical. His lack of mental and moral coordination never made the box scores.

Chase was almost maudlin with joy over seeing Doc Barrett, who had trained the New York Yankees (then the Highlanders) a quarter century before when Chase was the manager. Though Barrett spoke the only language he knew,

Chase couldn't talk. Even his once sharp and cunning mind was bobbing and weaving with stumbling, shambling footsteps. Words were strangers to his tongue. Not until I asked him about first base did he square his bony shoulders and look me in the eye. "Sisler was the next thing to me," he said simply, and there was a hint of bragging in his voice, "but I could go get that old apple."

A shudder went through me at the sight of this object lesson. Somehow this fellow in all his years in big-league baseball had never learned the art of honesty. Oblivious to the ugly rumors, accusations and open charges, he had believed that his matchless skill was all that mattered. Eventually even that was unwanted. No one had made a bum out of Hal Chase but Hal Chase himself. He was one of those strange characters who spend a lifetime scheming ways to outsmart everybody and wind up outsmarting only themselves.

The Ace of Spads

My admiration for the chauffeuring sergeant, Eddie Rickenbacker, became adulation during the winter of 1917-1918 in France. With each tale of his exploit I'd picture a helmeted racing driver zooming through the sky in his automobile, leaving a trail of havoc. He was my kind. He still is today.

We thought of those World War I pilots as intrepid, daredevil-may-care gamblers. Perhaps some were, but not Rickenbacker. He calculated each risk with the mental slide rule he used for a brain. Once he had to slip inside the German defenses to get at one of their troublesome observation balloons. Knowing them as creatures of habit, he used their consistency as a gauge by flying in just when he figured they'd be filling the big bag.

He was right on schedule. Gliding toward the target, he tested his motor to make sure it would start up when needed, only to find that one of the two magnetos was dead. He could have, should have, banked and glided for home but just then, in the dawn, he saw the gas bag rising for an easy kill. Could he bring his motor to life on one magneto to escape? The question went unanswered as he glided silently over the balloon like a predatory hawk, dropped down and circled in level with it. He saw the black Maltese Cross on its side, looked over his shoulder for one more glimpse of perhaps his last sunrise and then sent fire-spitting bullets into the inflated sausage, closed his eyes and turned on the magneto with a prayer. The answer was a cough of combustion, a whir of propeller and up he went, barely clearing the flaming hydrogen as the clumsy sausage twisted to the ground.

I saw Rick again less than a year after our introduction at Neufchâteau in the mess hall of a flying field near Toul. A few other pilots—Raoul Lufberry, the "Lone Star" from Connecticut; the great and unfortunate Jimmy Meissner from Flatbush, Brooklyn; Reed Chambers, and others—were already glamour boys. They were there, laughing, drinking and deservedly enjoying their borrowed time. But over in the corner was the tall, solemn figure of Rickenbacker. What was he doing? He was calibrating bullets, one by one, into his gun to make sure that none missed fire, splintered his wooden prop or jammed. No "Fatty" Göering was going to jump him from behind a cloud and find his guns jammed.

Another rare quality in the man was that Rick never minimized the flying skill of the enemy—he knew what it took to maneuver any plane in a fight. Whatever Hermann Göering sank to, he was a top fighter pilot in World War I. We hear of the glamorous "Red Knight" Richtoefen, but Rick also remembers headaches in the skies named Milch and Udet in the yellow-bellied No. 2 Jagstaffels, and a German sergeant named Thorn, too crude to be an officer but crafty enough to knock Allied planes out of the sky from the ground. With equal humility, Rick will insist that America's greatest flier in World War I was Frank Luke, of Arizona, who handled his tiny plane like a cowboy on payday with his six guns blazing. I admired Luke and his courage, but I revered Rick, who made me recall the wise words of my understanding colonel in Texas. Frank Luke died for his country; Rick lived for it.

Master Sergeant Rickenbacker came out of the war as Commander of the 94th. He had the rank of Colonel, but preferred to be called Captain. With twenty-six enemy planes to his credit, he was *the* American ace in everybody's eyes but his own. A grateful nation awarded him every possible honor including the DSC and the Congressional Medal of Honor, and France gave him the Croix de Guerre and nominated him for the Legion of Honor.

Returning home, he faced the soldier's usual struggle—making a living. When his automobile company failed, he went into aviation, first with Fokker, then American Airways Aviation Corporation and finally as general manager and president of Eastern Airlines which he built into a major and model carrier.

Many hours of his companionship and quiet wisdom have been my privilege for many years, and each one has served only to deepen my respect. I have sat beside him in one of his Eastern Constellations when the cough of a motor or propellers slow to synchronize brought him forward in his seat like a mother hearing a whimper from a distant nursery. He's still a grease monkey at heart.

Great as his prestige and position finally became, Rickenbacker risked it all for truth and principle. The general he had chauffeured, Billy Mitchell, was court-martialed and suspended for criticizing military shortsightedness on airpower and for insisting that America should have an independent Air Force. The old sergeant stood up to be counted and testified in behalf of the farseeing Mitchell. Today Rick has only one regret, that the General died in 1936, a few years before seeing affirmation of his pioneering beliefs in the wild blue yonder.

Handy Man with the Blues

That I occasionally commit a form of musical mayhem on a tune is not a gauge of my affection for it. My implements are to blame—we Missourians can't all be Helen Traubels. My only identification with music may be seen in a personal story told to me by a charming lady back in the mid-Forties. At a dinner party, she recalled, somebody mentioned that a famous singer had cut a record of "The Missouri Waltz" and because the new President, Harry Truman, had revived interest in the number, had sent a pressing to the White House.

"By the way," said one of the diners at the party, "who wrote 'The Missouri Waltz'?"

There was a silence and then another guest replied, "It must have been Bill Corum. All he does is write about Missouri."

Of course I didn't write the song, but I heard it before it was "written." If that sounds strange, it is no stranger than a big, bald-headed man named "Jelly" Sellers who became something of a legend in nearby New Franklin, Missouri. Jelly had hands—the biggest I ever saw—that were made to break a piano into kindling wood, which was something he could do without trying. Big Sellers improvised at the piano and there was a time that he had all the young fellows around that part of the state whistling a tune of his that he called "The Graveyard Waltz." Every young fellow except me, that is, because I never mastered the art of whistling.

One night Jelly went over to Moberly and started beating up a piano in the lobby of a hotel just to keep his fingers supple. A couple of traveling men heard him (who couldn't?), joined him and bought a bottle. When they heard "The Graveyard Waltz" they asked a lot of questions and Jelly confessed it was a little something of his own.

Jelly wasn't one to worry about publication, but one of the traveling men knew enough about music to make a stab at writing the notes as Jelly played. It may have been a coincidence, and I don't know which song came first, but not long after that "The Missouri Waltz" was published. I do know for sure that well before it appeared a lot of folks out my way could hum and whistle that melody.

I thought of this story whenever I visited Mr. William Christopher Handy. It was not often, and his passing makes the last visit a final one. There was a parallel to Jelly in Mr. Handy's life, because he neglected to copyright an early piece of his called "Mr. Crump." Its later title was "Memphis Blues."

This wonderful old gentleman, eighty-two and totally blind when I last saw him, lived on a well-kept acre between Yonkers and Tuckahoe, New York. There was a wishing well on the smooth lawn below his house of which he was very proud, and a bird bath that even a peacock wouldn't shun. Mr. Handy loved birds and their songs, for he remembered that as a boy on Handy Hill in Alabama he had listened to them sing and tried to imitate their song on his trumpet. It was an installment plan, side-valve trumpet costing $1.75 which it took him forty years to pay for, he said with a chuckle.

He laughed softly when he talked about his greatest song. "I was forty," he said, "when 'St. Louis Blues' came. I had a battered piano in a rented room off Beale Street in Memphis. It was a long job putting down the notes on pieces of scratch paper. My eyes were beginning to go even then. I picked up the papers and tapped out the melody on the piano. It was all right. Been all right for over forty years. Except for a minor change, it's the same music I set down that night."

After that one playing, Mr. Handy said, he slept a few hours and awoke to go out for a midday breakfast. Then, standing at the cigar counter at a place called Pee Wee's, he orchestrated the song and made harmonic lead sheets for the players in his band. That evening on the Alaskan Roof, so named to make it sound cool, "St. Louis Blues" was played for the first time. The dancers picked up the unusual and haunting rhythm slowly at first, Mr. Handy recalled with a sigh. They were hesitant, almost reluctant. Then it happened. The strains "hooked them." Before the night was done, in a stomping, wild acclaim during which the customers wanted nothing except his song, an epic chapter in musical history began.

As he told the story softly, smiling and seeming to see with his sightless eyes, the classic was drawing royalties from almost every country in the world. "Memphis Blues" composed three or four years earlier paid him nothing; nor were the strains of "Missouri Waltz" making Jelly Sellers any richer. Whether or not they "wrote" the songs, Mr. Handy laughed, they didn't "copywrote" them.

It was my privilege to bring Mr. Handy news of his favorite team, the Brooklyn Dodgers, and of his favorite player, Roy Campanella. He "watched" television by turning on the radio with it for more action, and he listened to the fights and to all the music he could.

He particularly wanted to add one more song to his long list. "The doctor tells me not to play the horn any more because it might cause a heart attack," he confided. "But sometimes when I can't sleep, I cheat a little at night, soft, so as not to disturb the neighbors. After all, it would be a good way for me to die."

I was in Kentucky when this fine and gentle man passed away, but I like to feel he is right beside Gabriel with his own horn, matching the archangel note for note.

The Tall Man of France

Paris in the Spring is all that the words imply, all that they say about it in song and story. It always will be, I hope, a place to inspire gay romance, for people in Paris are moved to believe they're in love.

Such thoughts came to me in the spring of 1958 when the statement of General Charles De Gaulle that "I hold myself ready to take over the powers of the republic by exceptional, but legal, means" was heard above the political chaos in France. Smaller men had tried to do the job after snubbing the hero more than ten years before. Just how De Gaulle will manage, I don't know, my knowledge of politics being too small to hazard a guess. But his return from self-imposed retirement came as no surprise to me. The tall man of France was always a natural leader and a hero to me after I had a couple of peeps at him and heard his voice while doing a small stretch of war corresponding thirteen years ago.

It was the first parade in Paris after the liberation—how the Parisians love a parade—and the crowds were enormous. The host of Parisians who flowed and eddied through the old, narrow streets and plazas were happy people and on that day, March 27, 1945, they were De Gaulle's people. His picture was in every window, his name on every lip. If the fervor exhibited for Clemenceau and Foch in the hour of victory after the war to end wars was not there, it should be remembered that many of these people were having their first look at the man who, in the black and bitter days of 1940, had insisted that "France has lost a battle, but France has not lost the war."

One educated Frenchman said to me, "Most of us don't know De Gaulle. He has just been one of our generals and we are a country of many generals. But for the last five years, if you were a Frenchman, it was De Gaulle or nothing. He was like a little island in a big ocean of despair and we were tired swimmers. If we did not reach out for him, we sank."

Agree with him or disagree with him, like him or distrust him, the fact remained that history never has produced another man like De Gaulle. But the politicians snubbed him, making his return after so many years particularly ironic. My feeling at the time of the parade was that De Gaulle was in the unhappy position of a crapshooter who has his last small chip on the line and who rolls a four for a point. Whereupon the crapshooter says, "Now gentlemen, I'll show you how to make it the hard way," and whango! to everybody's disbelief he throws two deuces, and from then on refuses to put down the dice.

Even his one-time patron and idol, Pétain, laughed at Charley's book on how to fight a modern war. "Tanks and Planes and more tanks and planes" was the proper prescription, he wrote—and this, mind you, was back in the peaceful 1930s. Mobility was the watchword, he believed: specialists with modern arms and mobility. Had he been a Tennessean speaking the language of Nathan Bedford Forest, De Gaulle would have said, "Get there fustest with the mostest armor."

The French brass hats laughed and wrote Charley off as a crackpot. Defense in depth was the pay-off, the Maginot Line was impregnable, and France had the greatest army on earth. But the Germans who had read the book by De Gaulle and believed it came swooping through the Low Countries and across France, and this time there was no taxicab army to be inspired by the ailing Gallieni, no "Papa" Joffre and no miracle of the Marne. The Wahrmacht rushed over France, engulfing her, and all the time the German High Command might have been saying, "Look, this is the way De Gaulle said it should be done, remember?"

There was, here and there, sporadic resistance, about like that of the Germans in their high, wide road of retreat to defeat a few years later. After that, as far as France was concerned, there was nothing—nothing, that is, save a little-known and unpopular general in London, Charles De Gaulle, standing still and cold by a banner on which was the cross of Lorraine.

All this is history now, but as I wandered through the close-packed Paris crowds that holiday Monday and saw the stands of tattered, decorated banners of past wars massed in the Place de la Concorde, I joined the multitude in believing that the tall man of France was going to be somebody to be reckoned with in the years ahead.

Little did I dream how long it would take or what desperation would have to be endured. However, I did have a feeling at the time that something should have been done to thaw out that cold, frosty spirit, to humanize and popularize the deeply religious French general. Thirteen years later, as De

Gaulle emerges to answer his beloved country's need, I still feel that even if he does the job better than anybody ever did, it's six, two and even he'll never be popular.

Champion of Champions

Yes, newspapermen meet such interesting people—but each meeting carries the hazard and price paid for all friendships. The price is paid with a friend's death, and when the death is premature the price is inflationary.

All of us are an army marching to the inevitable. But now and then the unexpected disappearance of one marcher leaves a permanent void in the ranks. From then on vagrant memories are little daggers that stab the mind. In sports writing you can't isolate recollections; they continue to be part of your work, for he who was fine and immortal in a special way continues to help you earn your living and your reputation. Your feeble efforts to repay him are limited to recollections set down in print.

Most poignant of all to me and to many others are the memories of the husky young dining-room helper I first met in the Sigma Nu Fraternity House at Columbia University in 1921. His mother, Christina Gehrig, was cook and dining supervisor of the house. She worked to help her only child get some higher education and to support her husband, then ill.

Many of us in Columbia marveled at the sight of those long drives that Lou Gehrig occasionally walloped at South Field, then Columbia's football, track and baseball field.

A few years later this muscular marvel began living a legend in human conduct, on and off the baseball field. He became a symbol of physical endurance, of dignity and deportment and of athletic greatness. He was known affectionately as "The Iron Horse" and those who "knew him when" swelled with indescribable pride.

Suddenly he was beckoned from the marching line. His place remained vacant, on the baseball field and off. It always will. On the evening of October 7, 1939, my column should have shouted about the New York Yankees winning their seventh straight World Series game. Their pitching was superb, their hitting murderous. They had beaten the Chicago Cubs in four straight games the year before, and they would surely take the disorganized Cincinnati Reds the next day to duplicate the feat of a decade before when the Pirates and the Cardinals lost to them in successive years.

But all this seemed so unimportant, so remote that it didn't occur to me. My scorecard and the marginal notes of the game had no meaning. It was more important that one of the great marchers was being called from the line. Here was the end of a memorable career, a moment so moving that it muddied my thinking and allowed me to consider only my own small world, my personal loss and the inevitable we all hate to acknowledge.

After an hour or so of torment, I handed the following copy to the Western Union operator:

LAST SWING

CINCINNATI, Oct. 7—Warm October sunlight hangs in a golden haze over the placid bosom of the broad Ohio. It is gay here in Cincinnati, with its little parks and many fountains and ancient beer gardens. Gay and festive.

The national convention of the American Federation of Labor is in session, debating problems that will eventually affect us all. But nobody cares about that now. At least not the folks of Cincinnati. For another World's Series has come back to the old city on its seven hills after twenty years. An honest World's Series this time.

Joe McCarthy's champion New York Yankees are jubilant, tasting already the joys of another short, sharp victory and the long Winter vacation to come. Then it will be Spring again. Springtime in Florida, where the bright red flowers bloom in March with the bright hopes of the new season. But not for quite all the Yankees.

Sitting tight-lipped and grimly smiling among the Champions day after day, with a haunted look about his eyes, is one who probably will not be making the old familiar swing again.

Once they called him the "Iron Horse." Now he is the Iron Man taking a pebble-game man's cut at the mysterious offering of the pitcher no human has ever solved. The pitcher known as Destiny. Taking his cut with chin thrust forward, eyes straight ahead and unafraid. Still the captain of the Yankees. Still the captain of his soul.

When he rolls his stockings down into the bottoms of his baseball pants tomorrow or Monday in that odd way that baseball players dress, it probably will be the last time that he will ever don a "monkey suit." The last time he will carry the number 4 on a back that once looked to be the most powerful and indestructible in baseball.

"See that number four?" opponents of the Yanks used to ask. "Well, that's the hard number."

Ruth and Gehrig, 3 and 4. Add them up and you have 7. But you will not have Babe and Lou again. The likes of them go by together only once.

I followed along behind Lou to some little steps in the Netherland-Plaza Hotel a while ago. He did not know I was behind him and I saw him edging over to put his hand against the wall as he came to the first step. So there were tears behind my eyes as I turned into the coffee shop and ordered a drink I did not want.

As I sat there, fanning with the waitress about the Reds because she wanted to fan about the Reds, my mind went back to the October twilights, when I used to watch from my dormitory window an awkward kid in an old pair of knicker-bockers shagging flies on South Field at Columbia.

To remembering a walk at least a mile from the Bienville Hotel to the Y.M.C.A. in New Orleans, to go swimming with that same young man. Walking, because money was scarce with him on that first Spring training trip of ours, and because he was too independent to let me, or Bob Boyd, another reporter, pay his fare.

To the day when wise little Miller Huggins startled us all by sending him out to play first base in place of Wally Pipp. Putting him into the game, as he first explained, for a few days. Then not being able to get him out again.

And of the long years while his youth and power and vigor, his determination to drive on to victory, were physical manhood personified.

Of another trip South together. This time to St. Petersburg, when I said to him idly: "Ever think of getting married, Lou?"

And he replied, "I think of it, but first I've got to know that Mom's all right. It takes a long time to save up when you're starting from taw."

Then there were the happy days that found him shyly courting in Chicago. Diffidently. For he's a timid fellow. There will be something of the sophomore about him always. Fame and modest fortune and untroubled happiness now, for a little while.

And the night in the Garden when he made a little speech out of his heart about America that shamed the high flown orators.

Then the strange sickness that came to worry and distress and baffle him. Of the deep and abiding friendship of a roommate named Bill Dickey. A stand-up sportsman, who played ball by day, and fought to kid and jolly his pal out of worries through the troubled nights.

Finally the unbelievable answer to what was wrong. Grim as it was, it was better than uncertainty. Then that touching, unforgettable day in the Stadium: "I am the luckiest man on the face of the earth."

And now what seem so likely to be the closing hours of the last Western swing.

It is gay in Cincinnati. The city is draped in flags and bunting. There is music, laughter. The sunshine is golden above the river.

But I wonder what one man is thinking as he looks out across the field through the Autumn haze from the shade of a dugout that is scarred and criss-crossed with the passing of many spikes.

Whatever it is, he smiles and says: "Did you see that Dahlgren lay the wood on that one?"

New heroes are in the making here. One more championship is being carved out for the long records. But so as not to be forgetting, may I give you my friend and my idea of the champion of the champions—Lou Gehrig.

THOROUGHBREDS: HORSES AND PEOPLE

*There is no book so bad but
something good may be found in it.*
                        Cervantes

The Greatest

You could not go wrong, in that spring of 1917 when the United States threw its weight on the side of the Allies, by naming a colt Man o' War. The spindly-legged, fractious, golden chestnut son of Fair Play, out of the Rock Sand mare Mahuba, could not have been more perfectly named, for he was to prove a veritable man o' war on the race tracks of this country and Canada.

He was a thundering torpedo, with a stride unlike that of any other horse we have ever produced and with a speed that no other horse of his time could match. Later they gave many of his sons and daughters apt martial names, and some of them were good ones—Crusader, American Flag, Scapa Flow (an ill-fated fellow, but one of the most beautiful I ever saw), Bateau, and Edith Cavell. The first Derby winner sired by Man o' War—who was not a Derby starter himself—was little Clyde Van Dusen, a colt so small for future breeding that they gelded him. The unwarlike name was in tribute to a great trainer.

One thing all Man o' War colts had in common was the ability to run in the mud. Of these and others, War Admiral came closest to his pappy, except in his deep brown color. He had twenty-one victories in twenty-six starts and won $273,000, about $25,000 more than Man o' War. As yet War Admiral has not sired a Derby winner, though he came close in 1957 when his grandson Iron Liege, out of Iron Maiden, won for Calumet.

Having seen this great golden boy run the heart out of John P. Grier in the summer of 1920, I thought I'd seen the greatest horse and greatest race of all time. But ten years later, on a bleak Autumn day in Baltimore, I changed my mind. The Pimlico Futurity was run over the old Hilltop course and the winner became my favorite. Though Jamestown previously had taken most of the important two-year-old stakes, the brown beauty, Equipoise, looked like perfection itself as he thundered through that final sixteenth over a mile. As I watched Twenty Grand do the impossible a few months later to take the 1931 Derby in record time, I wondered what might have happened had Equipoise been able to start. It was a year of outstanding three-year-olds, but Equipoise managed to win twenty-nine of his fifty-one starts and pick up well over 300,000 depression dollars, $70,000 more than Twenty Grand.

Only a few years ago I had another favorite, Swaps, a great grandson of War Admiral. I had seen him on bright mornings in Kentucky winging over an old track, saw him wandering, like a placid cow pony, around Mr. Tom Young's slip beds, casing the joint. He was a quiet golden colt, maybe a bit "touched," as Trainer Tenny said, "spooky now and then."

By and large, he was quite a gentleman the first time I ever saw him run, in a race before the Derby that was supposed to be between Nashua and Summer Tan. In a sprint that had been put on the menu for his order, Swaps suddenly turned into a golden blur 70 yards from the finish and then continued around the turn, working out after the finish the fastest I'd ever seen a horse run. He took Nashua by a length and a half and Summer Tan by eight when he won the Derby in time only two-fifths of a second slower than Whirlaway's 1941 track record.

As you may suspect, I'm a running-horse man and maybe in my heart I always was. But neither Man o' War, nor Millionaire Citation, nor Nashua, nor the close-to-my-heart Swapsie, nor the picture-gray trotter (what a picture!) Greyhound, nor all the horses that have come and gone in our country before my eyes ever quite left as deep a footprint as old Dan Patch, shuffling through the dust with his practiced, even pace in the happy, living-in-dreams America of the 1900s shuffling his feet in the dust of memory of a million kids of my generation.

Gentle Centaur

Sports writers have been lucky over the years, and especially in the Twenties, to have undisputed leaders in half a dozen major sports. This always makes writing easy, because the standout is so high on the pedestal that everybody can see him. Anything you say about such a man, fact or rumor, gets attention and fills columns.

We don't have them today, and I'm not sure why. I mean, for instance, a Paavo Nurmi whose best mile was 4:10 and a fraction, and best two miles just under nine minutes. He was alone as a performer in the 1920s when a four-minute mile seemed an unattainable pinnacle. Today we've developed a small army of milers who break four minutes.

We had one standout performer in sports who in my forty years of watching and writing about individual greats, I thought was the best at his game that ever lived. The acknowledged greats of his sport looked up to him, yet I and other sports writers wrote less about him than about any other champion. He was better at his sport than Dempsey in boxing or Tilden in tennis, better than Bobby Jones in golf, better than Babe Ruth or Ty Cobb in their game, better than the Old Man Mose of the racing saddle, Eddie Arcaro, whose supremacy is as plain as the nose on his face.

My guy was *always* supreme in his sport—no more than that. His name, as you may have guessed, was Thomas Hitchcock, Jr., my personal Beau Sabreur as an American gentleman, soldier, sportsman, athlete. Although I never really was close to him or saw him more often than he played in the International matches, I'm proud to say he was my friend. I can also say that I had a reverence for his skill that I couldn't express, privately or publicly, because I didn't know enough about polo.

But I know the movements and manners of horses. I know that you cannot fight a horse from his back, just because you happen to hold the reins. You can subdue the horse, but you can subdue anything from an elephant to a crime wave, and where does that leave you when you need the conquered animal, person or nation to work for and with you?

Wiser heads told me, and even I could see it, that this was the genius of Tommy Hitchcock. Every movement of his body—head, shoulders, arms, hands, seat, legs and feet—was a message to the polo pony, *before* the gentle tug on the reins. "The pony knew what Tommy wanted him to do by the way he used each ounce of his weight," said one of my informants. "The pull of the bit was confirmation."

Once I had a golden opportunity to discuss all this with Tommy for the first time. The sports world was doing one of those superduper radio broadcasts on behalf of the Red Cross. Tommy was my star to interview, and I planned to get him before the radio public and at the same time collect material for some columns.

Young Hitchcock was big, broad, dark-haired and handsome, like his father, and quiet, soft-spoken and easy-smiling. In spite of my own awe, I tried to put him at his ease, but I just couldn't overcome the feeling of hero worship which I have for the truly accomplished. The result was some of the worst radio minutes in microphone history.

My questions were carefully planned and somewhat intelligent, if I do say so. But his answers weren't; he just looked at me and blinked. After a full minute of waiting, I realized we should have had a horse of some kind in the little studio for Tommy to sit on. The engineer signaled frantically from the control room, whirling one hand in a circle for me to speed up. Quickly I phrased a question that required a simple yes, the kind I hate. "You sit facing forward on a horse, don't you?", I asked. Hitchcock's eyes bugged out, his lips tightened, and he *nodded* into the microphone. I cooked up a question requiring a simple no. He replied by shaking his head violently from side to side.

Perhaps I reflected these answers to our listeners, but I was so scared myself that I didn't know what I was doing. I wasn't smart enough to switch tactics and make him talk by calling some of his polo friends names or accusing him of using western spurs in a game. I simply babbled the questions and he only shook or nodded his head.

When the ordeal was over, and we were going off the air I heard him murmur, "Thank you, Bill." That was all the great unseen audience heard of Tommy Hitchcock, the greatest polo player who ever lived—and also the most modest and most frightened.

The awesome fact that Hitchcock had the maximum ranking, a ten-goal handicap, for eighteen years, answers all doubts about his supremacy. The game produced other standouts with that ranking—I think of the great Devereux Milburn, Monte and Larry Waterbury, and in later days,

Mike Phipps, Cecil Smith and the nearest thing we have to
Hitchcock, Stewart Iglehart. But imagine a golfer, ball
player, tennis star or boxer ranked at the very top of his
specialty, unchallenged for nearly two decades. Tommy
Hitchcock could have been on top for another dozen years,
but the modest, gentle centaur died in the night fogs of
London in World War II.

Up the Stairs to Doyle's

Often I have wondered how many of the millions of Americans who have played bridge day after day through the years
know that Tod Sloan, the jockey, brought the game to this
country. He introduced it in a Broadway billiard room, just
south of Times Square, owned by Jack Doyle, John J. Mc-
Graw and the prize fighter, Kid McCoy, born Norman Selby.
If this doesn't start arguments, especially among old players
of whist—a different game—let's try another. It was John Mc-
Graw who brought back from Cuba and helped popularize
the daiquiri, and who named a Havana restaurant just around
the corner from the American Club and operated by one Jose
Abeal, "Sloppy Joe's."

A reporter of the roaring twenties couldn't get such vital
information without going "up the stairs to Doyle's." There
he could find laughter, legends and stories without number.
Tales about Tod Sloan were always fascinating. One of Jack
Doyle's oft-told best concerned Tod's return from a trip to
Europe after scoring a great victory on one of the horses of
the King of England. He startled Broadway with the first all-

fur man's overcoat ever seen in the Times Square area. The garment had cost over $2,500, and all conversation halted when the coat swaggered through Rector's with little Tod inside, identifiable only by the inevitable cigar almost as big as himself.

"I recall the first time Tod came in here with the coat," growled Doyle. "It was glistening new. Every billiard game stopped and half the players asked if they could stroke the soft fur. The porter had put a mother cat and her new litter of kittens in a box on top of some burlap bags. It was a bitter cold night and before we locked up we checked the new arrivals. We were down the street, with the joint locked up for the night, when we noticed that Tod had left his coat upstairs. I wanted to go back, but Tod said it was okay. He continued on up Broadway to the Claridge Hotel, saying he'd pick it up next day. Well, he did, but when I opened the place the next morning, I found the coat where Tod had wrapped it carefully around the mother and kittens."

Doyle would explain "characters" quite matter-of-factly, defending idiosyncrasies to the limit. "Of course Sloan was broke," he said. "But who isn't at one time or another except a money magpie who hasn't got enough imagination or heart to help anybody? Tod rode everywhere, here and in Europe, for royalty and riches, but he had a blitz hand with a buck. You think he only rode horses? I once saw Sloan watching an angry driver trying to get a fallen dray horse up from the icy street. He pulled, tugged and cursed. Tod pushed through the gallery of ghouls, put his arms around the horse's neck, said a couple of words, clucked, and the horse got up on his feet. How the hell can a person like that be compared with us ordinary mortals?"

It was upstairs at Doyle's that I first met one of the most aptly named greats in sports, "Gentleman Jim" Corbett, the former heavyweight champion. Though he always exhuded the gentility of his nickname, Corbett did it without effort or ostentation. He was ramrod straight, polite, immaculately dressed, and usually smiling, which made his eyes disappear in the shadows of heavy brows. Being a master boxer, he was unmarked from nearly forty fights, and he spoke softly and listened considerately.

I've been lucky enough to meet two of America's greatest sports figures, and both acquaintances stem from Jack Doyle's. Corbett I met there, but the last time I saw him was when I visited his Bayside, Long Island, home on February 1, 1933. Corbett had taken to his bed, which faced a window looking out upon Little Neck Bay. He knew that the ten count was being tolled but he spoke of many things in the future, none of which he would see or do. As he talked of how beautiful the trees outside his window were in the spring-time, he knew that he would not live to see them burgeon again. The knowledge was there in his eyes, as plainly etched as the stark and barren boughs against the pane. The coura-geous refusal of Corbett and his devoted wife to admit to each other that the final parting was near after thirty-seven years of boon companionship and happiness made a lump in my throat. The end came only eighteen days later.

The other great sporting figure I met through Doyle was Christy Mathewson. Jack brought him to life with his tales about this pitching marvel who had once made me so sad in Robison Field, St. Louis, by beating my Cardinals. I met Mathewson in late September, 1925. Bill Farnsworth, my sports editor, sent me, along with Bill "Ironsides" Ironson, one of the top sports photographers, to Saranac Lake, New York, for a story and pictures. Matty wouldn't pose because he had lost so much weight during his long illness, but he did see us in what is now part of the Will Rogers Sanitarium.

It was twilight when we left the house and another day had slipped from Christy's meager calendar. As we walked away down the hill, Ironsides and I turned and looked back. Matty had lighted the electric light over his bed and sat propped up by an open window reading. A faint hint of fall was in the breeze that stirred the curtains and the little pines outside.

News that the end had come reached us in the press box at Forbes Field, Pittsburgh, just as Pie Traynor hit a fifth-inning homer for the Pirates' only run of the first World Series game. Walter Johnson's great victory was thrust into the background as we wrote about the passing of a man who personified a whole baseball era. Of course none of us could do it as well as the Sheriff, W. O. McGeehan of the New York *Herald Tribune,* did in the first and last paragraphs of his column:

> PITTSBURGH, Oct. 8—While the captains and the kings of baseball were gathered here last night after the first game of a World Series there died at Saranac the best loved of all the baseball players and the most popular of all American athletes of all time—Christy Mathewson. . . .
>
> If baseball will hold to the ideals and the example of Christy Mathewson, gentleman, sportsman and soldier, our national game will keep the younger generation clean and courageous and the future of the nation secure.

Taverns in the Town

I can't explain why, periodically, sportswriters patronize and help popularize certain new bistros and bars in town, or why we use our employers' valuable newspaper space to perpetuate some back-slapping host, manager or maitre d' as the new paladin of the pubs. For example, I've written thousands of words about Bernard "Toots" Shor as champion of the chop-house set. I could still write a book about him and his sports-writers' sanctuary. One reason prevents it—pal Tootsie might write a book about me, and since we have so much on each other we'd both have to leave town. In fact, an unconscious reason for this book could be that an autobiographer, by getting there first with the facts, can deny whatever else may be written about him later.

Bars and taverns—actually no more than hangouts—have been popular as long as sports writers needed reasons for not going home at a respectable hour. My old friend, Sid Mercer, used to tell me stories of Manhattan's watering places. "You simply didn't rate," handsome Sid said solemnly, "until you had some difficulty at Jack Dunston's Round Table in the rear or the Battling Nelson bar up front, and were bounced by the flying wedge of waiters right out onto Sixth Avenue and Forty-Second Street."

Jack's went out shortly after prohibition became a fact on January 20, 1920, but was reincarnated on the south side of 48th Street, just east of Seventh Avenue. Called Billy La Hiff's Tavern, its doors were opened early in 1922. At the same time there began an era that has no parallel in sports—for which some of us may be thankful. Nighthood was always in flower, because nobody ever seemed to sleep.

The direct link between Jack's and Billy's was the bland and perhaps most widely known head waiter of our time, Jack Spooner. Some of the biggest names in politics, sports and show business cooled their heels or wet their whistles in the Tavern lobby while waiting for a table in the section called "Spooner's Corner." He had been a figure at Jack's, and at the Tavern he really took charge, always with a touch of the veiled insult, the slight affront or the false indignation. But no one ever took offense at the smiling, seemingly just-scrubbed face. Spooner's domination included bringing his own choice of food to a patron, rather than "letting him kill himself with a menu." More sports stories, news and intrigue came out of Spooner's Corner than the busiest publicity office. Tex Rickard negotiated some of his biggest deals there.

Proprietor Billy La Hiff was a slight, dapper and debonair fellow whose only obvious shortcoming should have made him a failure in his business. He couldn't remember names —even those of prominent people he had met more than once. His stock greeting, "Howya, little feller!" or "Hi-ya, big boy!" gave him time to spar with his memory for the patron's right handle.

Next to his family and his fabulous Tavern, duplicate of an oak-paneled English inn, La Hiff loved the theater best. His niece, beautiful Nancy Çarroll, became a film star and married into the theater. She was the wife of Jack Kirkland, who dramatized the long-run hit *Tobacco Road* while living upstairs over the Tavern. La Hiff also introduced Ruby Stevens, a pretty Brooklyn girl, to playwright Willard Mack, who was seeking a young lady for a part in his play *The Noose*. Ruby was never heard from again, because she reappeared as Barbara Stanwick.

Another of La Hiff's "discoveries" was a cute redhead named Peggy. He provided her and her mother with an apartment on Long Island and sent the girl to dramatic school. Before graduation, Peggy married a cloak-and-suiter and moved to California. After a while, she became lonesome and wanted to see New York and Billy again. She hadn't seen her husband for some time and didn't know where he was; could Uncle Billy send her transportation? Uncle Billy could and did. He rushed over to Sixth Avenue and mailed her a pair of roller skates.

On July 2nd, 1925, the Tavern was the scene of the strangest of all fights, one typical of the screwy times. Earlier that night Harry Greb had successfully defended his world's middleweight title against Mickey Walker in a Yankee Stadium fight that drew $375,000 for the Italian Hospital Fund. As was the custom, most of the principals wound up at the Tavern to crow or eat it. Nobody remembered how it started, but suddenly the victorious Greb and the thoroughly licked Walker were out on 48th Street shedding their coats. Two of the greatest fighters who had just boxed fifteen brutal rounds for a fortune apiece now were slugging each other for pleasure and pain. It was past midnight, which accounted for the poorest crowd either had ever drawn. They slugged each other halfway down the block before the fight ended as suddenly as it had started.

La Hiff followed Greb into the Tavern washroom where the champion doused a twice-bruised and bleeding face. Then Billy's stomach did a flip-flop, for Greb had carefully removed an artificial eye and placed it on the wash basin. Few knew that Greb had lost the sight of one eye from a deliberate thumbing three years before in Boston, and no one, not even Mickey Walker, had known that Greb had rushed out to battle in the street under such circumstances. One hard punch in the glass eye could have killed him.

One day James A. Farley, a patron of the Tavern from the days when he was chairman of the Boxing Commission, appeared with Governor Franklin D. Roosevelt. Of course they were seated in Spooner's Corner where, throughout the lunch, Jack addressed Mr. Roosevelt pointedly as "Mr. President." Whether this was by accident or design, I never knew, but I do know that it was in 1932, not many weeks before the Democratic Convention in Chicago.

Above the Tavern were apartments that La Hiff rented. The list of tenants was a Who's Who of the times; Walter Winchell and his family lived there in his early days, and Mayor Walker in his last and troubled days as the city's chief executive. A pair of Jacks, back to back, since Dempsey and Kearns weren't speaking at the time, lived there, as did Jimmy Hussey and master song-smith Walter Donaldson. After leaving Lindy's on Broadway, Damon Runyon invariably walked around the corner to La Hiff's office where he could always commandeer a typewriter. There the D-Man wrote some of his best columns and a few of his fiction pieces, too. It was from La Hiff's in 1932 that many of us went to the apartment of Ed Frayne, sports editor of the *American,* for Damon's wedding to Patrice Amati. Mayor Walker performed the ceremony, after which we returned to the Tavern for appropriate observation of the occasion. A La Hiff celebration for his friends was something to remember—though few of them could when they recovered.

Of course the Tavern was by no means our only hangout. It was simply the only one of its kind, but it wasn't nearly big enough for all those who wanted to stay up late and talk. Mother Leone's, on 48th Street west of Broadway, was a special favorite of the sports mob, and still is. Dinty Moore's, two blocks south, had a peculiar link to the Tavern, for Dinty's boy, Willie, ran to La Hiff whenever he had a row with the old man. After each run-in, Willie would hide away in a Tavern apartment. But Bugs Baer doubted the seriousness of the alleged family row. "I've been to Moore's," Bugs cracked. "The kid just comes here for the food."

Of all the fantasies and unbelievables produced by the Tavern in its twenty very odd years, it will best be remembered for developing a phenomenon called, for want of a better or worse term, Toots Shor. The big fellow, a native of Philadelphia, was first a glorified bouncer at Leon and Eddie's, then at the Tavern, which he also managed. Early in World War II he got enough backing to open his own place in a couple of benighted brownstone houses on West 51st Street bordering Rockefeller Center.

The stories began the moment Toots walked into his "joint" to take over. The details of financing, the splendid architecture (a Tavern touch), food and waiters had been a frustrating and costly experience. Dramatically reflecting the strain, Toots took every cent from his pocket—less than two dollars —and threw the change across the street "to the Rockefellers. I'll go in the joint broke," he announced. Unfortunately his petite wife, Baby, stopped in a while later for congratulations and money for cab fare home. Toots had to borrow from his captain, Joe Harrison.

In my book, Toots Shor's is an extension of Jack's and the Tavern both in food and in spirit. The Spoonerism has given way to the Shorism, a less delicate kind of sneer and insult, spiced by such terms as "crumbum." But the sports crowd beat a path to Shor's from the start, and they quickened the pace after May 10, 1940, the night Lew Jenkins knocked out Lou Ambers for the lightweight title. The conquering hero was barred from celebrating in the Stork Club for wearing a tieless sports shirt. Outraged by such an affront to earthly immortality, Shor ordered the new champion and his party to his place forthwith as honored guests.

"You can come to my joint in boxing shorts!" he declared.

This big, blue-eyed St. Bernard with the face of an overfed adolescent has given me thousands of precious hours and a million laughs, but never one more unforgettable than the time he finally got straightened out with the rationing board on a red-stamp rap. It was World War II and Tootsie was ruled off the meat course for three or four months. Meanwhile, his business had doubled because of sympathetic friends rushing over to help out "poor Tootsie" by eating his meat substitutes.

At last the ban ended. The baseball crowd was in town for the start of the World Series and he could serve meat again. He was ecstatic as we walked the darkened streets after closing his place; the next day he would reward his loyal patrons with "the biggest, juiciest and best steaks I can get." He raved on and on about the big tenderloins and roasts of beef he would serve until I stopped him cold. I said, "I guess only your type could do such a thing on Meatless Tuesday." His pardon had come through on a Monday in that period when Mayor LaGuardia was asking folks to help the war effort each week by not buying, selling or eating meat on Tuesdays.

Shor's saloon prospered and he was able to use the building next door to enlarge the place. He wound up with three big floors, a fabulous volume and a national reputation. Underneath it all, though, he wasn't much different from when he first showed up at La Hiff's. He was a little wiser maybe, but just as liable to give the place away, drink by drink. We had a tough time with him in the summer of 1958 when he sold his two buildings, the last ones standing in a full half block needed for a new hotel. Though Toots had a million dollars for the first time in his life and a full year to vacate, you'd have thought from the way he blubbered all night and threatened to drink all the brandy in stock that Baby had left him and taken the kids.

Actually, I think Toots was overcome by the thought of not having a place to hang out at night with the gang. You may think I'm exaggerating, but that's the way he is and always has been. After he had sold the place, our biggest worry was that he'd find some way to get rid of the money. I know from experience that he's one of the quickest to reach with the ready remedy when a friend is in trouble, and I don't know anybody I've rushed quicker to help.

We had something of an argument on this score on Thanksgiving Day, 1958, which I spent with Toots and his family in their beautiful home. I had come out of the hospital pretty sick, but well enough to enjoy a holiday dinner of eggnog. Tootsie insisted that I needed money. I insisted that I needed only appetite and some weight, since I had liberal hospitalization coverage and two good jobs paying me well for doing nothing—though I was writing the column against orders. In fact, I was in a position to lend him a little scratch, if his big check bounced.

We laughed. After so many years of touch and go and of digging down with mutual aid, here we sat, both loaded, with no way to help each other.

Symphonies in Ebony

The first sports writer, a little before my time, covered the old, *old* Olympic Games and wrote good poetry. His name was Pindar and he once said, "Refrain from peering too far." Whether he meant forward or backward I don't know, but to name the best in anything you have to peer back. In the case of a couple of prize fighters and a baseball player, my memory of them at their best could never be too far back to see. Equally indelible are my memories of their beginnings, which I was fortunate enough to witness. As the theater program says, they'll be named in order of appearance.

I saw my first big-league fight, Dempsey against Carpentier, on July 2, 1921. But my feelings about the heavyweight division were first aroused eleven years before that. A man named Jack Johnson knocked out Boonville's adopted martyr, Jim Jeffries, at Reno, Nevada, on July 4, 1910. Though I'd never heard of professional boxing before that, I hated Johnson with all the fury a fifteen-year-old could muster. The news, received early in the evening because of the time dif-

ference, took all the sparkle and color from the rest of the
fireworks. I've been following boxing ever since, and in all
that time there are two men who stand out above the crowd.

Joe Louis (Barrow), the heavyweight champion, was almost
without faults in the ring, but he never expressed his superiority except with his two fists. He was strictly a fighter, the
greatest fighter of all time in my opinion. I'd have no hesi-
tancy in saying this if he were fighting Jack Dempsey at
Dempsey's best, or Gene Tunney at his best, for I saw them
both. Before that—well, if Johnson, Jeffries, Fitzsimmons,
Corbett or Sullivan were resurrected and reconditioned for a
fight with Joe Louis at his peak, my money would still have to
go on Joe.

This opinion is based partially on the fact that Louis was
one of the few outstanding fighters to bring *two* great hands
into the ring. You don't have to go much further, but I will.
He had a devastating hook and cross in either hand, and the
most destructive jab that boxing has ever seen. The jab is one
punch for which there is almost no defense. The feeble claim
that he "couldn't take a punch" is silly. Even sillier is a fighter
who can take them. Louis simply avoided them with a skill
that was the equal of Tunney's or Corbett's. That he didn't
have to take punches, and continued to deal them out with
either hand, made him a champion longer than any other
heavyweight. Like Tunney, he retired an undefeated champion in 1949 with only one loss on his record. Like Tunney's,
it was a real beating.

The buttals and rebuttals from the foregoing declaration
would fill a book. In the past, they have filled a number of my
columns—for which I was always grateful—but this is for the
record and I set it down with aforethought and no malice.
While any dissenter is recovering from his shock, let me add
that Joe Louis' superiority wasn't limited to the ring. He was
as great a person and an American as he was a champion.

I never heard an ugly word spoken about Louis. In this he was unique among almost all sports figures, especially fighters. I'll never forget the growls, groans and hisses at the announcement of Dempsey's name, or the contempt for Tunney because he had read a book and perhaps too often allowed his tongue to linger lovingly over three long words where one short one would have done a better job. I'll never forget Ring Lardner's comment when, soaking wet, he reached press headquarters after Tunney had taken Dempsey's title in Philadelphia. He announced, as only Lardner could, "Tunney will be the most popular champion since Tommy Burns!" (Burns' title was always clouded by Jim Jeffries' retirement).

No one ever said such things about Joe Louis because his simplicity, sincerity, integrity, deep-seated pride and complete lack of pretense made it impossible. From the very beginning, we knew him as an uneducated boy whose words came from his heart, not his head. For instance: "We'll win because we're on God's side." Or: "I ain't fightin' for nothin'. I'm fightin' for my country."

After the knockout by Schmeling: "Ma, he just whupped me."

To his trainer: "Chappie, you gotta go into the ring with me. But I promise you won't have to walk up the ring steps but one time."

About Billy Conn's speed: "He can run, but he can't hide."

About his race: "I want to put up one more fight to help my people—the best of my career. The hardest fight I ever had was against prejudice and intolerance. My people know what I mean."

When Louis came out of retirement and licked Ezzard Charles for seven of ten rounds, then lost the last five and the decision, I wrote hopefully on my scorecard, "Joe's last fight." There were tears in my eyes, and maybe in my voice, as I signed off the radio broadcast for Don Dunphy and myself. No other fighter could affect me this way.

Joe Louis had left more than the memory of a has-been champion under the pale and murky moon before a tiny crowd that looked like a crap game huddled around the ring in the vast emptiness he had filled so often. He left a legacy of honesty and dignity to a sport with which those two words are not synonymous. He fought for sixteen years without uttering a word of alibi for himself, or of disparagement for an opponent, or even of reproach for those who failed so shamefully to guard his financial future.

The strains of my second symphony are far less somber, because Ray Robinson could never stimulate the feeling of sympathy and admiration that Louis inspired. Yet Sugar Ray, the sweetest piece of fighting machinery of my time, is superb among fighters and, in his division, as great as Joe Louis. His technique has a pattern of rhythm and grace, an explosive fire. He also has, I've always believed, a constitutional defect that causes him, now and then, to "run out of gas."

But if there is real art to the so-called sweet science of boxing, then Robinson, whose right name is Walker Smith, stands as a top artist of all time. He can do more things better than any fighter I ever saw, and as for punching speed, only Louis could flick a jab as quick and fire a punch of *any* kind with as much explosive suddenness as Robinson.

In this respect, Louis and Robinson stand alone in the boxing world, with weight the only deciding factor in supremacy between them. This evaluation has nothing to do with the sort of soldier Robinson was or wasn't, with whether he always has kept his word, or respected his signed contracts, or with whether he has tried on occasion to play both ends against the middle and ducked around corners when an honest, straightforward and Joe Louisan approach would have been to his ultimate advantage. These things have no bearing on his matchless skill in the ring, where he could duck and dodge or meet the issue with a solid wallop in either hand. He had so much natural class and acquired skill that he lost only one fight in his first ten years as a professional. Provocative, annoying, sometimes maddening, he has been the greatest of welterweight and middleweight champions, and came within six minutes of being the greatest light heavyweight champion on June 25, 1952, when, in 100-degree heat, he ran out of gas.

I saw my first big-league baseball game well over fifty years ago, but I didn't believe Willie Mays the first time I saw him in a shivery night game at Parkway Field, Louisville. The 1951 American Association season had just opened. The visiting Minneapolis team was the top farm club of the New York Giants. My old friend, Horace Stoneham hadn't flown a championship pennant at the Polo Grounds in fourteen years and I was more than interested in his main source of supply for the future. During the six or seven innings I watched Willie Mays that chilly night, he hit two home runs and a triple. He made a couple of noncircus catches, difficult catches that the Joe DiMaggios and Tris Speakers would have made look easy. Willie made them look easy, too.

From then on, radio broadcasts prevented me from forgetting what I'd seen. After doing the play-by-play of Louisville games, the announcer would give scores and details of other baseball activity. At first I tuned in before going to bed just to get the big-league scores. But I can't tell you how many times I heard the announcer say, "Willie Mays hit a home run," and I developed the habit of saying to myself with a chuckle, "Willie's done it again."

When I returned to New York from my Kentucky Derby chores in mid-May, Willie was hitting close to .500. Stoneham's scouts, who were supposed to know, said he could make it at the top, but only in centerfield. That presented a problem, because the Giants had a fine centerfielder in Bobby Thomson. We writers got the idea that Willie couldn't "play the lines," until Leo Durocher was considerate enough to explain it.

"The fact is, Bill," he said in confidence, "he's just about as good in center as you can find. Playing him anywhere else would be stupid. We can't say that. We can't say he's better than Thomson, but he is. He may be the best, but we can't say that, or anything except that he'll play center."

It was a time of crisis in my personal life, and I had to stay close to a telephone. Practically every day my mother and I would sit before the television set watching the Giants' game or, when they were on the road, watching the Yankees and listening on the radio to the Giants' game. Needless to say Willie did it again . . . and again . . . and again.

What did Willie do? He hit, yes, but he didn't break any fences or records. He had weaknesses, especially for the high, outside fast one that could have been taken for a ball. He fielded well, was great on some catches, but on none that any great centerfielder wouldn't have made. He lost his cap regularly and at first stopped to pick it up before chasing the batted ball. He threw hard, and often too hard to the wrong spot. He ran bases fast and often, but perhaps not with finesse and sometimes at the wrong time.

At first, *what* Willie did was important to me. But while watching him that first year, and seeing the Giants do the impossible, thanks to Bobby Thomson's playoff-winning home run, the most spectacular base hit in all baseball history, *how* Willie did it counted most. That's why I began to rave about him from the start, and have never quit. For Willie Mays, from the very start until 1958 when he missed his second batting championship by .003, has been a natural ballplayer, completely unconscious in every move he made. Because he has the reflexes, eyesight, knowledge of the game, and the urge to win without fearing the consequences, there is no limit to the distance he can go.

That is why I believe him to be the greatest of all ballplayers. Mind you, I saw Ty Cobb, and he was alone in his fashion. So was Babe Ruth. Joe DiMaggio was the picture player, as fine a person and companion as he was a ballplayer. But very early I sensed in Mays a rare quality, a natural, uninhibited way of expressing himself physically that is the hallmark of the creative artist. It is that strange gift of moving without thinking, of doing first and then thinking, a habit that got me into plenty of trouble as a kid because I wasn't an artist and too often did the thing wrong.

But when the artists do it—a Rubinstein or an untutored Jelly Sellers, a Maria Callas or an Ella Fitzgerald, a Fred Astaire or a Bill Robinson—they do it without conscious thought. The lightning strikes a writer once in a while, especially when he knows his theme and feels it. Oh, how those columns run out of the machine, like music, like magic—you feel as though you're stealing your employer's money. But there are so few of them compared with the blood-sweat-and-tears pieces that are sent downtown—also with a feeling that you're stealing money.

Willie Mays has had that lightning from the start. There is no limit to the fantastic heights he can reach, so long as he retains that inner magic of unconscious, unafraid expression. Whether Giant players realize it, they sense this magic and depend upon it. I saw it happen with Babe Ruth. We wrote, "As Ruth goes, so go the Yankees"; what we meant was that Ruth's functioning as an artist was contagious. So it has been with Mays from the very start, and it is one more reason why he is great. His natural ability adds points to other batting percentages, extra steps and effort to the movements of other players.

This priceless ingredient is rare in baseball today but I have never seen it work so effectively in more than fifty years of watching big-league baseball. For all these reasons I have never seen a greater baseball player than Willie Mays.

One for the Book

It is strange, but gratifying, that the greatest thrill of the countless big-league ball games I've seen should have been provided by my favorite pitcher, Grover Cleveland Alexander. He was my favorite long before that October Sunday at Yankee Stadium, 1926, when he shuffled in from the bull pen in the seventh inning and, with the bases full, struck out Tony Lazzeri on four pitches.

"Old Pete" denied that he was tipsy when he went in to save the National League and my sagging hopes for the St. Louis Cardinals. I'll take his word, but if he didn't have a morning-after-the-night-before head it was no fault of the crippling stuff they bottled in New York at the time. The truth is that Alex hadn't the faintest idea he'd be called on to pitch in the Sunday game. Nor did Manager Rogers Hornsby expect to call on him, for he had beaten the Yankees in the second game, 6–2, and had tied the Series by winning the sixth game, 10–2. He had held Ruth and Gehrig to one single in fourteen times at bat.

To play it safe, though, Hornsby left Coach Buzzy Wares behind at the Alamac Hotel to rout Pete out of bed and get

him to the Stadium by game time. The chore took some doing, Buzzy reported later, because each time they'd start, Alex
would find an excuse to go back to the room. Suspicious,
Wares followed him the third time. Alex had located the hidden pint of whiskey right where he had left it, under some
soiled towels. Wares took charge of the bottle and suggested
food. Alex insisted he could beat the Yankees on an empty
stomach—besides, who would have the heart to call on a
thirty-nine-year-old pitcher who had won his second Series
game the day before?

But Buzzy managed to pick up a ham sandwich, which was
the extent of Pete's eating up to game time. At the start of the
game, he trudged down to the bull pen with Bill Sherdel, the
left-hander, Henry Vick, a catcher, and others. There Alex
tipped his wrinkled cap forward and stretched out on the
bench to sleep a bit in the left-field sun.

Jess Haines, the starting pitcher, began to develop a sore
finger in the fifth. The Yankees got their second run in the
sixth, to make the score 3–2. Haines was shaky in the seventh,
and Hornsby waved frantically from his second-base position
for bull-pen action. Sherdel responded; Alexander continued
to sleep. With the bases full and two out, Hornsby called
time, looked at the blister on Haines' pitching finger, and
beckoned to the bull pen. Sherdel picked up his sweater and
started. Hornsby waved him back.

"He wants you, Pete," Sherdel said.

"Not me," Alex grunted. "You."

Sherdel started in a second time, only to see Hornsby slap-
ping his right shoulder to indicate a right-hander. So they
hoisted the reluctant hero from the bench and pointed him
toward the Yankee Stadium pitcher's mound.

"I took all the time I could getting in from the bull pen,"
Alex said later, "because I knew the wait wasn't going to hurt
me and it might bear down on a young fellow like Tony. I

warmed up with three or four sinkers and soft ones, while Lazzeri stood at the batter's box and watched them float by. I signaled Severeid that I was ready and Tony stepped in there to take his cut."

Meanwhile, Combs, Ruth and Gehrig waited on the bases. "I fed him three low curves around the knees. He fouled them, and one went out into the left-field seats, but foul by a foot. Then I took a deep breath and fired away with my fast ball across his letters. He swung and missed and I left for the bench."

There were two more scoreless innings, but that was the ball game for me. The dream of a lifetime was a reality at last. The Cardinals had won a world championship, and that shuffling man with the battered cap had made it come true.

I wish the Alexander story had ended there but it seldom does for his kind. He had long been an alcoholic and a problem to managers for years. The Cardinals had picked him up from the Chicago Cubs earlier that season for the $4,000 waiver price. In his first start he beat the Cubs 3–2 in ten innings before a record crowd in St. Louis.

What has bothered me most is Alexander's final victory in the big leagues three years later, on August 10, 1929. He relieved in the late innings of a game at Philadelphia and held the Phillies. The Cardinals tied the score, 9–9, in the ninth, and then put over two to win in the eleventh, 11–9. It was one of baseball's biggest days, all the newspapers cried, because Old Pete with 373 victories had passed Christy Mathewson's lifetime total of 372 for National League pitchers. Cy Young, whom I saw pitch in the skintight suit, red cap and red stockings of the early 1900s, holds the mark of 511 victories for two leagues, and Walter Johnson's total of 414 was made in the American League. Matty had died at Saranac Lake four years previously. Alex was now the National League champion and his new mark would last forever.

"I cautioned Alex against well wishers and celebrants," said Manager Bill McKechnie in recalling the big day. "We were leaving for games in New York and Brooklyn. I warned him that if he made one wrong move there'd be a ticket back to St. Louis for him."

Old Pete nodded his red head, for he understood, but he was a sick man and a weak man as a result of his sickness. He disappeared for two days and McKechnie ordered the traveling secretary, Clarence Lloyd, to buy the ticket. When Alex finally appeared, he was sent to St. Louis and from there to his home in St. Paul, Nebraska. He was paid full salary to the end of his contract.

Branch Rickey traded him with a catcher to the Phillies for a pitcher and an outfielder, but Alex couldn't win for the Philadelphia manager, Burt Shotton. He drifted into the minors, won a game at Dallas, and became something of a public charge. He was once found lecturing at a flea circus just off Times Square, New York. When he died in late 1950, it was learned that Singing Sam Breadon, the Cardinals' owner, had long been paying him $100 a month through the National League office.

One of baseball's mysteries is the disappearance of Old Pete's distinction of being the biggest winner of all National League pitchers. In 1939 someone as yet unidentified supposedly found in old newspaper box scores another victory for Christy Mathewson. It was quietly added to his lifetime record without fanfare or even explanation, thus creating a tie with Alexander. The error was blamed on the loosely kept accounts of 1901 and 1902, but it was never explained even by an asterisk.

Presumably the same statistical archeologist has, for the past twenty years, been digging into Alexander's distinguished pitching career with the same care and zeal in search of another victory in his behalf to restore the honor of which he was deprived. But it will take more than records sneaked into the book to dim my admiration of Grover Cleveland Alexander, an artist, a master at his trade, a foolish unfortunate, and a great contributor to the legend of the game. Will we ever see his equal?

Three Barristers in Brooklyn

MacPhail to Rickey to O'Malley spanned twenty years of Brooklyn baseball. This is twice as long as Tinker to Evers to Chance in Chicago, and the Dodger triarchy may have been twice as smart, since all three are wealthy. As I recall, the three Cubs achieved only wealth of immortality, chiefly from a sports poem not written by Grantland Rice.

I venture to say that future fans of baseball will look back upon the two Brooklyn decades with more admiration than anger or incredulity. All three mouthpieces of Montague Street, as different as night is from day and from dawn, are my friends, I'm pleased to say. Some would censure them, individually or collectively, for what they did to or for Brooklyn baseball. Why not? They even censure each other, and at this writing a couple of them aren't on speaking terms.

But to me denunciation is less interesting, and much harder work than delineation, especially since I know a lot of good and delightful things about all three. I never had time or inclination to check their alleged evils, except to learn that all three were once practicing attorneys.

When Leland Stanford MacPhail took over the Brooklyn

Dodgers in October, 1937, his red head was bursting with ideas. This chronic condition was previously responsible for his making baseball history in Columbus and in Cincinnati, Ohio. Both cities had bankrupt, second-division ball clubs when MacPhail arrived. When he left they were first-division teams with enough manpower to bring pennants and prosperity.

Whether bankrupt or not, MacPhail's Dodgers were certainly bank-held throughout his tenure. The team had finished in the second division for the five preceding years. Under MacPhail's stewardship, the next five finishes were seventh, third, second, first and second. His last team lost out on the final day of the 1942 season, by which time he had re-enlisted as a Colonel. He told me then, "I owe Uncle Sam sixty-four thousand dollars in taxes and this war had better get over fast, or I'll never get even."

Newsclips of MacPhail's five years in Brooklyn are a riot, or rather, colorful reports of a five-year riot. The players fought with each other and with sports writers (who fought among themselves), and MacPhail took on all comers including his own employees. There was never a newsless day. During this five-year turmoil the Dodgers became truly big-league for the first time. While daffiness was a hallmark of Dodger doings on the field and off, MacPhail used it to camouflage sound planning, horse sense and hard work.

At Columbus, Ohio, MacPhail had set attendance records with night games and by blanketing the area with radio broadcasts. At Cincinnati he had installed the majors' first lights and again created new interest with broadcasts. He installed lights in Brooklyn and brought East a radio voice belonging to Walter Lanier "Red" Barber. (I won't hazard a flock of friendships by saying that Red is the best sports announcer, because he may not be, and he'd be the first to credit somebody else with that nebulous honor. But after nearly twenty years in this town, Barber is still right at the top.)

MacPhail rebuilt and refurbished Ebbets Field, set up a lavish "Yacht Club" for thirsty writers, installed an electric organ (he is an accomplished organist), and placed before it the talented Gladys Goodding. Of these and other innovations, he is proudest of his pioneering move in Brooklyn to combat the bean ball. "With the help of Al Rainey, of A. G. Spalding, and the counsel of Doctors Bennett and Dandy, of Johns Hopkins, we developed a protective baseball cap. After Joe Medwick was nearly killed we made it a club rule that no player could go to the plate without wearing this protection. It was unheard of then. Today, I'm glad to say, the movement has spread throughout the game."

There are a couple of other items about this restless redhead that I'd like to record. Many know that MacPhail was a top football official, but few know that he was the first to use, and perhaps created, the semaphore system of conveying information on penalties to the press and radio from the field during a noisy football game. Even fewer know that Mac-Phail was a fighting private at the start of the first World War and a captain at the end of it. Commanding a Field Artillery battery of the 114th Regiment, he and his whole crew took a thorough gassing in the Argonne. It left its awful scars, so the redhead and I belong to the same club. One good thing about mustard gas is that it leaves soldiers' eyes too weak to see each other's faults.

Wesley Branch Rickey came to Brooklyn in late October, 1942, and remained exactly eight years. During that time he developed the best-known baseball club of all time. The Dodgers became a household word, a dirty word in places of ignorance and bigotry, and a symbol of democracy in action.

Branch and *Rickey* were two wonderful words to me during my teens, for in that time he guided the destinies of both the St. Louis Browns and the Cardinals, and his farm-club system made Missouri the baseball capital of the world.

Branch Rickey was my personal hero then, but he became one of our great Americans in late October, 1945. I wrote:

> This column would like to commend Branch Rickey, one of baseball's wisest and most thoughtful leaders, for having signed former Lt. Jackie Robinson to a Montreal contract.
>
> It would also like to congratulate Robinson. And finally it would like to suggest that this would be a good time for all concerned to emulate the young man who appears to have had almost nothing to say about his being the first Negro ever signed to play in organized baseball.
>
> To make a *cause célèbre* of the matter, to stir a tempest in a teapot, can do nothing or nobody, including the Negro race, baseball, Chandler, the Rickeys and, in the end most important of all, our country, anything save harm.
>
> Two obligations are imposed by the inevitable bringing of Robinson or some other Negro star into baseball. One is for baseball and the fans to accept the fact with common sense. The other is for the Negro race to behave with equal good sense.
>
> Good luck to Rickey! Good luck to Robinson! Good luck to baseball, which may be a little slow on the uptake, but which usually gets around to doing the sensible thing in the long run.

Rickey became an even bigger man in my eyes when the controversy about Robinson was confined to whether or not he could play baseball in the minor leagues and, if he succeeded there, in the major leagues. The question of who would eat in whose dining room or whose daughter would marry whom was never allowed to be part of the integration of the Negro into organized baseball.

Rickey's stature as a human being loomed even larger in 1947 when he lost two of his Dodger coaches to the Yankees, and his manager, Leo Durocher, who was suspended by Commissioner Happy Chandler. I lost a little, too, for publicly calling the action against Durocher "Nonsense Piled on Nonsense." That was how I saw it, but I was barred from broadcasting the World Series for the Gillette Company and a fat fee. Had the fee been ten times what it was, the price would have been cheap for the privilege of saying in print what I sincerely believed.

Rickey remained silent all season in obedience to the Commissioner's gag on "all parties to this controversy," but immediately after the World Series, in which his Dodgers participated, he fought the Commissioner for the right to re-employ Durocher. He won, and Durocher's contract for 1947 was reinstated for 1948.

Through many long meetings with Rickey (there are no short ones), I have come close to the heart of the man, and my admiration for him is boundless. A few years ago he wrote me an expression of appreciation that said: "When the day comes that you look back upon a career of writing, you can have the satisfaction of knowing that a thread of fairness, colored with much kindness, ran through all the years. And if someone were to say that to me, I would consider it the highest compliment I can think of. And I mean it that way for you too."

Naturally, I was grateful for this response to a column I had written about Rickey's attendance at the trial of a fellow who had written a threatening letter to Ralph Kiner. The story does more than anything I know to explain the most puzzling side of Rickey—his inability to desert anybody in trouble—and it may help those unfortunates who hate Leo

Durocher to understand why he stuck by his manager. Rickey wrote me:

I didn't volunteer to say a word at the trial. I was subpoenaed as a witness and was sitting back in the courtroom when the judge asked me to come up to the bar as a friend of the court, and then asked me for my recommendation. It was the quickest extemporaneous speech I ever made in my life. It was very brief and I ended it up by saying that I just couldn't "send this boy to jail." I couldn't and that was it. Why the press fastened on to it, I don't know. Really, it was not worthy of mention anywhere. The judge knew very well that it would have ruined that boy if he had sent him to jail and he would have made the same decision, I know, regardless of anything I said.

This story reminds me of the remark made by one of my oldest racing friends, Sunny Jim Fitzsimmons, about the so-called bad actors among thoroughbred race horses. He said, "There are no bad horses. There are only good horses, and horses that have been neglected."

Walter Francis O'Malley, third of the three Brooklyn barristers, can credit his half ownership of the Dodgers to the MacPhail administration. By doubling the attendance and concessions income of the previous five years and by selling broadcasting rights MacPhail enabled the bank to pay off all existing obligations except the Ebbets Field mortgage. The bank retired as administrator of the Ebbets estate and was free to help finance the sale of the Ebbets holdings to O'Malley, Rickey and John L. Smith, industrialist, in 1945.

I have always known O'Malley as a truth-telling fellow. He went to night school at Fordham University for his law degree, he is a fine father of two wonderful children and a devoted husband, who has never heard his wife talk because of a life-saving removal of her larynx before their marriage.

Walter began to speak about a larger place for the Brooklyn Dodgers long before he bought out Rickey's 25 per cent interest in late 1950. Just how sharp a businessman he is I cannot say, because I've never wanted to buy anything he wanted to sell. I only know that long before the stalemate with New York's Mayor Wagner he told me that the Dodgers "can't play in Ebbets Field much longer. It may be profitable, but it's not good business with so much at stake."

In January, 1957, O'Malley told me in confidence that the Giants were playing their last season at the Polo Grounds. They might be going to Minneapolis, but the better guess was San Francisco. He reported his conversation with Horace Stoneham to me. He had said to the Giants' owner, "You and I are rivals in baseball, but through the years the rivalry between our teams has been one of the most important factors in each of our businesses. We are also friends. I'll put my cards on the table, if you are willing to put yours there."

"Sure," said Stoneham bluntly. "I'm leaving."

Good story that it was at the time, I had to respect O'Malley's confidence. But when he released me from the confidence six months later I began writing about the possibility of New York losing not one, but both National League clubs. I was accused of being "O'Malley's sounding board."

I cannot evaluate the terms that Walter proposed to Mayor Wagner and Park Commissioner Moses for remaining in New York. Perhaps they were on the stiff side, but if baseball is desirable to a community he, not the city, had the bargaining position. O'Malley played it square with me right to the finish, and I relayed everything I could to warn my readers and the city that we might have little more than a "ghost" baseball town.

In one of our last meetings Walter said as sincerely as I

have ever heard a man talk, "I've always wanted to stay in Brooklyn, and I want to stay in Brooklyn now. It's a thing inside me that I want to stay and keep the Dodgers here. It may sound corny, but it's been my dream."

O'Malley and the Dodgers left for Los Angeles where the horizon is wider and the business potentials greater. In years to come I think we will look back and marvel at all three Brooklyn barristers: at MacPhail for his big-league ideas and intrepidity; at Rickey for his greatness as baseball man and human being; at O'Malley for his foresight and the guts to do something about it.

SCOOPS

I wouldst thou hadst my bones, and I thy news.

                    Shakespeare

Little Notes about Big People

When I crashed this delightful profession I decided I'd rather write for a daily paper than do any other sort of job. What I know best about the newspaper business is that nobody could have kept me out of it. I'd rather be a bad newspaper man than the president of a great bank, and from the very start my only worry about scribbling sports was that some day I'd be found out and put back to work.

As I've implied, most of us who write these daily columns are accidents—sometimes shocking catastrophes—and there isn't a living man who could tell somebody else how to go about getting and holding such a job. Writers able to turn out splendid, polished prose have been dismal failures as daily commentators, while others of us who must laboriously yank each sentence out by the hair of its frowzy head have managed to get by.

Perhaps a story about my old coworker, Ford Frick, now the Commissioner of Baseball, will illustrate this intangible quality. While on the *Journal*, Ford was selected to broadcast news. He was a good broadcaster, as I learned when I followed him, so good and so natural that Liggett and Myers hired him to announce their program for $1,000 a week. In his first show the Indiana farm boy showed the sponsors how smart a Hoosier can be by giving them a city-slick vocal veneer that brought the agency man out of the control room on the run. "What are you doing, Ford?" he gasped. "If we wanted that type of stuff, we'd have hired Brokenshire. Give us that homespun Hoosier stuff with your natural nasal twang!"

Doing what comes naturally is more than a song title. It's the key to most success in the newspaper business. Otherwise, how could a man like Bill Curley, my managing editor, have tolerated the hair-whitening likes of me for all these years? The newspaper world has always been different and exciting because of the people who work in it. Men like Curley, Carr Van Anda, Tom White, Walter Young, young Bill Hearst, Joe Mulcahy, Joe Connolly, Ed Swasey and the lovable Rod Boone bear no relation to the blaspheming, screaming-mimi type of editor you see in the movies. My heroes are cool and calculating fellows who react instantly to a crisis.

All newspapermen are different; each is a rank individualist. Some people think Westbrook Pegler eats a few small children on a half shell to start his day. Others think him a bushy-browed, crusading saint, but to me he is a newspaper man whose heart and soul is in the business and who deeply believes that few things in the world are as important as a first-rate piece for his paper. As a sports writer, the only thing that set Peg apart from the rest of us was that he sweated more over his stories than we did. As a result, they were frequently better than ours.

Of all the writers I have known and been associated with, Bob Considine turns out the fastest copy and often the best. But Frank Conniff, the conscientious Ed Sullivan, Frank Graham and Red Smith are all sweaters, though their columns conceal it better than a woman hides her years.

Only the late W. O. McGeehan could outbleed Pegler over the start of a story. I once watched him litter an entire hotel room in Atlantic City with balled-up sheets of discarded copy paper before giving up and asking me to write his column. He stood aside and handrolled a cigarette while I did the sweating. It wasn't much of a piece when I finished, and it certainly wasn't McGeehan, but it did have what I always felt was a minor virtue in our business—it got into the paper.

Under Full Sale

Any newspaperman worthy of the term is a little proud of scoring an occasional beat on a story. He's correspondingly remorseful when a competitor skins him, but without benefit of statistics I'd guess that even a good reporter will get scooped about as often as he does the scooping.

News beats can't be blueprinted. They always come unexpectedly and unless there's a direct pipeline you depend upon good luck, friendship or the whispering of some man with an angle who hopes to store up reasons for asking favors later on. The oldest rules for beats have never changed: be ready for the break and get it into type and on the streets or somebody else will. I was ready in 1945 for one of the sweetest and best I ever enjoyed, but getting it on the streets in a hurry created a ticklish situation.

Soon after the death of Col. Jacob Ruppert in January, 1939, I wrote a column headed, "Empire for Sale." It was the first flat statement that the powerful New York Yankees baseball organization was on the market. But the news was not exactly secret. The government demanded cash for inheritance taxes—it had no interest in barrels of beer, Fifth Avenue real estate or even choice tickets to the Yankees' annual World Series games. Large holdings had to be liquidated and the baseball assets were most expendable.

My first announcement that Larry MacPhail and his group would buy the Yankees caused scoffing and ridicule, though I had simply printed the information and its source. I ended my piece by saying that while I certainly wasn't trying to sell the Yankees, there was no doubt that Colonel MacPhail and his associates were trying to buy them—and not for the first time. Six months before, MacPhail had procured enough ready cash from prominent racing people in Maryland to buy the Yankees from the Ruppert heirs. When Commissioner Landis frowned upon horse-racing money as a fountain of finance, MacPhail had to locate a new one.

If I sounded sure of myself in January, 1945, it was because my information had come from the best possible source. But MacPhail had told me very little. The rest of my knowledge came quite casually from a banker, Horace C. "Hap" Flanigan, who was impressed by what passed for "inside" information in my column. "You're on the right track," Flanigan said, complimenting me on the story. He satisfied my curiosity by explaining that his bank, the Manufacturer's Trust, was handling the sale as trustee of the Jacob Ruppert Estate.

"Well, when it's ready," I suggested timidly, "I'd like to be in on it, if possible."

"Sure," he said, "but forget it till you hear from me."

It was just as casual as that. A few weeks later we happened to be table neighbors at the Banshees Luncheon, which Flanigan usually attended and for which I hustled up guests from the sports field. During Hap's quest for sports autographs the sight of me reminded him of something.

"By the way, Bill," he said, "I'm selling the Yankees this afternoon."

"What time?"

He glanced at his wristwatch. It was 2:45. "In about an hour. We're signing the papers downtown."

"Thanks," I whispered.

"But don't go with it till you hear from me."

I agreed and returned to my table. At my side was Jim Farley, the former postmaster general, and an old friend. When I said, "Jim, it looks like you've lost the Yankees for good. They're sold," his head lowered and his ruddy features actually sagged. One of the biggest dreams of his life had exploded. Only a year before, almost to the day, he had come close to telling me the whole story. By coincidence, we met at a turkish bath, and during our conversation I learned that Uncle Jim would probably be the purchaser of the Yankee diamond empire. He had even laid his plan before Commissioner Landis: Ed Barrow, George Weiss and Joe McCarthy were to run the organization.

There was one fly in the ointment which Jim didn't mention—one of his financial backers was a Brooklyn contractor who owned race horses. Nevertheless, it was hard to imagine how professional baseball could possibly do better than to have a man of Jim Farley's character and national importance associated with the sport.

I had rooted hard for him, but now it was over and we both knew it. I jiggled with impatience, for by the time I had alerted my sports editor, Max Kase, and reached Flanigan for confirmation it was late afternoon. Now our problem was a big one: should we "fudge" the news for the final edition or gamble and hold the hottest exclusive of the year for the next day's city edition?

By fudging, our exclusive would reach about fifty thousand *Journal-American* readers, then fall into the laps of the morning tabloids with multimillion circulation. While we were vacillating, I gave the news to Bob Considine, of the Hearst-owned *Daily Mirror*, to protect the "family" in case of a leak.

"Let's gamble."

This weighty decision came from Harry Glaser, of our sports department, one of those keen, unsung editorial brains on every sports page whose light is hidden under a bushel of anonymity. Jake Karpf was another one, and I'd list those I happen to know on dozens of papers in New York and across the country if I weren't afraid of hurting some great ones by omission. These unsung heroes are often a by-liner's conscience, and their copyreading spares him public shame and ridicule.

The decision to gamble increased the problem. First I had to call Considine again; I told him that a story was a story and that he could run it if he wished. He showed his stature as a newspaperman by saying, "I have no story, Bill. It's yours."

I've never forgotten that. The next jolt came from my managing editor who wanted to know how authentic the story was. He was unimpressed that my source was the vice-president of a bank, and for good reason. An M.E. is paid not to surrender his front-page headlines and lead columns without a fight—you have to earn 'em.

By now Kase had agreed to take over the story as a by-line project, which showed how smart I can be at times. MacPhail and Topping were well known. But who the devil was Del E. Webb? Max had the job of writing about a completely unknown new major-league club owner. If you ever meet Kase, you will notice that one ear is flatter against his head than the other. It happened when he spent almost the whole night on the telephone trying to track down Del Webb, satisfy the managing editor on authenticity, and write the biggest sports scoop in years.

My biggest kick came from a stab in the dark after we had learned that Del Webb ran a large construction business in Phoenix, Arizona. He was asleep in the Ambassador Hotel in New York when Max Kase hoodwinked the poor switchboard operator into arousing Webb by giving him the message that "the man from Phoenix is on the 'phone. Just tell him it's the man from Phoenix." In fairness to the young lady, it took a lot of hoodwinking.

"Mr. Webb!" said Max quickly when the gruff voice answered. "This is Max Kase, sports editor of the *Journal American*. We're doing a story on you as the new part owner with Mr. Topping and Larry MacPhail, of the Yankees. Can you give me some background on yourself?"

There was a long pause, and then something that sounded like, "Well, I'm a son-of-a. . . ." It was blessed assurance that Webb was a principal.

Kase had reserved a two-column top spot on the front page, and all his first sports page. He had even sent scouts to the Astor Hotel, where the New York Baseball Writers were rehearsing for their annual show, to make sure that none of them had the story. The clincher came around 3:30 A.M. when Max pulled the unpardonable, but understandable. A sleepy National League president answered the telephone in Bronxville when he called Ford Frick.

"I don't want any facts," Kase pleaded. "But I'm sitting on a keg of dynamite, Ford. We've got the whole story—MacPhail, Topping and Webb as purchasers of the Yankees for two and a half million, with Ed Barrow's share still to be sold. I apologize for this call, but I'm sure you wouldn't want to see your old buddies left holding the bag."

Whether Frick broke down in tears at this, I don't know, but he did give Kase some magic words: "Why don't you take a chance and print it?"

There may be prettier sights than your favorite newspaper scooping town and country on a big story, but if so, you don't see them right away. Not until the tingling excitement subsides can you notice other items. Only one piece of front-page news was easier on the eyes that January 26, 1945, than our YANKEES SOLD TO MACPHAIL, TOPPING GROUP. The other headline was 91 MI. TO BERLIN. Our Russian allies were fighting as though they wanted to beat us into the German capital. As it turned out, they did.

Even the New York Yankees themselves were scooped—and no little irritated, too. The rest of the town's newspapers and press associations began calling when our city edition hit the streets. Half-hearted denials were soon followed by demurrers and finally by an impromptu press conference in which our scoop was verified in every detail. Max Kase had left no alternative. The clincher was a background story on Del Webb, the unknown partner in the deal.

That gentleman, who has been well known and well liked ever since, gave us the biggest kick of all when he strode toward us and snarled, "Which one of you is Max Kase?" Max pleaded guilty, and we both prepared to duck because Webb was tall, athletic and standing. Max and I were short, unathletic, and sitting; even with two against one it wouldn't have been a fair fight. Max, a quick thinker, grabbed Webb's right hand before it could become a fist, and started pumping.

Of course it was unnecessary. After grumbling at Max for waking him, Webb whispered, "How the hell did you find me? Not a soul outside our office knew I was in town!"

Catalogue at Campobello

In January, 1958, a fine piece of theater called *Sunrise at Campobello* opened on Broadway. The play by Dore Schary dramatized the ordeal and raw courage of Franklin D. Roosevelt, a fine physical specimen not yet forty, who was stricken and crippled at the threshold of a promising political career.

The play reminded me of an unpublished scoop from the 1944 Democratic convention in Chicago. Following the nomination of Truman for Vice-President, I filed my column and returned to the Blackstone Hotel to resume loitering in the lobby. Postmaster General Frank Walker came along, delighted with the convention results, and as always, we fell to reliving a few of the endless absurdities encountered at Shelby, Montana, twenty-one years before. While talking, we greeted passers-by, and one I waved to was an old fight-camp friend, Teddy Hayes, who quit boxing in 1923 to be Jack Dempsey's trainer and secretary. Teddy was with an old friend of Walker's, Edward J. Flynn, long the Democratic leader in Bronx County and a coworker in all the Roosevelt campaigns since 1932.

We exchanged greetings, then Walker said good night and excused himself. Flynn asked me if I was busy, and I said no, that even my column was on the wire.

"Why not come upstairs and relax?" he suggested.

Flynn had a suite on one of the higher floors with windows facing busy Michigan Avenue. The lake in the distance was dotted here and there with the shimmering lights of craft slipping by in the night. He slumped on the big divan that faced the windows and sighed. A tall man with prematurely gray hair, he was more bushed than his florid face indicated. He motioned for me to rest my bones beside him and we relaxed with small talk and a pair of scotch-and-sodas that Hayes produced.

Looking back now, I can see that Flynn gave a lot of thought that night to President Roosevelt's physical condition. At that time F.D.R. was defying the elements and conditions of war to visit faraway places. Flynn expressed no fears, of course, but he paused several times in the early part of the conversation to stress the man's past courage under a major physical handicap. Hayes was prompt with refills as we talked on. I did most of the listening as Flynn began to talk about the late twenties when, in recognition of the importance of Flynn's Bronx County leadership, Governor Roosevelt had made him Secretary of State.

In working with this physically handicapped man, said Flynn reverently, he learned the meaning of dedication. Roosevelt revealed the birth of a whole new political philosophy and talked about it in a manner that inspired awe in all those close to him. The awe was not for his politics, with which anyone has the right to disagree, but for the years of meticulous care and planning that obviously had gone into their construction. Here was a power to be reckoned with, chiefly because Roosevelt had worked longer and harder than anyone before him in laying his political plans.

"The culmination of his plan," said Flynn, "was to seek the presidential nomination at Chicago in 1932, nearly two years away. He wanted me to handle the preliminaries—go to every state and city, to almost every county and town. There I would meet every leader at all levels, down to the district man. When I expressed doubt that anybody could meet and talk to so many people without knowing who or where they were, he laughed and produced the most amazing thing I'd ever seen.

"It was a catalogue, a big card-index file, holding thousands of names, addresses, last-known phone numbers, businesses and other pertinent items. It covered every state in the Union, cities, counties and hamlets he had mentioned. There were the names of Democratic leaders, businessmen, workers, captains—women as well as men. When I asked him how in the devil he had made such a list, he tapped the braces on his legs, and said, 'At Campobello beginning *that* summer, Ed. I had to do something with the time.'"

Flynn told the unforgettable story of an educated, wealthy man, married sixteen years, with five children, who was stricken with polio on a remote island off the northeastern tip of Maine. Instead of moaning in despair, he began scratching his way out of the deep valley by work and hope, by writing letters and telephoning. He continued through the winter in the city developing the widest contacts any politician had ever enjoyed. All he needed now was someone to visit these people and deliver the message of the would-be candidate.

"It was out of the question for me," recalled Flynn with a sigh. "We had too much at stake in the Bronx, and I felt that leaving it might weaken a solid political situation. I thanked him for his trust and the opportunity and suggested that he consider Jim Farley who seemed ideal for a job that called for meeting people. Jim was liked by everybody who knew him. . . ." Flynn paid high tribute to the fine job that Farley had done, but his deepest admiration was for the monumental task that the courageous Roosevelt had essayed at a time when lesser men would have chucked it all.

It was sunrise, not at Campobello but at Chicago when we surrendered to weariness. We watched a while in silence as the red ball of July sun lighted up the sky over Lake Michigan, reminding Chicago that while the convention was over, the heat wave wasn't.

Ten months later I was in Paris. It was April and there were blossoming chestnut trees heavy with catkins along mile after mile of shaded avenues. Flowers were everywhere, lilacs, small red roses and vari-colored lilies, and the perfumed air convinced you that Coty and Chanel were distilling milady's come-hither potions right around the corner.

In the Club Français it was after midnight, and Charles Trenet was singing his foolish songs to a well-dressed audience. Suddenly the piano stopped playing and people stood up mechanically as the manager made the ominous announcement to his guests. The unbelievable had flashed across 3,000 miles of ocean to stun a nation and, indeed, the civilized world. Franklin Delano Roosevelt had died early in his fourth term as President of the United States. Missouri's Harry S. Truman picked up the reins of history on Friday the thirteenth.

Alpha and Omega

In the early twenties my constitutional consisted of walking up Broadway from 43rd Street to Lindy's original place next to the Rivoli Theater on Fiftieth Street. There I scanned the morning papers, had a snack and some conversation with the kind and understanding Leo Lindy, then rode home on the West Side subway to 110th Street.

One night I shared a car with a clean-cut young fellow about my age and build, give or take a few muscles. He had sharp brown eyes and a healthy, firm complexion. I was pale by comparison because my only sunshine came from a bulb over the sports copy desk of the *Times*. There was nobody else in the car—it was close to dawn and all decent people had checked in long ago.

We both got off at 110th Street. As the train pulled out, the man proceeded ahead of me with a crisp step. The place was mostly shadow, which made what happened more of a surprise. Suddenly two silhouettes leaped from the darkness and jumped my companion. The action was in full swing before the ticket seller was awake.

I simply couldn't stand by and see a nice young fellow set upon by two bigger thugs, even if he was landing a surprising number of effective punches despite his tight-fitting overcoat.

I waded in, though my size and natural pacifism threatened to lessen the young fellow's chances. I became a busybody, pulling at the attackers and keeping out of range of flying fists. My friend landed more and more effectively; he managed to whack both thugs several times in the face, and I heard one give a loud "Oo-o-o-o-f!" after taking a punch in the breadbasket. In a few second both muggers ran off and the ticket taker woke up and came out blinking like a mine mule in the gloom.

"What's goin' on?" he asked sleepily. "Any trouble?"

"No," said the young fellow. Turning to me, he said, "Thanks for the help."

"Don't mention it. You handled yourself pretty well."

He looked at his hands, rubbing them as we left the station and paused on the Broadway sidewalk. "I should've done better," he apologized, holding out his hands palms down, "but I couldn't risk these. Fighting is my business."

"You looked familiar," I said. "My name's Corum. I'm in the sports department of the *Times*."

"I'm Benny Leonard," he replied, shaking my extended hand.

The lightweight champion of the world, one of the greatest and cleanest of all time, walked a block with me before parting. Though we didn't meet often thereafter, we always greeted each other as friends.

My story skips almost twenty-five years to the day, to April 18, 1947. The story of Leonard's ring brilliance in the intervening years can be found elsewhere, particularly in a fine volume, *Leonard the Magnificent*, written by my good friend Nat Fleischer. I'm concerned here only with the Omega part of my tale, which is as bizarre as the beginning.

As usual, I had helped Don Dunphy broadcast the main event at St. Nicholas Arena that Friday night, providing color between rounds and trying not to second-guess. Benny Leon-

ard, who refereed the entire program, did his usual, expert
job. He worked with understanding from the fighters' side
and without flash. His warnings were soft-spoken for the
benefit of the boxers, not the spectators. In the ten-round feature, he gave Eddie Giosa, Philadelphia lightweight, a one-
sided victory over Mexican Julio Jiminez. The judges con-
curred, though not so enthusiastically.

Though he complained of the heat after the fight, Leonard
appeared to be in fine shape. He was overweight and the last
time we had talked he told me about a wonderful new diet.
With a smile, he cast a meaningful glance at my own battle
of the bulge—which I was losing—but I ignored the observation. After all, I had no complaint.

As a relief from the heat that night at St. Nick's, Benny removed his necktie and loosened his shirt collar before entering the ring to handle the semifinal between Mario Ramon of
Mexico and Bobby Williams of New York. Following the usual
introductions and instructions, the bell rang and the boys
began taking each other apart. Hardly a minute of the first
round was over when the figure of Leonard toppled to the
canvas-covered ring floor inches away from me. I could have
reached out across the ring apron and touched him. My first
thought was that he had slipped and I was just about to say to
him over the air, "Why, Benny, you stood up better than that
when you were fighting," when I saw his eyes and knew it
couldn't be a slip.

Fortunately help was at hand. Dr. Vincent Nardiello, of the
New York State Athletic Commission, moved quickly from his
seat near the corner and reached the stricken Leonard
within seconds. But nearly all of the twenty-five hundred fans
charged the ring too, refusing to believe tragedy was so near.
They milled about the ring as Dr. Nardiello tried to diagnose
under the worst kind of conditions. Unable to revive Benny,
he called for a stretcher. My fears rose fast while talking into

the microphone, as I saw the telltale signs I had learned to recognize as the inevitable. It was the first time that any radio broadcaster had the unwelcome opportunity of reporting such a tragedy over a national network. Later I was told that Benny's wife had learned the news from me, but as a reporter I had to say that the fallen referee seemed to be in serious trouble.

As they carried Leonard away, Dr. Nardiello leaned over and said, "I'm afraid he's out for good." He was dead when he reached the dressing room five minutes after his collapse. Later Dr. William Benenson, assistant medical examiner, announced the end had come from coronary thrombosis.

The unfinished Ramon-Williams fight was canceled.

Surprised Party

It was a private gathering, held by the New York Yankees, but sports writers were welcome if they could find it. Now there is hardly a party that I can't find, especially if it's a possible source of news. The Yankees always are, so on October 5, 1948, the night before the opening of the Braves-Indians World Series in Boston, I strolled into a private dining room at the Ritz-Carlton. Seated around a table were Mr. and Mrs. Dan Topping, George and Hazel Weiss, Mr. and Mrs. Eddie Werner of the Ritz-Carlton, and the great outfielder, Al Simmons, who was coach of the Philadelphia Athletics that year. I was greeted warmly and offered a glass and a chair. It's always like this before anybody loses a World Series game. Twenty-four hours later you can't find people from the losing league with a brace of bloodhounds. But right now I had merely stopped by to say hello. Maybe I hoped to pick up an item, but I didn't intend to crash, or to remain and banter.

However, I don't think the Yankees had ever recovered from our scoop about the sale of the club in January, 1945. Of course they never mentioned it, but now it was around midnight, the grape was running and I was viewed as a good target for a little ribbing. Dan Topping said, "Well, well! Here's the man with all the exclusive stories. What do you have this time?"

Frankly, I had a glass of their bubbly. Still standing, I lifted it in acknowledgment of the hospitality for which the Yankees have always been justly famous. But it didn't stop there.

"Maybe he can tell us who's the new Yankee manager." This taunt came from the usually reserved George Weiss, astute general manager of the club, and it really started the teasing. Other voices chimed in.

"Yes, tell us," Topping echoed. "Come on, Bill, let us all in on the exclusive. Who's the new manager?"

All kinds of rumors about the successor to the ousted Bucky Harris were flying about press headquarters. I drained my glass and set it on the table. "You're making fun of me," I complained good-naturedly.

"Oh, come on, Bill. Tell us who's the new manager."

"Well, I just came from Western Union," I said, "and I'm sure you all know. But if you don't, I'd advise you to buy tomorrow's *Journal-American*. I wrote in my column that the new manager of the Yankees is Casey Stengel."

That did it. The color rose in George Weiss' rotund face until it was an angry red. Topping's swarthy complexion darkened and his brown eyes glared. The others, especially the women folks, may not have known because they just looked at each other, but the news was written on the all-revealing features of Weiss and Topping. It was a confirmation devoutly to be wished, so I backed out the door with a bow, a happy smile and a murmur of thanks for the liquid cheer.

How could I be so lucky? I wasn't bluffing; I had added a last-minute "shirttail" to my column as follows:

> Out of a matter of 10,000 rumors going the rounds of the assembled baseball men and scribes here for the Series, we pick this one as our longshot special.
> That the inimitable Casey Stengel, who won with Oakland in the Pacific Coast League this season, will be named as the new manager of the Yankees.

Behind this item were many hours of chasing the will-o'-the-wisps that most tips turn out to be during a World Series. All sports writers were alert for any possible development in the choice of a new Yankee manager; in fact, earlier that evening we'd held a sort of communal check. Nobody knew anything that everyone else hadn't heard, and with deadlines approaching we had fanned out on our own. On the prowl, I wandered and gabbed and greeted, not so much in hope as on the theory that even a blind hog comes up with an acorn now and then. Little did I think that I'd come up with a whole tree.

The last person I talked to before making my deadline was a fellow Missourian, Bob Hannegan. He had taken the post of postmaster general in 1945, resigning in late 1947 to purchase control of the St. Louis Cardinals in partnership with Fred Saigh. He had just completed his first full year as an owner, and I paused to greet and congratulate him. "The hottest question around here," I said casually, "is who's going to be the next Yankee manager. Have you heard anything?"

Hannegan's brows arched. "I don't see how it can be anybody but Casey Stengel," he replied quietly. I restrained my nervousness as he said, "I just flew East with Del Webb. He seemed pretty happy about things."

We exchanged a few more words, and then I hurried away to find the New York morning-paper writers to whom I had said I knew nothing. I hunted particularly for Jim McCulley of the *Daily News,* because he had met me a second time to ask the question. I couldn't find him, but I did meet Rud Rennie, of the *Herald Tribune,* and told him that I had a strong tip on Stengel as the new Yankee manager. He stared at me, then laughed.

"Maybe so, Rud," I said, "but I'm going with it."

And so I did, to Western Union, where I added it to my column—after which I hunted up the Yankees' private party.

Four days later I wired New York:

> CLEVELAND, Oct. 9—The writer received confirmation from an unimpeachable source that Casey Stengel will be manager of the New York Yankees for 1949. The deal is all set and wants only official announcement from Yankee officials.

On October 12, the day after the Indians had won the six-game Series in Boston, the Yankees called a press conference at the Twenty One Club in New York to announce that Casey Stengel had signed a two-year contract as manager.

Voice in the Night

The clear, piercing voice of Leo Durocher was recognizable before he mentioned his name, but the hint of concern in it was surprising. His Brooklyn Dodgers had just climbed out of last place in the National League by beating the Giants in a Sunday Fourth-of-July game at Ebbets Field. Leo had tried to reach me all evening, and was calling to ask if he could come right over. I begged off. I had no paper for two days, but it had been a big holiday with a Monday celebration coming up. Couldn't it wait a day?

"We go over to Philly tomorrow for the holiday double-header," he pleaded.

"Then how about an early breakfast here? You can still make North Philly by eleven-thirty."

Durocher was at the Park Lane Hotel before seven the next morning. Neat grooming failed to camouflage the nervous, hounded man beneath. Before the food appeared, he was pouring out his tale of woe and his fear of the quicksand that threatened to swallow him and the Brooklyn baseball club. Most of what he said wasn't new, and none of it was surprising. My last piece had been a pretty strong column about the shake-and-serve system of Dodger lineups. In it I had taken a crack at Durocher's habit of playing catchers behind the plate, at first and at third. Both the manager and Branch Rickey were catching it from press and public.

Billy Southworth had the Boston Braves in first place, partly by virtue of being allowed to use a lineup with players in their normal positions, win or lose. With his strategy Durocher had made stick-to-the-book managers like Bill McKechnie and Eddie Dyer look like wild-eyed radicals. Leo was playing "scared pool," the worst kind when the chips are down. I wrote, "Leo seems to have lost his one-time touch even more completely than his batters have lost their batting eyes."

If so, it wasn't hard to understand. For eighteen months Leo had been through a wringer of circumstances that have not been explained today, more than ten years later. It was a wonder he had any wits at all left. Commissioner A. B. Chandler had climaxed a period of utter nonsense in the

1947 Spring training season by handing down, in my opinion, the most unfair ruling ever perpetrated in organized baseball. He suspended Durocher as manager of the Dodgers for one year. I could find no reason given in the official decision; there were only a couple of glittering generalities such as "unpleasant incidents" and "detrimental to baseball." But Chandler has never revealed anything to justify such a penalty, and his ruling boiled down to the silly implication that Leo was acceptable in 1946, not acceptable in 1947, and acceptable again in 1948.

"Now they want me to quit!" Leo exclaimed at breakfast that morning.

"Who does?"

"I'm not sure. Rickey, I suppose. Parrott showed up in the clubhouse during yesterday's game and said, 'Leo, the Boss wants you to resign!' "

"What were you doing in the clubhouse during the ball game?"

"I was chased in the fifth inning. It was a lousy call—"

I interrupted him and got him back on the subject of the resignation. Harold Parrott, the traveling secretary, was a good friend of Leo's and obviously carried a message from the club president, Branch Rickey, who had been hospitalized for a week.

"Branch called me over to the hospital the other day," Leo went on. "I thought to myself, this is it. I expected to be fired. Instead, he read a lot of minor-league statistics from averages scattered over the bed, talked about how I should play Gil Hodges, talked about everything."

"Except resigning."

"Not a word. Well, I won't quit. I told that to Parrott. I said if the boss wants me to resign, let him tell me himself. I'm not a quitter."

"Then don't quit," I said. "Go on over to Philadelphia and win some ball games so they can't fire you."

"That's what I told Parrott. I said, 'I'll make it so tough for Branch that he won't be able to fire me.'"

Durocher perked up through the remainder of breakfast and by the time he left the old swagger had returned and he was breathing fire at the world. He was grateful for the cheering up and insisted that I should write any story I pleased, quoting him freely about anything and anyone. I thanked him and assured him he wouldn't be quoted at all.

A few hours later the Dodgers took a ten-inning thriller from the Phillies, then romped home in the second game of the holiday double-header. The next day I wrote a bristling column in which I laid the frenzy in Flatbush right in the laps of the Dodger owners. Durocher was not a part of the Brooklyn team as other managers were a part of their teams. There was prejudice against him, as almost everyone knew. To keep his job, he could not afford to make a mistake, could not ride out the sort of slump that came to all managers of all teams at some time. He was on a spot, knew it, and knew he wasn't going to get another chance.

"Durocher is all but out as manager of the Dodgers," I wrote. "Nothing can be gained by not being frank about it. When the final word of his firing comes, as it may any day—even at any hour—the announcement may be signed by Branch Rickey, but it will not be Rickey's doing."

I pointed out that while Rickey wasn't the easiest man in the world to count on in a spot like this, he had never in his career fired a manager. I suggested that perhaps his unexpected and somewhat brutal firing by Sam Breadon in 1925 as manager of the Cardinals may have had something to do with his reluctance not to give any manager a full run for his white alley.

Rickey's partners in the ownership of the Brooklyn club

were John L. Smith, head of the Charles Pfizer Company, and Walter O'Malley, an attorney. I saddled them with part or all the responsibility for the "Durocher situation." How would these owners, or the Brooklyn club or baseball as a whole gain by the firing of Leo Durocher?

The days of human sacrifice had ended thousands of years ago, I wrote. "Today we don't even use live animals in the ritual. With or without Durocher—and it may be without him quicker than you think—the time has come for frankness, plain speaking and on-the-table dealing in the Brooklyn baseball situation. All of baseball can be hurt by the sort of thing that is taking place over there now. Men don't send an underling to tell a man his job is forfeit if they want to stand up in the public eye as men should."

On the day of this critique, July 6, the Dodgers made it three in a row over Philadelphia and a total of five straight wins. Returning to Ebbets Field, they beat the Braves in eleven innings for a string of six. My telephone began to ring with calls from Brooklyn. Branch Rickey tried in vain to get me to lunch at the Union League Club. I ducked him; I had a pretty good story and I didn't want to hear the other side just yet. There were mitigating circumstances—of that I was sure—but none could be strong enough to remove the stigma that the "frenzy in Flatbush" had brought to one of the game's best baseball towns. To the fans of Brooklyn, to me, and to the country at large there was only one real question: was Durocher the same good manager as he was before his suspension? I believed that he was and that he could prove it if given a chance to be the alert, hard-fighting, smart manager he had always been on the field. My mail indicated that more than three-fourths of the general public agreed with me.

More than a week went by and the situation simmered down to a question of whether Branch Rickey could produce enough good players to keep the Dodgers in the race. He certainly didn't have enough pitchers; at one time before the requested resignation, Durocher took his team West with only seven pitchers—and one of them had a sore arm.

Then came the shocker, one of the biggest and best news items in the history of sports. It broke on the Wall Street ticker, but the *Journal-American* had it in its earliest edition, headlined in red on page 1 as follows:

DUROCHER TO MANAGE GIANTS
Demote Ott;
Brooks Run
By Shotton
By BILL CORUM

Well, it broke.

In this order. . . .

Leo Durocher will become the new manager of the New York Giants.

Burt Shotton will take over as pilot of the Brooklyn Dodgers.

Mel Ott resigned last night in Pittsburgh as Giant pilot and will take a job in the Giants farm organization under Carl Hubbell.

Ott was on his way to New York for a meeting today in the offices of Horace Stoneham, who owns the Giants.

These fast-breaking developments were to be announced officially at noon.

Durocher's contract with the Giants will run for the rest of this year and through 1949. "The Lip" is assured a considerable future in his new job, and probably will receive a new contract for more money next year.

It definitely won't be for less dough.

Shotton is now with the Dodgers in Cincinnati and is expected to take over control of the Brooklyn Club immediately.

Branch Rickey, president of the Dodgers, left Brooklyn last night to meet Shotton there.

Durocher is here in New York for today's meeting. Leo left the team in Cleveland before the exhibition game Wednesday night, and then went on a scouting trip to Toronto and Montreal for the Dodgers.

Ott has never had any other club than the Giants. He started in 1925 and took over as manager in 1941.

Considering the importance of the subject it wasn't a long story, but even at that I had to stretch it—which accounts for one or two inaccuracies that nobody noticed in the confusion. They were corrected in a later, longer story that occupied a two-column spread for the rest of the day, headed by an eight-column, double-line banner in 90-point, above which was a blazing red attention-caller: "Bill Corum's Story. . . ."

I don't remember ever telling anybody how I got this scoop. Naturally it astounded all concerned, especially my old friend and coworker, Garry Schumacher, who is still an assistant to Horace Stoneham.

When the managerial change was finally settled at 1:30 A.M., after about twelve hours of secret work, all concerned agreed on a news release at 11:00 A.M., Eastern Daylight Time. Rickey wanted time enough to fly West by private plane so that he could break the news personally to Brooklyn writers at 10 o'clock Cincinnati time.

Schumacher, who had escorted Leo and Laraine Durocher to Rickey's office for the resignation and acceptance of the new offer, remained close to his quarry after they left Brooklyn. At least Schumie thought he did, and he and others remain mystified to this day about how I managed to wrap up the preliminaries of the story before dawn and got it into type.

It wasn't too hard once I had the basic story. Nobody

broke any confidences, but I was able to call a couple of contacts and wring out some related items for my front-page splash. In view of the threats and tension surrounding Leo, it was a happy story to write, for I knew that one of the best things of his zigzagging life had happened to him.

How did I get the story? In the early hours of that memorable July 16, 1948, there was a brief telephone call through the Park Lane switchboard. The caller used no name. He spoke only a dozen words and then hung up before I could say anything. But those words were spoken in clear, piercing tones that I could recognize anywhere on earth.

The strident voice simply said, "You're now talking to the new manager of the New York Giants!"

BLUEGRASS BUGLES

We will sing one song
For the Old Kentucky Home,
For the Old Kentucky Home
Far away . . .
                    Stephen Foster

Learning at Latonia

The horse race that introduced me to Kentucky was to decide, among other things, the three-year-old championship of 1923. In my opinion, the supremacy had already been settled by the stout-hearted Zev who had won the Derby and almost everything else of importance that year. The brown beauty had lost only one of a dozen starts as a three-year-old by running out of the money in the Preakness. But all this couldn't prevent opinions from differing which, as Mr. Twain so aptly put it, makes horse races. It certainly made this one because, on figures alone, it was no contest.

I agreed with the experts on this point the evening before the fifth running of the Latonia Championship. I wanted no enemies on my first trip to these beautiful hills where the grass wasn't quite as blue as I expected—but also not nearly as green as Handicapper Corum. I couldn't see how Admiral Cary T. Grayson's My Own stood a chance in the race, but I was thankful that others thought so because it was the reason for this nice trip with another pocket full of *Times* expense money.

While Zev and My Own were claiming most of the attention, Kentuckians were insisting that In Memoriam who had finished eleventh behind Zev in the Derby could win. Bob Gilmore, his trainer, wouldn't be written out of the race before it was run. "If the track is fast," he said, "In Memoriam will lead the others to the judges' stand. Even if it's slow, he'll still have an outside chance to win."

This optimism was laudable but somewhat foolish stacked against Zev's victories in the Derby, Withers, Lawrence Realization and Belmont Stakes, and against the English horse Papyrus. Not only Handicapper Corum believed him to be invincible; the whole Rancocas stable contingent thought so too. The rumor was that Harry Sinclair, the owner; attorney Col. J. W. Zevely, for whom Zev was named, Sam Hildreth, his trainer, Earl Sande, his jockey, and all the Rancocas stable grooms and their brides poured it in big that day on Zev to win. The total was put at $75,000, which may or may not have included the $10,000 side bet made with the My Own stable, horse for horse. Whatever the exact amount, it was an enormous sum for those days. Zev was a 7-10 favorite the night before the race with My Own at 2-1. The other entries were all long shots.

The early November day broke gray and a mist collected in the valley through the morning. But it couldn't stop the stream of traffic from the surrounding hills and from Cincinnati across the Ohio River. The picturesque little park was filled to overflowing with forty thousand people by post time. The long stretch run flanked by people on both sides sent away the small field, all carrying a hundred and twenty-six pounds, with the roar that only a real racing crowd makes.

It was Zev's race, as we expected, for he had good early speed and staying power to hold them off over the mile and three-quarters. He succeeded through a mile and a quarter in shaking off My Own, when out of the hovering mist came another bay to challenge the galloping brown. Neck and neck they ran, stride for stride, with a neighborhood boy, M. Garner, looking the great Earl Sande right in the eye. They galloped that way for a full fifty yards, and then the brown horse broke. In Memoriam responded to the whip

and opened the gap in that final quarter to win by six lengths
and take down the fat purse of $50,000. My Own was fourth
behind Rialto, thoroughly beaten.

The home folks, justifiably mad with joy, made the hills
ring, for this was the greatest upset in racing since the defeat
of Man o' War as a two-year-old four years before. It came
as a shock to all except the Kentuckians who were rushing to
cash in their mutual tickets at $23.60 for $2.00. Handicapper
Corum was not among them, only partly because I was
pounding out a long story which I learned after returning
home made the first page of the New York *Times* Sunday
edition.

In finishing the piece I had to rush to interview jockeys,
trainers and owners. Only after that did I go to a window—
the Western Union window, to wire Boonville for "getaway
money." For while watching Zev falter in that extra quarter-
mile, I also watched all my expense money evaporate into
thin air. New York writers were big and understanding. W. J.
"Bunk" Macbeth, Vince Treanor and Eddie Curley, who had
shown me around, were quick with offers of help upon learning that I had "bought my checkered vest," as they termed
a clean-out.

I never forgot the gesture but I declined, for I had plenty
of scratch in Boonville, where my father had banked my re-
mittances sent back from the war. Still, it was a dismal day
because if ever a horse was superior before a race, Zev was.
Unfortunately, his superiority ceased a quarter of a mile
from home.

The winning jockey, listed on the program only as M. Garner, must have thought me a strange sort of newspaperman.
If so, it made us even; he was strange to me, too, being the
first jockey I'd ever spoken to in my life.

"Mr. Garner," I said politely to this kid of twenty-three,

"I'm a newspaperman. Will you tell me how you rode the winner? How you happened to beat Zev and Sande?"

Through pale, watery-blue eyes set in deep, dark circles he looked at me as though he was being kidded. "I guess I just had the best horse. In Memoriam was a pretty good sort of horse today."

What else could he have said? Had I expected him to quote the horse? I imagine that, young as he was, Garner sympathized with me and did the best he could. Thereafter, Andrew Mack Garner—Uncle Mack he was called when other Garners followed him—was rather special to me in his field. He rode nearly eight thousand races and 1,317 winners in twenty-two years of booting. Starting at the age of fourteen he rode the leaky roof circuits. He brought them home at beautiful Belmont Park, he rode Blue Larkspur for Col. Edward R. Bradley and Osmond for Joseph E. Widener, and that lovely, shining darling of the bluegrass, Miss Joy for Montfort Jones.

When interviewing Garner after his only Kentucky Derby victory astride Cavalcade, I remember how we laughed in recollection of our first meeting in Latonia. His sudden, dramatic passing only two years later, in 1936, came as a sharp, personal loss. Mack rode four races on the last day of his life at River Downs, one of them a winner.

"Boy, but I feel awful," he said to his buddy, Jockey Earl Pool, after slipping down from his fourth mount. He loosened the cinch. "It must've been something I ate."

"Maybe it was something you drunk, Bo," replied Pool with a wink.

Mack Garner dressed, hung his tack on its peg, got into his car and drove home from his day's work, even as you and I. He was met at the door by his wife, two daughters and two sons, and ate his dinner. A few hours later he answered the last bugle in his Covington home only a short distance from where he had galloped In Memoriam out of the mist to pass Zev and make me a native of "Death Valley" on my first visit.

They Laugh That Win

Little Latonia had earned the name "Death Valley" by being a graveyard for odds-on favorites and a constant nightmare for chalk-eaters. It was the place to encourage the believer in hot tips, which I can assure you after many years of observation only the suckers will play. It took me twelve miserable years to learn this, but I finally grasped what any sane man would have known from the beginning—that tips on horse races are the bunk. Even a tip that pays off is worthless because it whets the appetite of the believer and sets him up for the next six or a dozen bad ones. At the end of these twelve years my knowledge, gained from sad experience, was that I knew nothing about horses. Nor had I found anyone else who did. In the dead of night I studied the business of tips and managed to glean a few constructive observations.

For instance, nobody has ever conversed with a horse. No one has ever found a way to learn whether a horse felt like running on a particular day or at a particular distance.

Secondly, how do tips or "good things" originate? If a Ben Jones, Jimmy Fitzsimmons or John Gaver can't get such information from the feedbox end of the stable, who can? Yet you never hear Mr. Fitz, or Ben or any respectable trainer saying even to his owner, "Equinity is a shoo-in today." At least, I never got anything like that, and today, after thirty-five years of many close associations, I'd get mighty suspicious if any racing friend tried to give me such information. If the trainer can't get feedbox information, the owner can't, because the owner has only one source of information. That fountain of knowledge is the trainer who is never too optimistic in talking with his owner. Pessimism reduces the disappointments. The average owner is simply the fellow who puts up the money—and what a sleighride some of them take!

The third possible source for tips is the jockey. But did you ever talk to an average jockey? I'm not talking about a Sande, a Garner, Arcaro, Atkinson or a McCreary; I mean the run-of-the-mine, school-skipping pigskin artist. If you've met one of these, you know he's lucky to know enough to come in out of the rain. Not until they get the smart Aleck slapped out of them and learn to keep their mouths shut are they worth listening to. Of course by then they don't talk. If a jockey exercises a horse, as many do for experience, exercise and pay, he is apt to know as much as the next person about how the horse will run. What he doesn't know is anything about the horse under another exercise boy.

The horse can't talk. The trainer rarely does, and is never impartial. The owner doesn't know. And the "talking jockey" spells cat with a "k." But you will find hundreds of thousands of otherwise sane people in this land of ours throwing away hard-earned money on race-horse "stable information."

More important than gullibility, I believe, is that many more people than we realize simply like to gamble. They may be secretly ashamed of gambling for gambling's sake, and seize the tip to authenticate or dignify the urge. We talk of gambling fever, which exists and is a dangerous thing socially and morally, but what we conveniently overlook is that to many people "everything is sweetened by risk." There exists in human nature a desire to be part of uncertainty, and it can't be wiped out by love, law or losers.

The gambler can be wiped out by overdoing it. But that goes for anything that any of us does or overdoes. It all comes down to a question of whether we can be "temperate in all things," and since most of us are on the frail side in the field of will power, overindulgence becomes catastrophic now and then. But that's not the fault of anyone except the victim himself.

With horse racing, you do or you don't, and if you don't it isn't a taste that you are ever apt to acquire. Horse racing has always been a gambling game, and anybody who argues to the contrary is trying to kid you. Everything about it, from breeding to racing, is a gamble. In the case of a wobbly foal on spindly legs, it is a $25,000 gamble just getting him to a barrier.

But there is more to horse racing than any other gambling game and if properly conducted it is the sport of sports. I have never been unduly frightened of the bogey that all horse players die broke. Dying broke probably isn't so bad. It's living broke that's tough, and horse players, lacking security, always seem to contrive to have going-about and going-into-action money. It's amusing to hear some worried, rainy-day-tomorrow soul groan, "Look at that poor fellow. He's been going to the races for twenty years and hasn't got a dime." The groaner invariably overlooks the fact that the dimeless gentleman probably arrived on the racing scene in exactly the same condition. Another obvious fact is that a lot of guys who have been going to the library for twenty years haven't a dime to show for it either.

This is no brief for all kinds of racing at all times and places. The sport can be cheap and sordid. It can fall into the hands of grasping promoters who want to pump the last dime out of it and who make it harmful to the community. But racing can also be fine and thrilling and beneficial to a community. Ask any citizen of Louisville, Kentucky, what brought his city back after the bank closings of 1932, or the great spring flood a few years later. He'll reply without hesitation, "The Derby!" Ask the people of Texas who once voted racing out of existence because of certain unhappy experiences, but who were soon sorry and quickly moved to vote it back in again. During that period I saw a sign nailed on the main entrance of one of the abandoned tracks in Texas. It read, "No horses! No mutuels! No gambling! No fun! No Nothing!"

Twenty years ago, in 1938, I helped launch the campaign for mutuel machines in New York City because I felt that some supervision of the public's urge to gamble on horses would return a profit to the city and perhaps relieve other taxes. While governors and other officials in high places attended New York races and wagered on them, it was still illegal to slip Joe the Bookie two dollars outside the premises. This was all right, so long as Joe the Bookie didn't operate. But he did operate—and so successfully that a lot of his patients died. With the campaign for mutuels, I also suggested an act of law that would permit a limited number of reputable "commissioners" to accept bets within the law. This would relieve the hypocrisy of a state that took money with one hand while the other held a ruler to rap the hand clutching two dollars to bet with Joe the Bookie.

I've never made a plea in behalf of merely gambling. Gambling has always been a bum racket. But it has been going on for quite a while, and you can't tell a gambling dollar once it's in the cash register or the church collection. To me gambling for a livelihood would be a fate worse than debt. I know professional gamblers who seem to enjoy it, but I don't envy any part of their lives except their ability to hide their feelings. The pro looks as though every ticket is a winner, but that, I've learned, is part of the complicated code by which the gambler lives.

I don't suppose that in the previous pages I've cured a

single reader of addiction to gambling, so for the benefit of all betters I offer some of the ironclad axioms by which professional gamblers live:

When you're a winner, go to dinner.

After winning, never quit a loser. (Stash some away; don't send it all back on the next race, or the next roll of the dice).

Disregard the "mud marks" on a racing or scratch sheet. Many tracks have mud that differs, and horses can't read.

Never switch handicappers in the middle of a race meet, and among the first four selections of the handicapper you are following play the horse with the biggest odds across the board.

Always stick to the rule of three and don't be afraid to parlay the bulk of your winnings three times, but never more than that.

These are only a few of the basic rules that the professional gambler observes unconsciously. His ability to disregard outside influence, unconfirmed information, hysteria and tips makes him a professional. Those who haven't the will power to conform are amateurs and suckers—I know from experience.

Number One Man of Sports

The late Col. Matt J. Winn would have entered a disclaimer against the way I've catalogued him. With his cherubic face flushed in embarrassment, he'd have protested, "Now, Bill, you know a man only does the best he can."

I know, and that's why I say it. The clean and thriving sport of thoroughbred racing may give thanks today because this old gentleman of unique talent and vision "only did his best" and became the nation's outstanding sports promoter. Half the states of the Union should be equally thankful, for they are collecting the prettiest penny from the sport. The staggering take has reached an all-time high at this writing. Of course all the blame for this bonanza—two billion dollars in the past eighteen years—can't be laid at the late Colonel's door. But I wouldn't try to say how much of it was *not* due to his half century of constructive influence, for Matt Winn pioneered and built the sport in five of today's most prosperous racing states: Kentucky, New York, Illinois, Maryland and Louisiana.

Colonel Matt was operating the Latonia, Kentucky, track for his syndicate, the Kentucky Jockey Club, when first I was introduced to him in 1923. Meeting him, I understood how a little track could become for one November day the horse-racing capital of the world. His large, lumbering frame, easy-smiling blue eyes and soft Kentucky speech radiated personality, kindness, understanding, integrity and an abiding love of horses. A keen showman and promoter, he had built a genuine horse controversy to attract the top three-year-olds and the "Big Apple" writers. In the day of the 100-cent dollar the Latonia Championship paid a purse of $50,000. That this race in 1923 produced a major upset of two three-year-olds of proved class was a sample of what usually happened when Colonel Matt did the staging.

The Colonel's affinity for horses may have come with his birth in Louisville of Irish parents, Patrick Winn and Julia Flaherty. If not, it developed soon after because on May 17th, 1875, six weeks before his fourteenth birthday, young Matthew saw the very first Kentucky Derby from the tailboard of his father's grocery wagon. Fifteen horses dashed away to the sudden boom of Col. W. H. Johnson's starting drum. The race was a mile and one-half, the true Derby distance (both men and horses seem to have been more rugged in those days of the reconstruction period). Nobody broadcast that first Derby and no reporters were sent out from metropolitan dailies to write high-falutin' stories about it, but Col. Henry Watterson's *Courier-Journal* had a writer on the press bench to report the color of the betting ring and the results of the race.

At any rate, the starters galloped off to the shouts and screams of the "hard boots" and their ladies, and when the winning line was passed Aristides, the favorite at 2 to 1, was acclaimed and toasted in mellow bourbon as the first Derby winner.

Matt Winn saw seventy-four more of these historic races and promoted the last forty-eight of them by which time he had become a living symbol of the classic race. So strong is the association of Winn and Derby that we never think of him in any other career. But for quite a while after leaving St. Xavier College and business school in Louisville he was a tailor and merchant. It was not until he was past forty that he and a half-dozen associates took over the New Louisville Jockey Club at Churchill Downs.

The original Jockey Club had been organized in 1875 by Col. M. Lewis Clark with capital of $32,000 and on land owned by John and Henry Churchill. When Colonel Matt took charge, a group called the Western Turf Association was playing a cozy game of freeze-out in the matter of racing dates. Matt formed the American Turf Association and thawed matters in a hurry by making Churchill Downs attractive to horse owners. The battle continued through the early years of the century, but the Colonel led an expansion movement by buying the Churchill Downs land in 1904 with four associates. Three years later another corporate arm took over Douglas Park in Louisville.

When opposing forces tried to stop him by having book-making outlawed, Winn studied the Kentucky statutes and found no legislation against betting machines. Legally in the clear, he hurried to New York and bought half a dozen old French pari-mutuel machines, installed them for the 1908 meeting and won that skirmish. The system has been in use ever since.

After World War I, the Churchill Downs group absorbed courses at Covington (Latonia), Lexington and several in Illinois—Fairmont Park in East St. Louis, Washington Park and Lincoln Fields in Chicago. Between seasons before the war Colonel Matt operated tracks in Mexico City and in Juarez across the Rio Grande from El Paso.

The winning battle at Churchill Downs had drawn the attention of James P. Butler, the wealthy owner of a New York grocery-store chain famous for its green fronts. Butler's efforts to operate a major track in Westchester County, New York, had been blocked by the ruling Jockey Club headed by August Belmont. Butler sought Winn's help at Chicago in early 1907. At first Matt declined, but friendship was inevitable since both were considerably Irish and Matt had been an apprentice in his father's own grocery store.

What drew the two men together was the autocratic handling of New York racing by the powerful Jockey Club. Butler's Empire City track was going begging for racing dates. Matt Winn's ruddy face turned ruddier and by early summer he was in New York, sleeves rolled up, defying Belmont and his wealthy associates. By August Colonel Matt had a major racing meet in full swing and in competition with upstate Saratoga. New York fans saw a new lineup of horses and jockeys; Matt had persuaded the Western stables to ship East and join the fight. Empire's success from the start threatened the existence of tracks at Sheepshead Bay and Gravesend. Eventually they closed, but Empire went right on.

Within a year, Matt Winn had won a war, not of competition, but of diplomacy. August Belmont said, "Had we known you were going to conduct racing on such a high plane, the dates would have been allotted." Full cooperation of the Jockey Club followed, and Empire City became part of the "Big Apple." Matt tried to leave New York, but Butler persuaded him to remain and build. The Colonel stayed chiefly because he hoped to interest Eastern owners in making Churchill Downs part of their program. Success crowned his efforts in 1915 when he persuaded Harry Payne Whitney to take a whack at the Kentucky Derby. Mr. Whitney did more than that; his chestnut Regret won the race and $11,450, and stands today as the only filly to reach the wire first. Though there was peace in New York racing, Mr. Whitney had the added satisfaction of beating two other Eastern owners, Butler and Parsons. He entered regularly after that and won again with Whiskery in 1927.

For those years of supervision and reconstruction of the Empire City track, Matt Winn took no salary or payment from Butler. He received only room and board at the old Waldorf-Astoria. His simple explanation was, "I owed it to racing."

Despite the countless thoroughbreds and the seventy-five Derby winners he had seen, Colonel Matt was an Exterminator man to the last. He admitted to being sentimental, but he was that way about all horses. No sir, "Old Bones" was special, and it had to be charged to dependability. "A hundred times, Bill," he would whisper, shaking his head. "A hundred times that fella went out, and brought back money eighty-four times."

" 'Whirly' went out sixty," I reminded him, "and came back fifty-six. . . ."

"Donerail went out well over a hundred," he broke in. "Rosebud won half of eighty starts. But 'Bones' won half of his hundred. Ran everywhere. Ran our race here in the worst mud and Escaba caught him at the top of the stretch and took a neck lead. But Willie Knapp touched him with the crop and he sloshed on to make up the neck and a length more. A hundred times he went out, Bill, and was never disgraced."

There wasn't a problem, personal or professional, that you couldn't discuss with this unusual man and come pretty close to a solution. Over the quarter of a century that I had the privilege of knowing him, he helped me solve many of them. Once I had an option on many acres in Flushing Meadows, New York, where I hoped to build a race track and call it Greentree Park in honor of a great stable. Colonel Matt's encouragement was based on only one factor—easy access by the public.

"Breeders, owners, horses and jockeys make the race, Bill," he said softly, "but I never saw a successful one without people watching and cheering, most of them with a dollar or two at stake. The ideal track is on a trolley line, as close to town as you can get it."

When he died in November, 1949, Matt J. Winn left a permanent void in thoroughbred racing and in American sport. But he also left a symbol, a heritage to challenge all who would continue where he left off. It is a worthy goal, perhaps unattainable, and an indictment of those who would ignore it. He also left a fine family and a grandson, Matt Winn Williamson, who bears a striking resemblance to what I'm sure the Colonel looked like in his thirties. Young Winn has the florid face, the easy, blue-eyed smile, and with a little more effort he can easily achieve his grandpappy's corpulence. He ably represents the family interests as a director of Churchill Downs, Inc.

Will Winn ever be another Matt Winn? To answer that I'd have to echo one of my old sports writing friends, Bill Slocum. Back in 1937 some kid asked Bill if he didn't think rookie Bob Feller was as great as Walter Johnson. Bill's face reddened as he controlled his anger, for he had seen the great Johnson struggle through year after year of 1–0 defeats and victories, always uncomplaining.

"That's a good question," Slocum finally said. "Tell you what, meet me here twenty years from now and I'll give you my answer."

Let's say that right now young Winn is a rookie Bob Feller—which isn't anything to be ashamed of.

The Sun Shines Bright

There is always an air of curtsy and crinoline about the Kentucky Derby. Its surroundings of gables, spires and balustraded porticoes whisper of the time of forebears who hewed a new civilization out of the "dark and bloody land." (That's what "Kentucky" means in the Indian language.) The "long hunters" in the early days were mainly Virginians, horse lovers by inheritance and habit who took West a few horses of good stock. The native bluegrass that grew plentifully even in the woods was ideal for pasturage and there was thoroughbred racing in the territory long before it became a state in 1792.

To some of us the echoes of the old starting drums still linger over the ancient Downs. The rustle of taffeta, the sense of a world apart, the gentle laughter, the Rebel-scarlet silk of the Lost Cause and the reverence for the thoroughbred are there like an unseen mist, an unforgettable aura when you're part of it for the first time.

The first time for me was 1926. I was covering the Giants in St. Louis, where John McGraw was starting to break up his once invincible team, when the assignment came. I wrote a follow-up for the *Journal* on the release of Art Nehf and Heinie Groh, and took a sleeper on the Southern for Louisville. I could continue East after the race and catch the team in Cincinnati.

At this writing my total of Kentucky Derbies numbers over thirty. If written words alone make a book—and I know from this one that they don't—I've already turned out a few volumes about The Race. And little wonder, because it's the best copy of all sports spectacles, the easiest to write about.

The eye opener of my first Derby was the runaway of two horses with the same silks, the green and white of Colonel Edward Riley Bradley. It had happened before when Sir Barton and Billy Kelly won for J. K. L. Ross in 1919, and Bradley's Idle Hour Farm horses had done it in 1921 when Behave Yourself and Black Servant ran tandem. But here was Bradley a second time, with Bubbling Over five lengths in front of Baggenbaggage for $56,000 and the $5,000 gold cup. Twenty-two years passed before Citation and Coaltown finished one-two for Calumet.

I remember all the finishes—though not just of the horses —very well. I can see the ground-eating Twenty Grand, almost last at the clubhouse turn, thundering past the 1931 field on the backstretch and heading for home to break Old

Rosebud's seventeen-year-old record for the mile and a quarter. He was in complete command all the way. But a more indelible memory is of an elderly gentleman racing through the infield to the finish line, tossing his hat into the air as he ran. He was the overjoyed father of "The Flying Dutchman," Charley Kurtsinger, who had jockeyed Twenty Grand to the fifty grand and a record.

The hysterical father crossed the fast track and chased his boy right to the clubhouse. Charley's mother was also at the race, and a brother and three sisters—and aunts and uncles too, I imagine, because they all lived in Louisville. Charley was born just over the hill you can see from the press box. Sixteen years before, in 1915, this barefooted kid had watched from the infield rail as Regret raced to glory.

The finish of the 1933 race remains to blot out many of the others. A poor horse beat a very good horse when a jockey simply reached over, grabbed the good horse's bridle and held him back until his own poor horse had won by a nose. I've never seen anything like it since, and never will. Though racing officials are notoriously disinclined to allow claims of foul in important races, no judges or stewards will ever again overlook the outrage that Don Meade, riding Broker's Tip, committed against Head Play and a little boy named Fisher. For fifty yards Meade hung on in plain sight of everybody, as Fisher struggled in vain to beat him off with the whip and to break free the hand on his horse's head.

They fought it out in the jockeys' room afterward—at least Fisher, half-hysterical, made three attempts to fight. But the race was over. The other jockeys dressed in a strange and strained silence, though it was easy to tell from their looks and actions where their sympathies lay. They felt sorry for the little boy, and contempt for Don Meade.

Of Colonel Bradley's four Derby victories, this was his

last and surely the one he enjoyed least, sportsman that he was. He sent nearly thirty entries to the post in twenty-six years and Broker's Tip, a winner, was probably the worst. He won only one race in fourteen starts, and that by a palpable foul—but it was the coveted Derby.

Derby memories of horses, people, and the stories they made possible have been graphic, sad and joyful. They add up to a sizable box of jigsaw pieces. There are also a few recollections that were used unfairly against my judgment in picking horses. The stock charge is, "He picked Red Rain, didn't he?" Of course I did, though not to win the Derby— luckily he wasn't a starter. Because Red Rain had looked so good winning the Hopeful Stakes in 1935, I thought he'd sweep the boards as a three-year-old. I picked him to win several important stakes the next year, but he never won another race. Good old Crimson Downpour, as I used to call him in an effort to forget, made people forget that I picked the 1934 Derby one-two with Cavalcade and Discovery. Only the small matter of Agrarian finishing third and Mata Hari fourth, instead of the other way around, prevented me from predicting the first four places.

But I've only hit eight Derby winners in twenty-six years. I won't say what I played, but the picks were made at the risk of public embarrassment and I've usually had the good fortune with my Derby selections to have them "there or thereabout" even if they missed getting a whiff at the necklace of roses. However, nobody will ever know how really good I might have become as a Derby picker, because my best effort in 1949 also turned out to be my last.

Many claimed it was luck. One fellow I've never located called it "science." I said nothing; I didn't have to. I'll admit a certain amount of luck was involved when I spied the little roll of bills in front of the Brown Hotel in Louisville, a day or so before the Derby. Luck, and speed too, because just as I grabbed the little wad, a voice behind me said, "I saw that money, too."

"But your boarding-house reach was short," I said, and we exchanged wry smiles.

Walking along with the fellow, I peeked at the money—four one-dollar bills. He said, "Let's split it." But an inner voice said to me, "Keep it," so I told the fellow it was needed for my mutuel benefit the next day. He went on his way and I went to my room in the Brown Hotel. Seated at my desk, I stared alternately at my typewriter and out the window. Then I wrote the name of a different horse on each of the four bills, numbered them 1, 2, 3, 4, and began my column. I called it "Against Advice of Counsel," and I wrote:

. . . Now that the checks are about to go down I must wind up with the stable that seems to have this horse racing business solved best.

I'm going to bet Ponder, if only because I don't believe a Trainer Ben Jones entry should be held at 15 to 1, even if Ben was running an old brown billygoat off a dump heap.

And Ponder's a heap better than that. Better off his past performance sheet than either the owner Wright or the trainer, Jones, seems to think.

I should note here that Jones had laughed a few days before when I expressed a liking for Ponder. "We're just in there trying to grab a little of that third or fourth money, Bill," he insisted. "Ponder's a nice little horse. But he ain't enough horse to win this race. He's outmatched with Olympia's kind."

He was a running horse at the finish of the Derby Trial. He comes from the winningest outfit there is, from a Derby stable trained by a Derby trainer, and he strikes me as having had just about enough racing this Winter and Spring to make him cherry ripe.

So, here we go, good friends, and it's strictly against the book.

1. Ponder. 2. Capot. 3. Palestinian. 4. Old Rockport.

Twenty-four hours later I was filing my report of the race from the press box, trying not to look too smug.

LOUISVILLE, Ky., May 7—Absence makes the heart grow PONDER.

It has been a whole year since owner Warren Wright and trainer "White Hat Ben" Jones have been in the Kentucky Derby winner's circle here at Churchill Downs.

The whole of a long year, just think of it.

They must've got mighty lonesome for that Derby man himself, Col. Matt J. Winn.

But today, in intermittent sunshine and shadow before a throng of 115,000 madly cheering souls, the two gentlemen from Calumet got to hear the Colonel's soothing tones again. Soothing to the tune of $91,600, the net to the owner of the Derby winner, the diamond studded gold cup and the red, red roses.

For out of the clouds on the racetrack and just as the setting sun burst through the clouds overhead again, came the little dark-horse, Ponder, proudly bearing the devil's red and blue.

Away most tardily of all and last at the quarter and the half, with one laggard back of him at the three-quarter pole, the deep bay son of the Derby winner Pensive swept to a three-length triumph in the Diamond Jubilee Derby.

Greentree Stable's Capot, which broke the heart of the favorite and pace-setting Olympia (and maybe a small piece of Eddie Arcaro's heart, too), finished second and was, in turn, four and one-half lengths ahead of the Brooklyn colt, Palestinian. Palestinian wound up two lengths before the plodding Old Rockport. . . .

Some of the boys wanted to give me a saliva test or search me for mirrors and magic dust—which was all right as long as they didn't take out my few winning tickets on Ponder. He had paid a mere $34.00, $11.60 and $6.20.

The first and most welcome of many congratulatory messages came over the press wire from my old side-kick and sports editor, Max Kase:

CONGRATS ON DERBY YOU HAD IT ONE TWO THREE FOUR IN FRIDAY COLUMN YOU'VE MADE EVERYONE HAPPY HERE ALSO WITH MAX FIRST   REGARDS

MAX

Greater love hath no sports editor than that he lay down his cash to back his columnist's selections. All I got from the Derby press box were looks of deep suspicion from the chalk-eaters who had to explain why Eddie Arcaro had failed to hold the 4-to-5 favorite, Olympia, in front after hitting the mile pole with a length lead.

A most gratifying compliment came the next morning from the Negro lady who had tidied up my room at the Brown Hotel. You could count all thirty-two of her white teeth as she said, "I sho am a happy girl today."

"Yes?"

"Yes, indeed. I bets a dollar on that there 'Pander' you gimme and today I buy my mammy the biggest box of candy in town for Mother's Day."

I didn't have the heart to tell her that betting on the races was a terrible habit and could bring her trouble.

My New Kentucky Home

Five months after his seventy-fifth and greatest Run for the Roses, Mr. Kentucky Derby himself passed on to his eternal reward. I just can't imagine a man like Matt J. Winn earning anything less than the best.

I don't think that the owners of Churchill Downs, headed by their chairman, William Veeneman, expected to fill the void by asking me to occupy Colonel Matt's position as president of the Downs, nor was I silly enough to imagine that I could. Just by "only doing my best" for nine years I've proved that the void is permanent. But luck dogged my heels from the very start, the luck of having good friends and understanding employers. The job couldn't have been done without the cooperation of Veeneman's associates—Stanley Hugenberg, Brownie Leach, Tom Young, Russell Sweeney and others. Even more important was the permission and counsel of my Hearst employers, Bill, Jr., Bill Curley, and J. D. Gortakowsky. They agreed that in addition to my month's vacation I could take four weeks' leave of absence without pay each year.

Thanks to the understanding tolerance of the Gillette company I was able to continue broadcasting the fights with the brightest light ever hidden under a bushel, Don Dunphy, for nearly four more years. In one of the happiest associations of my life we had worked together at ringside for eight years, beginning with the first Joe Louis–Billy Conn fight of June 18, 1941. With the last "color job" in June, 1953, Dunphy and I had broadcast more than five hundred fights, and had become the Amos 'n' Andy of the ringside by surviving twelve years for a single sponsor.

My unwillingness to change the Matt Winn pattern of Derby operation has always been charged to sentiment. I admit being blessed with a lot of it, but I also had sense enough not to tamper with the winning lineup that the Colonel had established. I never said so, but I anticipated that my handling of the job would be like the complicated pieces I used to play on the pianola in Boonville without ever using my hands or head—just my feet. That was a foolish exaggeration, as I learned when I reported for duty in mid-March, 1950. Of course, having attended twenty-four of the Derbies I knew my way around. On hand to greet me was the faithful Thomas, an aged Negro. A combination cook and chauffeur, he has never broken the habit of shutting his eyes, regardless of heavy traffic, whenever he drove past the nearby cemetery.

I believe it was Thomas who first mentioned 6:00 A.M. as rising time. Well, I'd seen morning workouts many times, but always by leaving some café or gathering place on Broadway or in Saratoga around dawn and hurrying to the race track. It hadn't occurred to me that people actually went to bed early and got up at that time. At first I tried staying up until 6:00 A.M., which didn't last long because I began dozing around noon when I needed to be awake. There was only one solution; I learned the art of retiring *before* midnight. Now I can do it easily for two months every year. Will power is a wonderful thing.

I like to think that the Kentucky Derby is still Matt Winn's race and that Churchill Downs is still his park. For two months each year I rattle around in a portion of his apartment at the track. It has half a dozen large and empty bedrooms, each with shower and a television set, but Colonel Matt is still there for I've tried my best to retain it as he left it.

Television is the one big change in the Derby. Colonel Matt and I had talked many times about televising the race. I brought him firsthand reports on baseball television and told him that I thought one day it would take charge of the living rooms all over the country. Sure enough, television has carried The Race, and all racing, into more living rooms than could have been imagined a few years ago. It has done more to popularize the Kentucky Derby than anything.

Except Matt Winn.

Finis

Well, that's the end of it. For me, accustomed to writing about four typewritten pages a day, six days a week, for the past thirty-five years, it's been a tremendous job of writing. What you, the reader, may think of it as an autobiography is another matter. All I will say is that unless memory's tricked me, every word of it is true.

It's pretty late as I come to the final period, but the doorman in the Foreign Legionnaire's coat on the desert sands in front of El Morocco has let me in later than this. So break out some of that galloping water in the black bottles, Host John Perona, for here I come "Off and Running."

B. C.

Index